Lecture Notes in Computer Science 15357

Founding Editors

Gerhard Goos
Juris Hartmanis

The series Lecture Notes in Computer Science (LNCS), including its subseries Lecture Notes in Artificial Intelligence (LNAI) and Lecture Notes in Bioinformatics (LNBI), has established itself as a medium for the publication of new developments in computer science and information technology research, teaching, and education.

LNCS enjoys close cooperation with the computer science R & D community, the series counts many renowned academics among its volume editors and paper authors, and collaborates with prestigious societies. Its mission is to serve this international community by providing an invaluable service, mainly focused on the publication of conference and workshop proceedings and postproceedings. LNCS commenced publication in 1973.

Orhan Konak · Bert Arnrich · Gerald Bieber ·
Arjan Kuijper · Sebastian Fudickar
Editors

Sensor-Based Activity Recognition and Artificial Intelligence

9th International Workshop, iWOAR 2024
Potsdam, Germany, September 26–27, 2024
Proceedings

 Springer

Editors
Orhan Konak 🆔
Hasso Plattner Institute
Potsdam, Germany

Bert Arnrich 🆔
Hasso Plattner Institute
Potsdam, Germany

Gerald Bieber 🆔
Fraunhofer Institute for Computer Graphics
Research IGD
Rostock, Baden-Württemberg, Germany

Arjan Kuijper 🆔
Fraunhofer Institute for Computer Graphics
Research IGD
Darmstadt, Hessen, Germany

Sebastian Fudickar 🆔
University of Lübeck
Lübeck, Germany

ISSN 0302-9743   ISSN 1611-3349 (electronic)
Lecture Notes in Computer Science
ISBN 978-3-031-80855-5   ISBN 978-3-031-80856-2 (eBook)
https://doi.org/10.1007/978-3-031-80856-2

This Springer imprint is published by the registered company Springer Nature Switzerland AG
The registered company address is: Gewerbestrasse 11, 6330 Cham, Switzerland

If disposing of this product, please recycle the paper.

Preface

In recent years, the increasing acceptance of wearable sensors has opened new possibilities for understanding the human body, including but not limited to applications such as Human Activity Recognition (HAR), emotion and stress recognition, pain recognition, sleep analysis, and nutrition medicine. Wearable devices, due to their ability to collect large amounts of data unobtrusively, have garnered attention from both academia and industry, driving the development of solutions for continuous human state monitoring in daily life, workplaces, or medical contexts. This growing interest has made wearable computing an active field of research, with ongoing investigations focused on creating user-friendly and unobtrusive systems that offer high-performance services. The international Workshop on Sensor-Based Activity Recognition and Artificial Intelligence (iWOAR) has emerged as a platform for sharing experiences, presenting best practices, and showcasing technical and scientific results in these domains. In 2024, organized by the Hasso Plattner Institute, iWOAR provided a forum for scientists, industry professionals, and users to exchange ideas and explore the latest advancements in HAR and wearable computing technologies. This year's workshop invited academic research papers and best-practice industrial research approaches in a range of topics, including HAR, affective computing, artificial intelligence for wearables, real-time activity recognition, synthetic data generation, assistive technologies, privacy and ethical considerations, pervasive and wearable computing, personalized diagnostics and therapy, quantified self/biofeedback, and design innovations in sensor networks. The paper contributions included the latest findings in the field of HAR, artificial intelligence, and the combination of these technologies. Special considerations of the energy efficiency of classifications were carried out, and current image analysis methods and the extension of artificial intelligence via spontaneous behavioral change (biological randomness) were presented.

For iWOAR 2024, we were pleased to welcome two distinguished keynote speakers. Thomas Plötz from the Georgia Institute of Technology delivered a keynote titled "Human Activity Recognition using Wearables after the AI Revolution – Are we done? What Comes Next?" His talk addressed the challenges of HAR using wearable sensors, particularly how recent advances in artificial intelligence could potentially solve long-standing issues in the field. He emphasized that while AI has introduced breakthroughs, HAR remains a challenging task, and further progress could be made by exploring opportunities such as cross-modal transfer and self-supervised learning. Plötz also discussed foundational concepts of HAR, drawing parallels between human activities and natural language to argue that activities can be learned and better characterized, which would lead to more generalizable and robust models.

The second keynote was delivered by Özlem Durmaz Incel, head of the Pervasive Systems research group at the University of Twente, on the topic of "Beyond the Basics: Enhancing Lightweight Models for Resource-efficient Human Activity Recognition." Her presentation focused on improving the performance of lightweight models for Sensor-based HAR, particularly in resource-constrained environments like wearable devices with microcontrollers. She shared insights on integrating convolutional block attention modules into various lightweight architectures to enhance recognition accuracy without compromising efficiency. Additionally, Incel discussed the potential of combining knowledge distillation and attention mechanisms to further refine model efficiency and presented a comparative analysis of different optimization techniques, including quantization and pruning.

iWOAR 2024 received 28 submissions, each undergoing a rigorous peer review process. To ensure high-quality content, each paper was reviewed by at least two, and in some cases, three, program cofmmittee members. The final program included 15 accepted papers, resulting in an oral acceptance rate of 54%. Additionally, 4 short papers were accepted, undergoing review by the organizing committee to ensure their relevance and quality. Submissions were received from a diverse set of countries, including Austria, China, Denmark, France, Germany, India, Italy, Sri Lanka, Switzerland, the UAE, the United States, and Vietnam. To ensure fairness and integrity in the review process, we followed specific conflict-of-interest (COI) guidelines. Reviewers were required to disclose any potential conflicts of interest, such as personal, financial, or professional relationships with authors, and were not assigned papers from the same institution as the authors. A bidding process ensured that reviewers were assigned papers aligning with their expertise while avoiding conflicts of interest. This approach allowed us to uphold high standards of quality and objectivity throughout the review process.

We look back at a successful iWOAR 2024 at the Hasso Plattner Institute in Potsdam and thank all participants for presenting their latest research, the fruitful discussion, and pleasant atmosphere. Special thanks goes to Kristina Kirsten for excellent local arrangements, and the Springer Nature LNCS team for publishing these proceedings.

November 2024

Orhan Konak
Bert Arnrich
Gerald Bieber
Arjan Kuijper
Sebastian Fudickar

Organization

General Chair

Bert Arnrich   HPI, Universität Potsdam, Germany

Program Committee Chairs

Gerald Bieber   Fraunhofer IGD Rostock, Germany
Arjan Kuijper   Technische Universität Darmstadt, Germany

Steering Committee

Gerald Bieber   Fraunhofer IGD Rostock, Germany
Arjan Kuijper   Technische Universität Darmstadt, Germany
Denys Matthies   Technische Hochschule Lübeck, Germany
Kristof Van Laerhoven   Universität Siegen, Germany
Marcin Grzegorzek   Universität zu Lübeck, Germany
Mario Aehnelt   Fraunhofer IGD Rostock, Germany
Thomas Kirste   Universität Rostock, Germany

Local Arrangement Chair

Kristina Kirsten   HPI, Universität Potsdam, Germany

Proceedings Chair

Orhan Konak   HPI, Universität Potsdam, Germany

Publicity Chair

Sebastian Fudickar   Universität zu Lübeck, Germany

Program Committee

Allal Tiberkak	University of Medea, Algeria
Arjan Kuijper	Technische Universität Darmstadt, Germany
Bert Arnrich	HPI, Universität Potsdam, Germany
Cong Yang	Soochow University, China
Biying Fu	Fraunhofer IGD Darmstadt, Germany
Denys Matthies	Technische Hochschule Lübeck, Germany
Frédéric Li	Universität zu Lübeck, Germany
Gerald Bieber	Fraunhofer IGD Rostock, Germany
Heike Leutheuser	ETH Zurich, Switzerland
Hrisitjan Gjoreski	Ss. Cyril and Methodius University in Skopje, North Macedonia
Kai Kunze	Keio University, Japan
Kimiaki Shirahama	Doshisha University, Japan
Kristof Van Laerhoven	Universität Siegen, Germany
Lars Kaderali	Universität Greifswald, Germany
Marcin Grzegorzek	Universität zu Lübeck, Germany
Özlem Durmaz Incel	University of Twente, Netherlands
Paul Lukowicz	Rheinland-Pfälzische Technische Universität Kaiserslautern-Landau, Germany
Sebastian Fudickar	Universität zu Lübeck, Germany
Silvia Faquiri	Fraunhofer IGD Darmstadt, Germany
Thomas Plötz	Georgia Institute of Technology, USA
Xun Liu	Shanghai Ubiquitous Navigation Technology Co., Ltd., China

Additional Reviewers

Szymon Sieciński
Sumeyye Agac
Egemen Isguder
Jacek Rumiński
Eliasz Kańtoch
Ruben Schlonsak

Contents

Advances in Human Activity Recognition

Fine-Grained Human Activity Recognition Through Dead-Reckoning
and Temporal Convolutional Networks 3
    Nicolò La Porta, Luca Minardi, and Michela Papandrea

Comparison of Deep Learning and Machine Learning Approaches
for the Recognition of Dynamic Activities of Daily Living 18
    Cassandra Krause, Lena Harkämper, Gabriela Ciortuz,
    and Sebastian Fudickar

An Experimental Study on the Energy Efficiency of Feature Selection
for Human Activity Recognition with Wrist-Worn Devices 40
    Susanna Peretti, Chiara Contoli, and Emanuele Lattanzi

Multi-modal Atmospheric Sensing to Augment Wearable IMU-Based
Hand Washing Detection 55
    Robin Burchard and Kristof Van Laerhoven

Equimetrics - Applying HAR Principles to Equestrian Activities 69
    Jonas Pöhler and Kristof Van Laerhoven

Applications in Vision-Based Recognition

Leveraging Vision Language Models for Facial Expression Recognition
in Driving Environment 81
    Ibtissam Saadi, Abdenour Hadid, Douglas W. Cunningham,
    Abdelmalik Taleb-Ahmed, and Yassin El Hillali

Analyzing Exercise Repetitions: YOLOv8-Enhanced Dynamic Time
Warping Approach on InfiniteRep Dataset 94
    Michal Slupczynski, Aleksandra Nekhviadovich, Nghia Duong-Trung,
    and Stefan Decker

Supporting Thermal Imaging for Activity and Health Recognition
by a Constant Temperature Device 111
    Gerald Bieber, Erik Endlicher, Christopher Wald, Peter Gross,
    and Bastian Kubsch

Estimation of Psychosocial Work Environment Exposures Through Video
Object Detection: Proof of Concept Using CCTV Footage 124
   Claus D. Hansen, Thuy Hai Le, and David Campos

Wearable Devices and Health Monitoring

Objective Measurement of Stress Resilience: Is RSA a Possible Indicator? 151
   *Erik Endlicher, Gerald Bieber, Edda Jaleel, Angelina Schmidt,
   and Michael Fellmann*

Robust Wearable-Based Real Life Cognitive Fatigue Monitoring
by Personalized PPG Normalization 169
   Adonis Opris, Mohamed Benouis, Elisabeth André, and Yekta Said Can

The Supervised Learning Dilemma: Lessons Learned from a Study
in-the-Wild 181
   *Kristina Kirsten, Robin Burchard, Olesya Bauer, Marcel Miché,
   Philipp Scholl, Karina Wahl, Roselind Lieb, Kristof Van Laerhoven,
   and Bert Arnrich*

Novel AI and Machine Learning Approaches

FlyAI - The Next Level of Artificial Intelligence is Unpredictable!
Injecting Responses of a Living Fly into Decision Making 199
   Denys J. C. Matthies, Ruben Schlonsak, Hanzhi Zhuang, and Rui Song

Raising the Bar(Ometer): Identifying a User's Stair and Lift Usage
Through Wearable Sensor Data Analysis 220
   *Hrishikesh Balkrishna Karande,
   Ravikiran Arasur Thippeswamy Shivalingappa,
   Abdelhafid Nassim Yaici, Iman Haghbin, Niravkumar Bavadiya,
   Robin Burchard, and Kristof Van Laerhoven*

Similarities of Motion Patterns in Skateboarding and Hydrofoil Pumping 240
   Michael Zöllner, Moritz Krause, and Jan Gemeinhardt

Short Papers: Emerging Topics in Sensor-Based Systems

SurfSole: Demonstrating Real-Time Surface Identification via Capacitive
Sensing with Neural Networks 251
   *Patrick Willnow, Max Sternitzke, Ruben Schlonsak, Marco Gabrecht,
   and Denys J. C. Matthies*

ShoeTect2.0: Real-Time Activity Recognition Using MobileNet CNN
with Multisensory Smart Footwear 260
*Ruben Schlonsak, Tengyunhao Yang, Marco Gabrecht,
and Denys J. C. Matthies*

Optimal 2D-LiDAR-Sensor Coverage of a Room 269
Noel D'Avis and Silvia Faquiri

Using Wearable Sensors in Stroke Rehabilitation 277
*Justin Albert, Lin Zhou, Kristina Kirsten, Nurcennet Kaynak,
Torsten Rackoll, Tim Walz, David Weese, Rok Kos,
Alexander Heinrich Nave, and Bert Arnrich*

Author Index 283

Advances in Human Activity Recognition

Fine-Grained Human Activity Recognition Through Dead-Reckoning and Temporal Convolutional Networks

Nicolò La Porta[1,2]($\boxtimes$) (iD), Luca Minardi[2] (iD), and Michela Papandrea[2] (iD)

[1] Faculty of Informatics, Università della Svizzera Italiana, Lugano, Ticino,
Switzerland
[2] Institute of Information Systems and Networking, SUPSI, Lugano, Ticino,
Switzerland
{nicolo.laporta,luca.minardi,michela.papandrea}@supsi.ch

Abstract. Human Activity Recognition (HAR) represents an important task for many healthcare applications. From the perspective of developing patient-specific solutions, it is clear how the use of artificial intelligence enhances the potential of HAR. The present work settles its roots in the context of early-diagnosis of neurodevelopmental disorders in children (Autism Spectrum Disorder, ASD) and in the evaluation of their motor skills. In this paper, we present an artificial intelligence-based approach for fine-grained HAR which relies on dead-reckoning applied to data collected through inertial measurement units (IMUs). This approach has been applied on a dataset collected through IMU-embedded toys in order to validate its feasibility in the inference of infants' fine-grained motor skills. The proposed solution's workflow starts from the estimation of the orientation and position of solid objects through dead-reckoning exploiting Kalman filters and moves to the extraction of informative features, which are then used to feed a Temporal Convolutional Network (TCN). The achieved training average accuracy of 89% highlights how such a non-intrusive approach reaches great performances on HAR tasks, even overcoming the limitations of most of the works already present in literature, based on wearable sensors and/or computer vision techniques. The presented work and achieved results represent a solid base for IoT-based systems aiming at supporting clinicians in the early diagnosis of ASD in children.

Keywords: Human Activity Recognition · Dead-Reckoning · IMU · Deep Learning · Temporal Convolutional Networks

1 Introduction

Human Activity Recognition (HAR) is a rapidly growing field of research with applications in areas such as healthcare, sports, and security. The present work settles within the context of digital phenotyping of Autism Syndrome Disorder (ASD) [1–4] which exploits clinical research, IoT, and computer vision to analyze

O. Konak et al. (Eds.): iWOAR 2024, LNCS 15357, pp. 3–17, 2025.
https://doi.org/10.1007/978-3-031-80856-2_1

children's play behavior and the motor peculiarities related to autism syndrome from different points of view: manipulation of the toy, posture, body movement, and exploratory activity of the surroundings. Many pedagogists and psychologists recognize that play is a fundamental way of learning [5]. Many models have been proposed to describe the relationship between children's play and their development [6,7] and it has already been assessed that neuro-developmental disorders, such as ASD, affect the typical development of play behavior in children. Additionally, existing studies on children's behavior have a strong focus on children's social, emotional, and cognitive development [8], while little attention has been dedicated to the sensory-motor aspect of play [9]. In this context, our mission is to advance the SoA by simulating and studying children's play behaviors from the perspective of sensory-motor developments exploiting a non-invasive approach based on toys inertial measurements to support the early diagnosis of ASD, and to allow the anticipation of the intervention, which has been demonstrated to be more effective. From this standpoint, our current aim is to break down play behavior into sequences of fine-grained motor patterns with the intention of identifying and classifying some specific play actions or gestures. In our previous research, we investigated which play actions resulted as significant and measurable for the identification of ASD in target age of infants between 9 to 15 months [2]. The purpose of this paper is not to propose a specific methodology for ASD automatic play activity recognition but in turn we intend to demonstrate the feasibility of automatic recognition from a subset of the aforementioned actions exploiting an innovative fine-grained HAR approach. Traditional methods for HAR often rely on sensor data from wearable devices or cameras, which can be used singularly or in parallel exploiting sensor fusion techniques, although using multiple sensors adds complexity in synchronizing different sources of data. In recent years, HAR deep learning approaches have grown in interest, despite the large amounts of labeled data and high computational power required, since they outperformed old machine learning-based approaches [10–12]. The present work's operational pipeline (Sect. 2) relies on inertial data to estimate positions that an object occupies in space exploiting the dead-reckoning approach. Dead reckoning is a fundamental process in navigation where external references, such as landmarks or GPS signals are unavailable. For example, it is crucial for Unmanned Aerial Vehicles (UAVs) because it can be used as a control technique assuming the current position estimate as accurate and calculating new control signals based on this estimate relative to a desired position in situations where GPS signal is lost [13]. For HAR purposes, this approach has not been deeply investigated in literature due to its challenging and intrinsic drift over time. Drift error can occur due to various factors such as changes in the user's walking speed, turning angles, or environmental conditions. These factors can cause the inertial sensors to accumulate errors over time, leading to inaccuracies in the estimated position and ultimately affecting the accuracy of the activity recognition. To mitigate the effects of drift error, various methods have been proposed in literature. These include sensor fusion techniques that combine multiple sensor modalities such as inertial measurement systems (IMUs) and GPS or cameras, when available, to improve the accuracy of the estimation. Alternatively, Kalman filters have been proposed to model the drift error and correct it in the estimation process. An example of usage of Kalman filters for HAR purposes can be found in [14], where the authors introduced a novel algorithm based on a quaternion representation, allowing accelerometer and magnetometer data to be used in an analytically derived and optimized gradient descent algorithm to compute the direction of the gyroscope measurement error as a quaternion derivative. We embraced the latter approach focusing our study on a single IMU sensor, whose signals are filtered and processed in order to obtain relative positions to feed neural networks and perform the classification task.

Section. 2 describes in detail the workflow followed in the present study, with a comprehensive explanation of all its steps. Section 3 contains the results obtained and contextualizes them accounting also for the time-dependent nature of the signals. Finally, Sect. 4 summarizes the findings of our work, expresses the limitations encountered, and provides some insight for future studies.

1.1 State of the Art

Different approaches can be found in the literature and many of them explored HAR tasks through deep learning models. Some methods rely on image processing. For instance, Ito et al. in [15] use acceleration and gyroscope values to compute a Fast Fourier Transform obtaining images used to feed a Convolutional Neural Network to perform classification. Instead, [16] aims to provide health monitor to patients through HAR. They started from raw acceleration data and exploited continuous wavelet transform to compute 2D images used as input of a Convolutional Neural Network.

There are also deep learning approaches based on raw signals such as [17], which fed a Long Short Term Memory network with raw accelerometer data to perform classification on WISDM Lab public dataset which includes coarse-grained activities (walking, standing, and jogging). Further, [18] forewent recurrent architectures and proposed a self-attention-based network on raw accelerometer data evaluating the network on different public datasets.

Other approaches are based on object tracking aiming at predicting the 3D position of an object with time. Several works involve pedestrian tracking through IMU sensors. This scenario introduces the possibility of using algorithms exploiting the intrinsic periodical frequency of the movements. For example, Fourati et al. in [19] introduced a foot-mounted Zero Velocity Update-aided IMU filtering algorithm for indoor pedestrian tracking. This algorithm assumes that the traced object (foot) assumes periodically a static position that can be used to adjust drifting errors. Hou et al. in [20] suggested that the head is a valid alternative to place the sensor on for pedestrian tracking, in fact, they provided a specific Pedestrian Dead-Reckoning method designed for head-mounted sensors. This method belongs to the field of Step-and-Heading Systems and aims to detect each step of the pedestrian by estimating its length and direction. Finally, it integrates every step to obtain a complete trajectory.

When the problem does not involve periodical movement, sensor fusion techniques are used, combining IMU and other long-term reliable sensors. Toy et al. in [21] used an improved Dead-Reckoning localization system using IMU sensor to improve Global Navigation Satellite System-based vehicle localization when the satellite signal is denied.

Brossard et al. in [22] proposed a method to track vehicles based only on IMU sensors. They used a Kalman Filter and a neural network to dynamically adapt the noise parameter. They evaluate the method on the KITTI odometry dataset reaching performances comparable to top-ranked methods which, by contrast, use LiDAR or stereo vision. Very few works about fine-grained HAR performed through not-worn sensors can be found in literature [3, 23].

The present work is focused on the development and implementation of a dead-reckoning-based system for human activity recognition. Dead-reckoning, a technique commonly used in navigation and robotics, will be employed to estimate the orientation and position of IMU-embedded toys (a car and a ball). The inertial data will then be processed and analyzed to recognize and classify various fine-grained human activities related to the play.

The goals of this work are: i) To demonstrate a methodology which enhances the accuracy and efficiency of HAR systems, particularly in environments where traditional methods, such as GPS, may be limited or unavailable; ii) To prove the feasibility of an approach which could be applied to ASD children, that are characterized by hypersensitivity and thus intolerance to wearable sensors. Moreover, the proposed approach does not rely on any computer vision technique, thus eliminating the necessity of cameras that record the space the subject is moving into. The outcomes of this research will potentially have a significant impact on fields ranging from healthcare and fitness monitoring to augmented and virtual reality applications.

2 Methods

The workflow followed for our purpose has been divided into three major tasks:

1. Dead-reckoning, to estimate position from inertial raw data
2. Feature extraction
3. Classification through neural networks

2.1 Dead-Reckoning

In navigation, dead-reckoning is the process of estimating the position of a moving object from IMU sensor only.

Dead-reckoning is a kind of path integration: by integrating the acceleration of an object twice, its position can be obtained. IMU sensors provide angular velocity and acceleration. The latter term incorporates a constant gravity component we want to get rid of. Since we do not know gravity's components

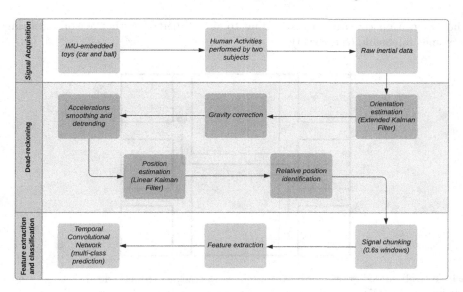

Fig. 1. Detailed workflow.

projections over the three axes of the IMU but only its magnitude, to retrieve the acceleration of the object it is necessary to find the orientation of the sensor and rotate it in the reference plane to isolate and remove gravity from the vertical axis, then rotate the sensor again and integrate the acceleration twice (see Fig. 2).

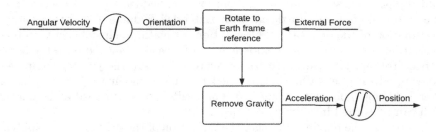

Fig. 2. Dead-reckoning pipeline: inertial measurements are integrated to obtain position and orientation [24].

Theoretically, dead-reckoning seems to work perfectly but, practically, the computation of integrals hides some challenges. In fact, the process involves three integrals: one integral for orientation estimation and two subsequent integrals for position estimation. Since the input of the integrals are sensor measurement values, the measurement error is carried into the computation and it grows in a nonlinear way. Moreover, the double integration for position estimation carries the integration constant, thus leading to signal drift. For this reason, tracking becomes infeasible (see Fig. 3).

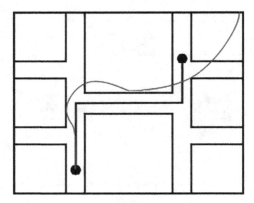

Fig. 3. Unbounded growing error on simple path tracking through dead-reckoning double integration [25].

The explored approach replaces orientation estimation with an Extended Kalman Filter and position estimation with a Linear Kalman filter. Kalman Filters are Hidden Markov Models that produce estimates of hidden and observed variables by predicting the next values merging an estimate of the following value with its effective measured value. The estimate takes into account the noise of the process and the noise in the measurement values. The dead-reckoning process takes advantage of Kalman filters by reducing its intrinsic drift error. The detailed pipeline is shown in Fig. 1. From IMU-embedded toys, raw acceleration values are collected and go through an Extended Kalman Filter that returns an estimation of the orientation. Orientation estimation helps obtain the object acceleration since the gravity component can be easily removed once the sensor has been rotated into the earth frame reference, where the gravity component is known. Then acceleration is smoothed through a moving average filter and detrended before going into a Linear Kalman Filter to obtain position estimation which can be turned into relative positions.

This part of the pipeline manages the limitation of the drift error, by applying a form of correction: every position is transformed into the relative position vector related to the previous position (see Fig. 4).

Processing is possible because the aim of the project is not tracking but activity recognition. By transforming each position into a relative position vector related to the previous position, the pipeline mitigates the effect of drift error. This approach is sufficient for activity recognition since the relative changes in position can still reflect the characteristics of different activities. Absolute position accuracy is not crucial in this context. What matters is the relative movement patterns, which can still be accurately derived despite some level of drift or position error.

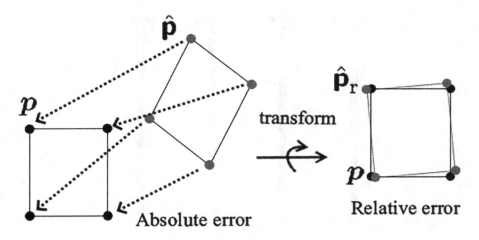

Fig. 4. Comparison of absolute and relative errors [26].

To correctly initialize the process noise covariance matrix of the Extended Kalman Filter we used the noise values along the 3-axes provided by the Shimmer3 IMU datasheet.

2.2 Features Extraction

The following step is to generate an *instantaneous displacement signal* where each sample represents the differential position with respect to the previous one. Finally, the signal is segmented into 0.6 s-long non-overlapping windows used as temporal support to build a signal representation suitable for neural networks. In particular, each window was transformed into an image in order to feed a particular type of convolutional neural network as explained in Sect. 2.3. Each image is built by stacking the three axial-vector components one upon the other (see Fig. 5).

2.3 Model Selection and Training

In [23], it was demonstrated that traditional machine learning approaches perform well on coarse-grained activity recognition but showed also a consistent performance drop when applied to fine-grained activity recognition. In this study, instead, we exploited a deep learning approach based on a Temporal Convolutional Network (TCN), a particular type of Convolutional Neural Network (CNN) that was first proposed by Lea et al. in [27] capable of capturing both spatial-temporal features like a CNN and high-level temporal information as a Recurrent Neural Network (RNN). Figure 6 presents the architecture of the model. A single TCN layer (number of filters = 108; kernel size = 6; dilations = 1,2,4 and 8; activation function = ReLU) output flows into two parallel pooling functions and then is concatenated. Batch normalization is applied and the

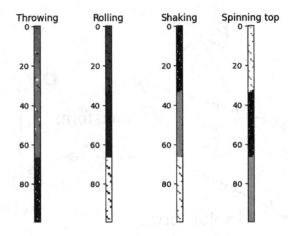

Fig. 5. Chunked signal image representation.

model is regularized through dropout. Then, there is a flattening layer and a series of dense layers until the output passes through a softmax function that returns a vector of probabilities.

The Dataset. A synthetic dataset has been collected using Shimmer3© IMU sensors by two different subjects (adults) simulating the play behavior of children with two different toys: a ball and a car. For each toy, a set of activities has been investigated (see Table 1), particularly the ones that resulted in the most frequently chosen by children in a previous study [2]. Each activity was recorded for 30 s from both subjects at a sample rate of 100 Hz. While the sensor embedded in the ball was placed inside of it, instead, the sensor embedded in the car was placed inside one of its wheels, in order to be able to differentiate among different fine-grained activities. These activities have been performed in an indoor environment.

Training Methodology. A training set (TRS) and a test set (TS) were derived from the original dataset, which was composed of 2'396 observations. In particular, TRS contained 75% of observations and TS contained the remaining 25%. In order to account for the temporal nature of the data, it was adopted a custom splitting approach which did not contemplate any shuffle of the data. It was decided to divide each window into two portions: the first one assigned to TRS and the second one assigned to TS. The network has been separately trained on the two toys using cross-entropy and ADAM as loss function and optimizer, respectively. The training has been done on 300 epochs using a batch size of 32. All the exploited hyperparameters have been properly tuned.

The code associated with this project is accessible via Zenodo at the following link: https://zenodo.org/doi/10.5281/zenodo.13623602.

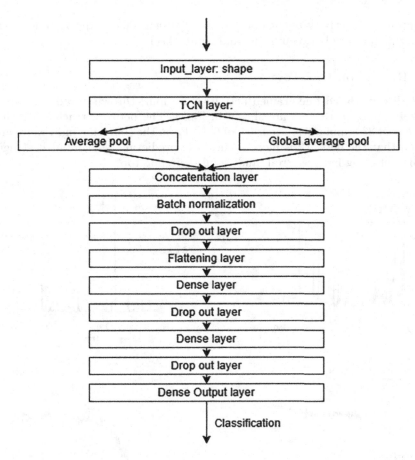

Fig. 6. TCN model architecture capable of capturing spatial-temporal features.

Table 1. Performed activities divided by toy.

Ball			
Throw	Roll	Shake	Spinning top
Car			
Flip	Slide	Hit	Spin wheels

3 Results and Discussion

3.1 Results on Car Toy

The car toy-related fine-grained activities are four: spinning wheels, knocking, flipping, and sliding (typical activities performed by Typical Development - TD and Not Typical Development - NTD children). Results are shown in Fig. 7. The network reaches a training accuracy of 89% and a test accuracy of 69%. From the confusion matrix, it can be noticed that the network is stronger in predicting 'hit' activity but it does not meet performance expectations when it has to differentiate between 'slide' and 'spin wheels'.

3.2 Results on Ball Toy

The ball toy-related fine-grained activities are four: throwing, rolling, shaking, and spinning top. Results are shown in Fig. 8. The network reaches a training accuracy of 83% and a test accuracy of 60%. From the confusion matrix, it can be noticed that the network is more accurate in predicting 'shake' but it struggles in differentiating between 'roll' and 'spin' (spinning top).

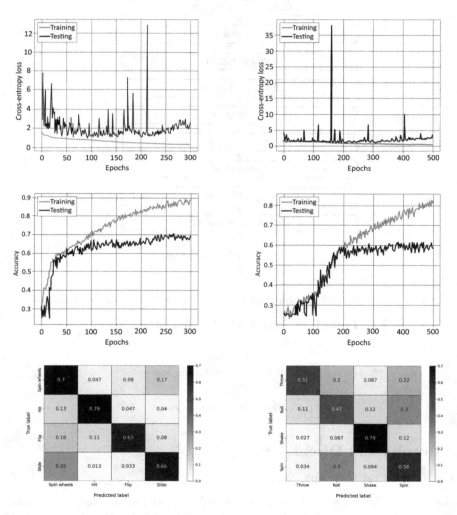

Fig. 7. Results on car toy. **TOP** Cross-entropy loss. **MIDDLE** Model accuracy. **BOTTOM** Confusion matrix.

Fig. 8. Results on ball toy. **TOP** Cross-entropy loss. **MIDDLE** Model accuracy. **BOTTOM** Confusion matrix.

As we expected, recognizing ball activities is harder than recognizing car ones because the sensor is placed inside the ball and the activities of rolling the ball and spinning the ball from the top are both based on a rotation of the toy but, while during the first the ball moves through space, instead, during the second it rotates with a fixed contact point on a surface.

3.3   Exploiting Time-Series Continuity for Predictions

The test accuracy is the canonical metric used for performance evaluation. It is the sum of all correct predictions over the total samples. Considering activities as chunks of signals completely independent from each other can be misleading because we lose the concept of temporal continuity of time series. We can exploit the intrinsic continuous nature of the signal for the prediction task. The idea is that for the ith chunk, the prediction is the most present value in a window centered over it. For instance, by taking advantage of this simple but effective technique it is possible to correct a prediction error caused by an occurrence of some activity, namely 'B', predicted within a sequence of another activity, namely 'A', in a certain period of time.

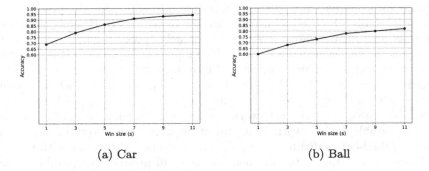

(a) Car   (b) Ball

Fig. 9. Continuity validation method. Test accuracy increases as the window size increases.

Figures 9a and 9b clarify how this simple practice significantly improves the performance of the proposed approach. On the y-axis there is the accuracy value while on the x-axis there is the window size. A window size of 1 stands for looking only at the raw predictions of the model, while the next values use the validation method explained before.

There is a positive trend in accuracy that tends to increase with the window size, in fact, the model has less possibility to return an error when it also considers the predictions in the chunk before and after the current one. This is true because the model is not random guessing. Given a certain increment in window size, the accuracy improvement resulted higher if the baseline accuracy was higher. In fact, given a window size of 3, the network trained for the car increased about 10% in test accuracy against the baseline, while the one trained on the ball increased about 8%. A window size of 3 is already promising, and larger sizes appear to be even more performant. However, longer window sizes result in higher performance only when the child engages in a specific play activity for a longer time. Such a case becomes increasingly implausible as the size of the window increases.

Summing up, it is clear how considering a wider window for activity predictions helps the proposed approach to identify the true activity in the current chunk.

4　Conclusions

The present work wants to be an alternative approach for fine-grained human activity recognition based on dead-reckoning and temporal convolutional networks. The proposed method aims to extract features from inertial data applying Kalman filter-corrected dead-reckoning and accurately classifying specific actions or gestures performed by individuals. The novelty of the present approach relies on the combination of Kalman filters and neural networks to successfully accomplish the HAR task using the former to mitigate errors and transform absolute positions into relative ones to train the latter. Moreover, for the present work the inertial dataset has been collected through smart toys (IMU-embedded toys) thus differing from many wearable-based approaches present in literature [28–30], which seem to outperform our approach reaching even more than 90% accuracy. However, this is an unfair comparison because of two main reasons: (i) many works in literature are based on non-hand-oriented activities, such as walking or going upstairs, which are intrinsically simpler to recognize with respect to the hand-oriented activities this works focuses on; (ii) the nature of data itself. In fact, wearable devices worn by a subject produce more deterministic inertial data than IMU-embedded toys since they are constrained to move with the subject himself. In layman's terms, these devices will produce comparable signals if the same activity is performed, while this assumption is not always true for IMU-embedded toys. In conclusion, our approach shows the potential of combining dead-reckoning and temporal convolutional networks for fine-grained human activity recognition in a different domain with respect to other related works. The presented approach can find many applications related to the broad spectrum of ASD. For instance, the identification of "lower-order" motor repetitions which include toys manipulation, repetitive play patterns, banging toys together, toy tranfer from one hand to the other, etc. [31,32]. From a clinical perspective, the last two belong to the milestones in children neurological development [33].

The main limitations of the presented approach rely on the reduced number of tasks analyzed, either in terms of activities and exploited toys. However, we remain confident that the present work can represent a solid base for future works in the perspective of developing IoT systems capable of supporting clinicians in the early diagnosis of ASD, and capable of distinguishing different phenotypes of autism with the intention of delivering patient-specific treatments [4]. Future works will focus on overcoming the aforementioned limitations. For instance, they could focus on further refining the dead-reckoning estimation process to reduce drift error and improve the accuracy of HAR or on training new networks for other activities in order to investigate more deeply the potentialities of this approach. Moreover, such a system could be integrated with computer vision techniques, such as the one presented in [28], in order to build multimodal diagnostic systems that provide new informative viewpoints and improve the treatment quality. The presented feasibility study assessed our methodology over data from adults, so, to further generalize it, we are currently collecting data to test the proposed pipeline over a wider and more variegated pool of subjects comprehending children with ASD.

Acknowledgements. This research is supported by the AI4Autism project (Digital Phenotyping of Autism Spectrum Disorders in children, grant agreement no. CR- SII5 202235/1) of the Sinergia interdisciplinary program of the SNSF.

Disclosure of Interests. The authors have no competing interests to declare that are relevant to the content of this article.

References

1. Faraci, F.D., et al.: AutoPlay: a smart toys-kit for an objective analysis of children ludic behavior and development. In: 2018 IEEE International Symposium on Medical Measurements and Applications (MeMeA), pp. 1–6. IEEE (2018)
2. Rossini, E., Faraci, F., Papandrea, M., Puiatti, A., Bernaschina, S., Ramelli, G.P.: AutoPlay: smart games for evolutionary screening under 14 months. In: Swiss Medical Weekly, vol. 149, p. 6S (2019)
3. Bonomi, N., Papandrea, M., et al.: Non-intrusive and privacy preserving activity recognition system for infants exploiting smart toys. In: EAI International Conference on IoT Technologies for HealthCare, pp. 3–18. Springer, Cham (2021)
4. Tafasca, S., et al.: The AI4Autism project: a multimodal and interdisciplinary approach to autism diagnosis and stratification. In: Companion Publication of the 25th International Conference on Multimodal Interaction, pp. 414–425 (2023)
5. Rodger, S., Ziviani, J.: Play-based occupational therapy. Int. J. Disabil. Dev. Educ. **46**(3), 337–365 (1999)
6. Page, J., Nutbrown, C., Clare, A.: Working with Babies and Children: From Birth to Three. Sage (2013)
7. Mulligan, S., White, B.P.: Sensory and motor behaviors of infant siblings of children with and without autism. Am. J. Occup. Ther. **66**(5), 556–566 (2012)
8. Carpenter, K.L., et al.: Digital behavioral phenotyping detects atypical pattern of facial expression in toddlers with autism. Autism Res. **14**(3), 488–499 (2021)
9. Suzuki, S., Amemiya, Y., Sato, M.: Enhancement of gross-motor action recognition for children by CNN with OpenPose. In: IECON 2019-45th Annual Conference of the IEEE Industrial Electronics Society, vol. 1, pp. 5382–5387. IEEE (2019)
10. Sharma, V., Gupta, M., Pandey, A.K., Mishra, D., Kumar, A.: A review of deep learning-based human activity recognition on benchmark video datasets. Appl. Artif. Intell. **36**(1), 2093705 (2022)

11. Gupta, S.: Deep learning based human activity recognition (HAR) using wearable sensor data. Int. J. Inf. Manag. Data Insights **1**(2), 100046 (2021)
12. Vrigkas, M., Nikou, C., Kakadiaris, I.A.: A review of human activity recognition methods. Front. Robot. AI **2**, 28 (2015)
13. Power, W., Pavlovski, M., Saranovic, D., Stojkovic, I., Obradovic, Z.: Autonomous navigation for drone swarms in GPS-denied environments using structured learning. In: Artificial Intelligence Applications and Innovations: 16th IFIP WG 12.5 International Conference, AIAI 2020, Neos Marmaras, Greece, 5–7 June 2020, Proceedings, Part II 16, pp. 219–231. Springer (2020)
14. Madgwick, S.O., Harrison, A.J., Vaidyanathan, R.: Estimation of IMU and MARG orientation using a gradient descent algorithm. In: 2011 IEEE International Conference on Rehabilitation Robotics, pp. 1–7. IEEE (2011)
15. Ito, C., Cao, X., Shuzo, M., Maeda, E.: Application of CNN for human activity recognition with FFT spectrogram of acceleration and gyro sensors. In: Proceedings of the 2018 ACM International Joint Conference and 2018 International Symposium on Pervasive and Ubiquitous Computing and Wearable Computers, pp. 1503–1510 (2018)
16. Nedorubova, A., Kadyrova, A., Khlyupin, A.: Human activity recognition using continuous wavelet transform and convolutional neural networks. arXiv preprint arXiv:2106.12666 (2021)
17. Chen, Y., Zhong, K., Zhang, J., Sun, Q., Zhao, X.: LSTM networks for mobile human activity recognition. In: 2016 International Conference on Artificial Intelligence: Technologies and Applications, pp. 50–53. Atlantis Press (2016)
18. Mahmud, S., et al.: Human activity recognition from wearable sensor data using self-attention. arXiv preprint arXiv:2003.09018 (2020)
19. Fourati, H., Manamanni, N., Afilal, L., Handrich, Y.: Position estimation approach by complementary filter-aided IMU for indoor environment. In: 2013 European Control Conference (ECC), pp. 4208–4213. IEEE (2013)
20. Hou, X., Bergmann, J.: A pedestrian dead reckoning method for head-mounted sensors. Sensors **20**(21), 6349 (2020)
21. Toy, I., Durdu, A., Yusefi, A.: Improved dead reckoning localization using IMU sensor. In: 2022 International Symposium on Electronics and Telecommunications (ISETC), pp. 1–5. IEEE (2022)
22. Brossard, M., Barrau, A., Bonnabel, S.: AI-IMU dead-reckoning. IEEE Trans. Intell. Veh. **5**(4), 585–595 (2020)
23. Pandurangan, S., Papandrea, M., Gelsomini, M.: Fine-grained human activity recognition - a new paradigm. In: Proceedings of the 7th International Workshop on Sensor-based Activity Recognition and Artificial Intelligence (2022)
24. Huang, C.J., Chi, C.J., Hung, W.T.: Hybrid-AI-based iBeacon indoor positioning cybersecurity: attacks and defenses. Sensors **23**(4), 2159 (2023)
25. Fallah, N., Apostolopoulos, I., Bekris, K., Folmer, E.: The user as a sensor: navigating users with visual impairments in indoor spaces using tactile landmarks. In: Proceedings of the SIGCHI Conference on Human Factors in Computing Systems, pp. 425–432 (2012)
26. Liu, Y., Wang, Y., Wang, J., Shen, Y.: Distributed 3D relative localization of UAVs. IEEE Trans. Veh. Technol. **69**(10), 11756–11770 (2020)
27. Lea, C., Flynn, M.D., Vidal, R., Reiter, A., Hager, G.D.: Temporal convolutional networks for action segmentation and detection. In: Proceedings of the IEEE Conference on Computer Vision and Pattern Recognition, pp. 156–165 (2017)

28. Kulsoom, F., Narejo, S., Mehmood, Z., Chaudhry, H.N., Butt, A., Bashir, A.K.: A review of machine learning-based human activity recognition for diverse applications. Neural Comput. Appl. **34**(21), 18289–18324 (2022)
29. Hou, C.: A study on IMU-based human activity recognition using deep learning and traditional machine learning. In: 2020 5th International Conference on Computer and Communication Systems (ICCCS), pp. 225–234. IEEE (2020)
30. Zhuang, W., Chen, Y., Su, J., Wang, B., Gao, C.: Design of human activity recognition algorithms based on a single wearable IMU sensor. Int. J. Sens. Netw. **30**(3), 193–206 (2019)
31. Caldwell-Harris, C.L.: An explanation for repetitive motor behaviors in autism: facilitating inventions via trial-and-error discovery. Front. Psych. **12**, 657774 (2021)
32. Tian, J., Gao, X., Yang, L.: Repetitive restricted behaviors in autism spectrum disorder: from mechanism to development of therapeutics. Front. Neurosci. **16**, 780407 (2022)
33. Dosman, C.F., Andrews, D., Goulden, K.J.: Evidence-based milestone ages as a framework for developmental surveillance. Paediatrics Child Health **17**(10), 561–568 (2012)

Comparison of Deep Learning and Machine Learning Approaches for the Recognition of Dynamic Activities of Daily Living

Cassandra Krause, Lena Harkämper, Gabriela Ciortuz$^{(\boxtimes)}$ ⓘ, and Sebastian Fudickar ⓘ

Institute of Medical Informatics, University of Lübeck, Lübeck, Germany
{gabriela.ciortuz,sebastian.fudickar}@uni-luebeck.de

Abstract. As a consequence of demographic shifts, the proportion of the older population is growing at an accelerated pace, resulting in a notable decline in cognitive and motor functions. This study examines the potential of wearables to monitor activities of daily living (ADL) and identify changes in behavior, thereby enabling early intervention to maintain the independence of the person. Eight dynamic ADLs were analyzed using data collected from eight subjects who were wearing a sensor belt that includes an accelerator and a gyroscope. The data were preprocessed and employed to train and evaluate two distinct types of classifiers: a deep learning and several machine learning approaches. Two data splits were considered: a subject-dependent model, which utilized data from all subjects for training and testing, and a Leave-One-Subject-Out Cross-Validation (LOSO-CV) subject-independent model, which excluded one subject from the training set for validation. The subject-dependent approach yielded high accuracies of 99.5% and 99.8% for the classification network and the best support vector machine, respectively. The LOSO-CV yielded accuracies of 77.8% for the convolutional neural network and 77.6% for the best support vector machine. While the classification network demonstrated marginally superior results, the support vector machine required significantly less training time, suggesting its potential suitability for practical applications.

Keywords: human activity recognition · machine learning · feature extraction · feature learning · convolutional neural network · support vector machine · activities of daily living

1 Introduction

As a consequence of demographic change, the number of older people is rising rapidly. In old age, individuals experience a decline in cognitive abilities and, most notably, in motor functions. To assess physical decline, the activities of daily living (ADL) are frequently evaluated through the administration of a

---

C. Krause and L. Harkämper—Both authors contributed equally to this research.

© The Author(s), under exclusive license to Springer Nature Switzerland AG 2025
O. Konak et al. (Eds.): iWOAR 2024, LNCS 15357, pp. 18–39, 2025.
https://doi.org/10.1007/978-3-031-80856-2_2

questionnaire. However, this approach often results in a considerable degree of measurement noise, as self-perception frequently differs from the actual measured reality. It would be more prudent to assess the ADL over an extended period to identify changes and implement preventative measures to delay dependence. Technical assistance would be beneficial, as the scarcity of medical professionals necessitates that such assessments be conducted independently to alleviate the burden on them [12]. Additionally, individuals exhibit disparate behaviors in their own homes than under the supervision of a medical professional. Therefore, it may be advantageous to implement home access systems or to use wearables to facilitate continuous monitoring [7,21].

This study examines the potential for measuring ADL using wearable technology. For this purpose, we self-designed and implemented all the steps of a Human Activity Recognition (HAR) system. The study design is depicted in Fig. 1. Once the research question was defined, eight dynamic ADLs were selected for analysis. Dynamic movements, such as walking or jogging, exhibit variations over time, while static activities like sitting or lying down produce relatively constant readings. We decided to incorporate dynamic activities - even activities that require higher levels of physical engagement, like jogging or jumping - into our analysis, in order to enable the identification of subtle behavioral changes at an early stage. Detecting these changes early, while the individual is still capable of performing such activities, allows for timely interventions. Interventions, such as targeted exercise and training, can help to extend the period during which the person remains physically active and dynamic, thereby maintaining their independence for a longer time. Studies have shown that especially jumping, which is a rebound exercise, improved the Timed-Up and Go (TUG) test results in the rebound group twice compared to the control group [20]. This significant reduction in TUG test times not only indicates an improved ability to stand up from a chair more quickly, walk faster with better balance, turn more efficiently, and sit down with greater control without assistance, but also underscores the importance of jumping in assessing functionality in older adults. Jumping challenges and enhances coordination, strength, and balance, which are critical components for maintaining independence and reducing the risk of falls in this population [19]. Our approach aims to recognize eight dynamic activities in order to address emerging issues before they significantly impact the person's daily life.

The activities were performed and recorded in a separate data set of eight test subjects. A sensor belt was employed to quantify acceleration and rotation. Following the preprocessing of the recorded data, two types of classifiers were analyzed: a deep learning approach (DL) and a machine-learning (ML) approach. In addition, two data splits were analyzed: a person-specific approach, in which the data from all subjects is used for training, and a LOSO-CV to ascertain whether the data from an unknown subject can be robustly classified. In order to facilitate the testing phase, the data pertaining to a single subject was excluded from the training set. These approaches are then compared with each other and the reasons for any misclassifications are explained.

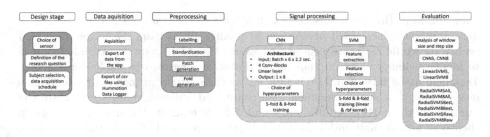

Fig. 1. Study design. The single steps of the study are presented, starting with the design stage, followed by the data acquisition, preprocessing and signal processing of the data. In the end, the evaluation steps are presented.

2   Related Work

In this section, we discuss the most common design choices of HAR system components for healthcare in existing work. HAR systems can be categorized based on the data acquisition tools used, classification methods employed and the complexity of the activities being analyzed [24]. We will briefly cover these aspects in the following paragraphs.

In terms of the acquisition tools, especially for healthcare applications such as activity monitoring of elderly people, wearable devices are preferred over cameras because of privacy concerns and because they satisfy the long-term usability of a monitored environment [15, 24].

Inertial sensor-based systems that employ accelerometers, gyroscopes and magnetometers can be easily integrated into wearable devices, which can be used to record movements on various body sites at the same time. However, the inconvenience and intrusiveness of wearing numerous devices can impose additional burdens on users, thus many studies prefer to use only one sensor, such as smartphones, which have become indispensable in people's everyday lives [8]. The authors in [14] proposed using one Inertial Measurement Unit (IMU) integrated into a belt to ensure effortless use and discreet sensor placement, particularly to allow an easy process of future self-assessments at home. The employed sensor must have the ability to model the motion information of the activities of interest so that it will be able to classify it [24].

Defining activities of interest depends on the target application or desired health-related outcome [6]. The authors in [13] proposed six activities - sitting, standing, walking, laying, going up and going downstairs, for elderly patients' monitoring of their general health status and dynamism. In contrast, we decided to use only dynamic activities, and not consider pose-related activities in our models.

Depending on the nature of the activity being analyzed - e.g. simple or complex actions, poses, locomotion patterns or ADLs - as well as the amount of training data available, various machine-learning models can be used for accurate activity recognition [17].

Traditional ML approaches like SVMs, decision trees and KNNs performed well across many HAR application areas [17] but require feature engineering to execute optimally [24].

Especially SVMs have been shown in [3,17] to perform well with data of unknown distribution and once its decision boundary is established, SVM proves to be a robust classifier and scales effectively for high-dimensional data. These facts motivated our decision to use the SVM in our research as the traditional ML approach of choice.

Traditional ML methods are increasingly outperformed by deep neural networks (DNNs), particularly in their ability to learn complex representations from multidimensional data [9].

Deep learning is the second big approach for HAR after traditional ML using handcrafted features but requires a substantial amount of training data to learn intricate features effectively. DL is an evolution of ML in that it uses deeper networks to autonomously learn and recognize more complex and hierarchical patters in large amounts of data without the need for manual feature extraction. Deep Artificial Neural Networks (ANNs) emulate the human neural system, with the primary goal of extracting non-linear relationships from data for classification, thus automatically extracting and learning the features instead of manually engineering and selecting them [10].

Convolutional Neural Networks (CNN) are powerful neural networks in image processing tasks using convolutions to learn representative spatial features [4]. CNNs perform well in recognizing locomotion activities like walking, cycling, sitting, or standing, but more complex activities made up of multiple simpler activities would require more specialized models like recurrent neural networks (RNNs) or hybrid architectures [2].

Since the collected dynamic activities are not very complex, and because CNNs have been shown to work well and converge faster on multidimensional time-series data when compared with RNNs [3], a CNN is selected as the deep learning model for the subsequent study.

3 Methods

In the following, the underlying methods of this study will be outlined. First, the recorded dataset will be presented. Subsequently, the deep learning and machine-learning approaches employed are outlined, along with a description of the experiments conducted.

3.1 Dataset

This study aims to examine the potential of deep learning and machine learning classifiers for the activities of daily living. To attain this objective, this eight dynamic activities were selected:

- Bend
- Walk
- Jump
- Jog
- Rotate left
- Rotate right
- Walking up the stairs
- Walking down the stairs

In this research, a self-acquired data set is employed. To attain this objective, we employed the SmarTracks Sensor DX5.0 Timing in conjunction with the TB40 belt. The data is recorded via an Android smartphone using the Smart Run app [16]. The Smart Run app paired with a SmarTracks DX5.0 sensor provides real-time timing results, which are streamed directly to your smartphone. The app also provides a way of exporting the raw data recorded with the Smar-Tracks Sensor, which we have used for our study. All subjects were introduced to the functionality of the device and were permitted to initiate and terminate the measurements independently. The smartphone was retained on the body throughout the recording period to ensure continuous connectivity with the sensor. The DX5.0 Timing comprises three sensors: a three-axis accelerometer, a three-axis gyroscope and a three-axis magnetometer. Each of the sensors was initiated with a sampling rate of 250 Hz. Eight subjects, designated S_i with $i \in \{1, 2, 3, 4, 5, 6, 7, 8\}$, were included in the study. In order to obtain standardized measurements, it is essential that the placement of the sensor belt and the position of the sensor unit remain consistent across all subjects. The belt was secured around the waist, between the L3 and L5 lumbar vertebral bodies, in accordance with the methodology described by Hellmers et al. [14]. Four of the test subjects were female, and four were male. The mean age of the subjects was 24.5 years, with a standard deviation of 3.2 years. The mean height was 1.71 m, with a standard deviation of 0.07 m. The cohort thus represents a targeted area of the population from 21 to 27 years.

Each subject was required to conduct each of the eight activities continuously for approximately two minutes, with the aim of achieving a balanced distribution of the activities. In order to facilitate subsequent data labelling, only the described dynamic activities were recorded, without transitions between different exercises. This approach enabled the assignment of one label to each whole measurement, alleviating the subsequent analysis.

As the accelerometer and gyroscope are capable of displaying movements with a high degree of precision, the magnetometer measurements were excluded from the subsequent discussion to avoid calibration and interference problems and to reduce the dimensionality of the data as it is also done in the experiments of Pesenti et al. [22]. As the test subjects conducted the measurements independently and there was a brief interval between the start of the measurement and the start of the activity, the initial and last five seconds of the individual measurements were excluded as the initial step in the preprocessing procedure. This was due to the fact that the subjects frequently placed the smartphone in their trouser pockets after initiating the recording process, allowing them to perform the desired movements with their hands free. For the two stair-climbing activities, the window was set to 2.5 s. This ensured that only the movement itself was presented in the data, as it was observed during the data recording that the subjects started to climb the stairs at a considerably faster pace than the planned five seconds.

The subsequent step involved standardizing the data across the three axes of the accelerometer and gyroscope, by using z-normalization, which is a standard preprocessing technique that can significantly enhance the learning capabilities of deep neural networks and also removes certain types of bias effects [1,5]. Consequently, the mean and standard deviation were calculated for all subjects. Afterwards, a windowing operation was performed in order to augment the data. After performing a search to find the optimal window and stride sizes, the width of the window was set to 2.2 s, while the stride was set to 0.1 s. The process of finding the optimal window and stride sizes is described in Sect. 3.4. The data after each preprocessing step is shown in Fig. 2.

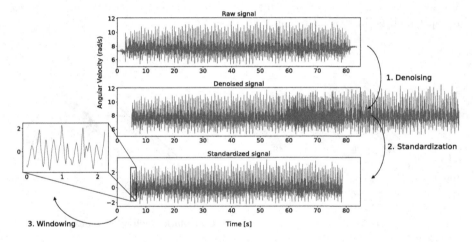

Fig. 2. Preprocessing pipeline of the data. A measurement of the gyroscope of the x-axis of subject S_1 of the activity *Walk* is shown. The data is visualized after each preprocessing step: after the denoising and the standardization (z-normalization).

Given the specified window length of 2.2 s and stride of 0.1 s, the resulting number of segments over all subjects amounts to 64164. The exact number of data, dependent on subject and activity, can be found in Table 1. The table shows that the segments of the classes *Walking up the stairs* and *Walking down the stairs* are significantly fewer than those of the other classes. This results in class imbalance due to the fact that the stair which was used is not particularly long, with each recording therefore being approximately ten to fifteen seconds in length. Furthermore, the first and last seconds of each recording have been omitted, which has also resulted in a reduction in the number of segments.

Table 1. A summary of the segments recorded per subject and activity, with a window length of 2.2 s and a stride of 0.1 s.

Subject	Activity							
	Bend	Walk	Jump	Jog	Rotate left	Rotate right	Walking up the stairs	Walking down the stairs
S_1	1173	1090	1119	920	946	1173	364	284
S_2	1119	1441	1115	898	1062	1124	847	781
S_3	1222	1427	1211	1020	1179	1173	989	751
S_4	1312	1086	1165	960	1116	1169	921	891
S_5	1169	1020	1234	1039	1211	1192	871	770
S_6	1180	1312	1169	1079	1188	1161	860	767
S_7	1103	1035	1161	1073	1138	1146	444	305
S_8	1222	822	1119	701	1010	756	476	383
Total	9500	9233	9293	7690	8850	8894	5772	4932

3.2 Classification Network

The deep learning approach utilizes a similar architecture to the one proposed in [23], which is illustrated in Fig. 3.

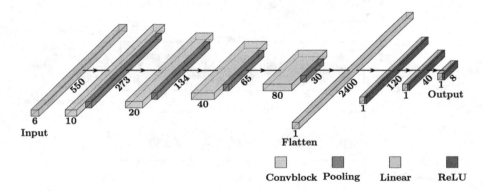

Fig. 3. Architecture of the proposed classification network. Four Conv-Blocks followed by max-pooling layers are used for feature extraction. Three fully-connected layers are used to obtain the output size of eight in order to represent the class probabilities of the activities.

The classification network receives a tensor of the shape $(B \times C \times N)$ as input, where B represents the batch size, C the number of channels and N the length of the sequence. Given that the input comprises patches of 2.2 s from three axes of the accelerometer and the gyroscope, the dimensions of the input tensor are $C = 6$ and $N = 550$. The classification network consists of four Conv-Blocks. Each Conv-Block comprises a convolutional layer, which doubles the dimensions, followed by a batch normalization and a rectified linear unit (ReLU) activation. A second convolutional block, comprising a convolutional layer, batch normalization and ReLU activation, is then applied, maintaining the number of channels. The Conv-Block is shown in Fig. 4.

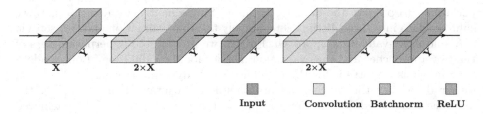

Fig. 4. Architecture of the proposed Conv-Block. The feature size is first doubled by a convolution, followed by a batch normalization and an activation layer. A second block of convolution, normalization and activation is applied, keeping the feature size.

Following each convolutional block, the dimensions are reduced by a factor of 50% through a max-pooling operation. Subsequently, the feature maps resulting from the final Conv-Block are flattened and fed through three linear layers, with the objective of achieving an output size of eight, which defines the probability for each activity class.

3.3   Support Vector Machine

In the ML approach, a support vector machine (SVM) was employed. As no features are learned automatically in this context, we utilize handcrafted features from the preprocessed segments that are suitable for IMU data [25]. Therefore, the following time-domain features are included:

- Minimum (Min)
- Maximum (Max)
- Arithmetic Mean (Mean)
- Standard deviation (SD)
- Variance (Var)
- Zero crossing rate (ZCR)
- Mean crossing rate (MCR)
- Positive peak count (PPK)
- Negative peak count (NPK)

In addition to a linear kernel, a Gaussian radial basis function (RBF) kernel is also analyzed. Given that this is a multi-class problem, the 'one versus rest' separation is employed.

3.4   Experiments

We describe our experiments in the following section as follows:

First, we present the search for the best stride and window length, which was performed to prepare the data for training. Subsequently, we describe how we split the data into three distinct sets, namely training, validation and test set, via a K-fold cross-validation approach. Finally, we provide the hyperparameters of the two approaches and the evaluation metrics for the validation of our models.

Since it is important for the classification of dynamic movements based on sensor data that the movements are completely contained in a window, the analysis of the window size is of great importance. Hellmers et al. [14] achieved the best results with a window length of 1.853 and a stride of 0.249 for dynamic activities. Therefore, we chose a range around these values to find out the best window length and step size for our recorded activities. For this purpose, we trained the CNN on a fold with 20 different window sizes ranging from 0.4 to 2.3 s with a fixed stride of 0.25 s and calculated the accuracy in each case to get the range of the sufficient window length. In the second step, a cross-analysis of window length between 1.8 and 2.2 and strides between 0.1 and 0.3 is conducted in order to identify the optimal pair of values. These are then employed in the subsequent analysis of all approaches, since related work has shown that the window and step sizes found for specific activities are optimal irrespective of the classification method [11].

Both the CNN and the SVM approach are validated through a K-fold cross-validation. First, a 5-fold validation is performed. For this purpose, the data of the individual activities is mixed across all subjects and equally distributed so that each task is presented with the same frequency in each fold. For the validation set, 10% of the training data was used at random. This resulted in an average training set of 46,200 segments, a validation set of 5,134 segments, and a test set of 12,830 segments. This approach may be beneficial in the context of subject-specific systems, which involve the adaptation of a classifier to a known set of subjects. In order to assess the generalizability of the classifiers on data from a subject, of which there is no previous knowledge in the training, an 8-fold cross-validation was also analyzed. In this case, one subject was excluded from the training set and used for testing across all activities. This resulted in the use of seven subjects for training purposes and one subject for testing. Additionally, 10% of the training data was randomly selected for validation, resulting in the following average quantities: A total of 51385 segments were used for training, 5710 for validation and 7069 for testing.

The classification network was trained for 200 epochs, with an early stopping mechanism built in to terminate the training if the validation loss did not improve for 10 epochs. Additionally, a batch size of 16 was selected. The Adam optimizer was used to optimize the weights with an initial learning rate of 0.001. A learning rate scheduler was applied, which reduces the learning rate by 0.1 every 20 epochs. The cross-entropy loss function was employed to quantify the error. Given that the classes are not balanced, it is necessary to address this issue in the classifiers. Therefore, the weights were assigned to the classes according to their probability of occurrence. The weights of the optimal network were utilized for the analysis of the test data set. In the following, the classification network with the 5-fold cross-validation will be referred to as *CNN5* whereas the one with the 8-fold cross-validation will be referred to as *CNN8*.

In order to identify the optimal features for the SVM, a random feature elimination (RFE) was employed. This involves training the SVM on the initial feature set and recursively considering an ever smaller feature set until only one feature remains, resulting in a ranking of the features. The lower the ranking, the more important the feature is, so the features with the lowest rankings are the ones that are selected. It is also necessary to address the issue of class imbalance in the SVMs. So the SVM with linear kernel was trained with weights automatically set inversely proportional to the class frequencies, thus compensating for any imbalance in the classes. The maximum number of iterations was set to 50,000. The dual parameter was set to false, as a greater number of segments were designated as features. A grid search was conducted to identify the optimal values for parameters C and *tol*. This resulted in a C of 10 and a *tol* of 1e-05 for the linear kernel. For the SVM with the RBF kernel, the automatic balancing of the classes was also applied, and a maximum number of iterations of 50,000 was selected. The gamma parameter was set to scale, and the C and *tol* parameters were also determined here using the grid search method. In the following, the SVM trained with the linear kernel on the best features resulting from the RFE with a 5-fold or an 8-fold cross-validation is labelled with *LinearSVM5* and *LinearSVM8* respectively. The SVM with the RBF kernel is trained with the raw data (*RadialSVM5Raw* and *RadialSVM8Raw*), on all hand-crafted features (*RadialSVM5All* and *RadialSVM8All*) and also on the best features (*RadialSVM5Best* and *RadialSVM8Best*) for the 5-fold and 8-fold cross-validation.

To validate the test dataset for both the CNN and the SVM, a confusion matrix was constructed based on the predictions and the ground truth. The following metrics are employed to assess the performance of the classifiers: accuracy, macro F1-score, precision and recall.

4   Results

This section provides the analysis results of the optimal window and stride selection and of the optimal feature selection using RFE. In addition, the results for the metrics accuracy, macro F1-score, precision and recall of the approaches *CNN5*, *CNN8*, *LinearSVM5*, *LinearSVM8*, *RadialSVM5All*, *RadialSVM8All*, *RadialSVM5Best*, *RadialSVM8Best*, *RadialSVM5Raw* and *RadialSVM8Raw* are shown.

4.1   Window and Stride

The results of the window length and stride analysis are presented in Fig. 5.

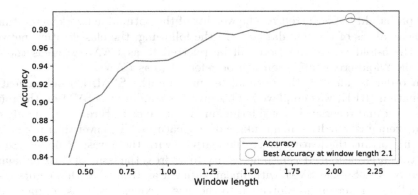

Fig. 5. Analysis of the optimal window length. The best accuracy was reached with a window length of 2.1 s (yellow circle).

It can be observed in Fig. 5 that the accuracy improves as the window length increases. When recording the data for the activity *Jump*, there were often small pauses between the jumps, which means that the required window must be large enough to cover the entire motion. The best accuracy values are between 1.8 and 2.2 s, so these values were used in the next step for a cross-analysis with the stride.

The results of the cross-analysis are presented in Fig. 6. The x-axis initially displays a fixed window length, after which the three strides between 0.1 and 0.3 are presented. It can be observed that the accuracy is highest for the smallest stride of 0.1, which yields the greatest amount of data, and then declines as the stride increases. The highest accuracy is achieved with a window length of 2.2 s and a stride of 0.1 s. These values will be used for all the approaches in the following.

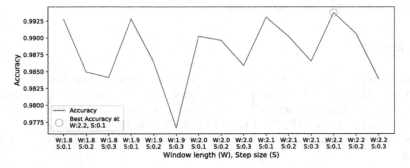

Fig. 6. Cross analysis of window length and stride. The x-axis first displays a fixed window length W, followed by three strides S from 0.1 to 0.3. The highest accuracy is achieved with $W = 2.2$ and $S = 0.1$.

4.2 CNN

The CNN was trained using K-fold cross-validation with $K = 5$ (CNN5) and $K = 8$ (CNN8). Table 2 shows the results of the metrics of CNN5 per fold, as well as the results averaged over all folds.

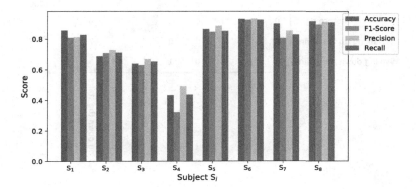

Fig. 7. Subject-wise scores for accuracy, macro F1-score, precision and recall of CNN8. Subject S_4 achieved notably lower scores.

Table 2. CNN 5-Fold comparison in terms of different metrics.

Fold	Accuracy	F1-Score	Precision	Recall
1	**0.996**	**0.996**	**0.996**	**0.996**
2	**0.996**	**0.996**	0.995	**0.996**
3	0.995	0.994	0.994	0.994
4	0.995	0.993	0.994	0.993
5	0.994	0.994	0.994	0.993
Average	0.995	0.994	0.994	0.994

Figure 8 shows that the tasks can be separated very well and there are only few misclassifications.

To show the extent to which the CNN generalizes even with a LOSO-CV approach of a subject, Fig. 7 displays the scores of the 8-fold for accuracy, macro F1-score, Review 1: Use consistent capitalization and recall. It can be observed that subject S_4 achieved notably lower scores compared to the other subjects. The scores of subjects S_2 and S_3 are also well below average.

As illustrated in Fig. 9, a diagonal can still be discerned in the confusion matrix, although there is a significant increase in misclassifications. It is noteworthy that a considerable number of tasks have been identified as *Walk*. Other

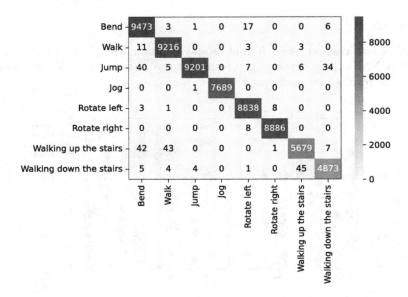

Fig. 8. Confusion matrix of CNN5. Only a few misclassifications have occurred.

common errors in classification included the misclassification of *Walk* as *Walking up the stairs* and *Jump* as *Walking down the stairs*. Furthermore, the activity *Jog* was often misclassified as *Jump*, and the activity *Rotate* was frequently misclassified as *Bend*.

In order to ascertain which activities can be classified as particularly well or poorly, Fig. 10 illustrates the accuracy for each activity. It can be observed that specific movements, such as *Bend* or *Rotate*, which differ significantly from the others in terms of execution, can be classified with the greatest accuracy. The activity *Walk* is the least well-recognized.

Table 3. Comparison of the average values of CNN5 and CNN8 in terms of different metrics

Model	Accuracy	macro F1-score	Precision	Recall
CNN5	0.995	0.995	0.995	0.994
CNN8	0.778	0.743	0.786	0.786

Table 3 shows the comparison of the average values of *CNN5* and *CNN8* in terms of different metrics. *CNN5* demonstrates superior performance, as the data exhibits greater variability across the folds.

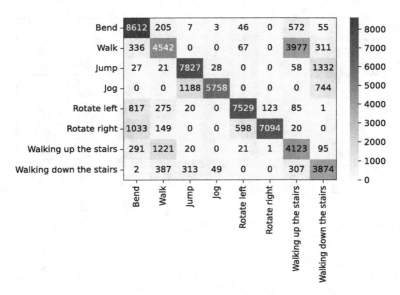

Fig. 9. Confusion matrix of CNN8.

4.3   SVM

The results of the optimal feature selection using RFE are shown in Fig. 11. The features comprise the nine statistical values for the six channels, resulting in a total of 54 features. The figure displays the summed ranks of the six channels for the respective statistical values. The lower the rank, the more important the feature is. Therefore, the mean crossing rate was identified as the most important feature, and the top five features were selected for further experimentation: mean crossing rate, zero crossing rate, standard deviation, mean and variance.

Table 4 presents the averaged results of the SVM models. In a manner analogous to that observed in the case of *CNN5* and *CNN8*, the outcomes of the 5-fold models are significantly better than those of the 8-fold models. In the 5-fold cross-validation, *RadialSVM5All* achieved the most favorable results, closely followed by *RadialSVM5Best*. In the LOSO-CV, *RadialSVM8Best* achieved the highest scores.

Figure 12 illustrates the accuracy of *RadialSVM8Best* task-wise. This analysis allows us to identify which activities may be classified more or less effectively. In comparison to *CNN8* (see Fig. 10), the results are notably more balanced; however, *Walk* is also the activity that is classified with the greatest difficulty. This phenomenon can also be observed in the confusion matrix of *RadialSVM8Best* in Fig. 13. Here, the activity *Walk* was most frequently classified as *Walking down the stairs* too; other misclassifications were similar to those observed in the *CNN8*.

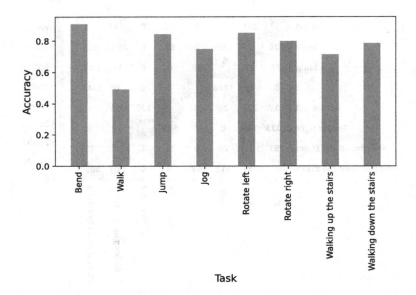

Fig. 10. Task-wise accuracy of CNN8.

5 Discussion

The objective of this study was to investigate the classification of activities of daily living based on self-recorded sensor data from a non-intrusive and easy-to-use sensor belt using a deep learning approach and a machine learning approach. Similarly to [15], we observed that our approach to recognize activities via a single inertial sensor worn at the waist, is both easily applicable and well-suited for recordings in a home environment.

One limitation in our study is related to the generalizability of our models, which were trained predominantly on data from younger individuals. Consequently, these models may not perform optimally when applied to elderly pop-

Table 4. SVM metrics

Model	Accuracy	F1-Score	Precision	Recall
LinearSVM5	0.983	0.980	0.980	0.979
RadialSVM5All	0.992	**0.991**	**0.991**	**0.992**
RadialSVM5Best	**0.998**	0.975	0.976	0.975
RadialSVM5Raw	0.985	0.983	0.983	0.983
LinearSVM8	0.771	0.728	0.769	0.759
RadialSVM8All	0.763	0.728	**0.788**	0.755
RadialSVM8Best	**0.776**	**0.731**	0.771	**0.766**
RadialSVM8Raw	0.699	0.653	0.695	0.700

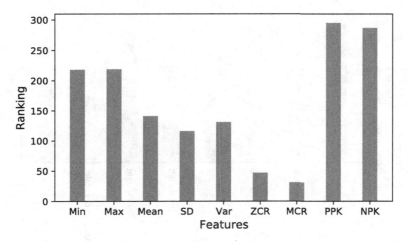

Fig. 11. Ranking of relevance of the handcrafted statistical features. The ranking was calculated using RFE. Lower rankings indicate a higher relevance.

ulations, as highlighted in [13,18]. To address this limitation we plan to include more diverse training data, particularly varying in age and mobility in the future. Still, our study serves as a foundational investigation, demonstrating the effectiveness of using a single sensor belt for activity recognition. This approach is promising and warrants further exploration with datasets specifically collected from elderly participants.

Both a person-specific system analysis and a LOSO-CV were conducted. In the person-specific system analysis, data from all test subjects was used for testing, while in the LOSO-CV, data from one test subject was used for testing. The following section will present a comparison between the deep learning approach and the machine learning approach. Subsequently, the misclassifications are analyzed.

5.1   Comparison of SVM and CNN

Table 5. CNN vs SVM

Model	Accuracy	F1-Score	Precision	Recall
CNN8	**0.778**	**0.743**	**0.786**	**0.768**
RadialSVM8Best	0.776	0.731	0.771	0.766

The results show that the 5-fold approaches, where all subjects were included in the training- and test data, yielded highly accurate results, with an average accuracy of 99.5% for the classification network and 98.95% for all SVM approaches. Only a few misclassifications were observed.

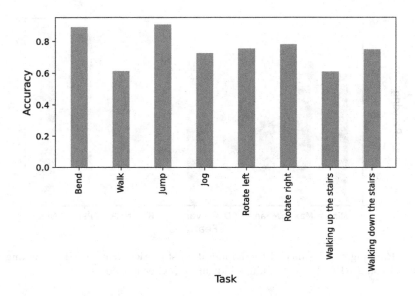

Fig. 12. Task-wise accuracy of RadialSVM8Best.

Table 5 presents a comparative analysis of the DL approach and the ML approach, demonstrating the performance of *CNN8* and *RadialSVM8Best* in terms of accuracy, macro F1-score, precision and recall. In contrast, *CNN8* demonstrates slightly superior performance, yet the SVM necessitates considerably less training time. Specifically, a single fold requires only a few minutes with the SVM, whereas the CNN requires approximately two hours for the same task.

The results of the LOSO-CV are presented in Fig. 15. A comparable trend can be observed in the case of subjects presenting a greater difficulty level (outliers), resulting in similar levels of inaccuracy across the board (subjects S_2, S_3 and S_4). Similarly, subjects S_6, S_7 and S_8 demonstrate the most favorable outcomes with both approaches.

Figure 14 illustrates the receiver operating characteristic (ROC) curve for both approaches in the optimal fold. The ROC curves of the individual activities for the *RadialSVM8Best* are displayed in the upper diagram, and those of the *CNN8* are displayed on the bottom. It is evident that the SVM curves are of a high quality, whereas the CNN curves demonstrate lower performance, particularly for the classes *Walk* (AUC of 0.79) and *Walking down the stairs* (AUC of 0.55). This is attributed to the presence of issues between the classes. Furthermore, the CNN exhibits superior results for the remaining folds in comparison to the SVM, suggesting that it may also be an outlier for this fold.

Nevertheless, the difference between the CNN and the SVM in the third decimal place is marginal, which is why they can be regarded as equally good. This can be attributed to the fact that the training set may not yet be sufficiently comprehensive for a DL approach, resulting in comparable performance

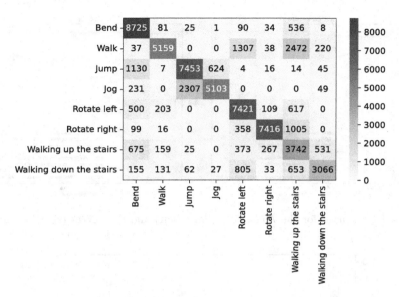

Fig. 13. Confusion Matrix of RadialSVM8Best.

between traditional and DL methods, which may be preferable in certain circumstances. These findings are consistent with the results of related studies that have employed a similar analytical approach.

This study did not examine more sophisticated DL architectures that are well-suited for temporal data. This may also be a reason why a traditional DL network is inadequate for processing this data.

5.2   Misclassifications

The two approaches (CNN and SVM) were trained with K-fold cross-validation, with $K = 5$ and $K = 8$, respectively. At $K = 5$, all subjects were distributed evenly across the folds, resulting in the absence of outliers. This explains the high scores and the low rate of misclassification.

In the LOSO-CV, one subject is omitted from training in each repetition, and the classifier is then tested on this subject. Consequently, it is possible to identify significantly larger differences between the folds. In particular, subject S_4 exhibits a notably low level of accuracy when classified with the CNN (see Fig. 7. It was apparent from the outset of the data acquisition process that subject three displayed a markedly unusual range of movements. These included a tendency to walk or run upstairs with a pronounced strolling gait, as well as a pronounced lateral movement when rotating. Consequently, his data exhibited a notable divergence from the mean, rendering him an outlier within the data set. This could be a potential explanation for the observed lower scores.

All experiments employing the LOSO-CV methodology demonstrate comparable misclassifications of movements. The frequent misclassification of the

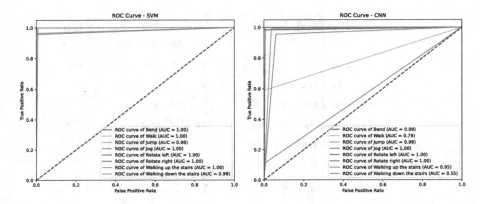

Fig. 14. ROC curves for the *RadialSVM8Best* (left) and the *CNN8* (right) of Subject S_7.

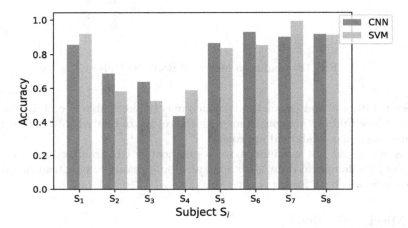

Fig. 15. Subject-wise accuracy of CNN8 and RadialSVM8Best. Subjects S_2 and S_3 and S_3 achieve the lowest accuracy.

activity *Walk* as a separate movement is likely due to the fact that this movement is often part of other activities, such as *Walking down the stairs* or *Walking up the stairs*. As a consequence of its inclusion in almost all other movements, it is arguably the most challenging to distinguish from the others.

The classification of *Walk* as *Walking up the stairs* was likely due to the presence of a plateau on the stairs and subjects' slow pace of ascent. Furthermore, the classification of *Jump* as *Walking down the stairs* was based on the observation of a similar acceleration on the z-axis and a gait that resembled jumping. Similarly, the activity of *Jog* was misclassified as *Jump* due to a similar acceleration observed on the z-axis. The classification of *Rotate* as *Bend* was likely due to the observation that a significant proportion of subjects exhibited a slight hip rotation when bending, particularly when only one arm was moved towards the floor.

6   Conclusion

In order to maintain the independence of older people for as long as possible, the activities of daily living should be tracked regularly so that changes in behavior can be detected as early as possible. In this study, the recognition of eight different activities was investigated using deep learning and machine learning approaches. For this purpose, a self-recorded data set of eight subjects was applied, whereby accelerometer and gyroscope data were recorded. A classification network and various SVM approaches were analyzed. Two data splits were examined: a subject-specific one, in which the training data consisted of all subjects, and a LOSO-CV, in which one subject was excluded from the training and was used for testing. The person-specific approach achieved accuracies of 99.5% and 99.8% for the CNN and for the best SVMs. Also, the LOSO-CV results in appropriate accuracies of 77.8% for the CNN and 77.6% for the best SVM. A number of misclassifications have been identified, some of which are attributable to data recording errors. In summary, the SVM and the CNN yield comparable outcomes, with the CNN demonstrating marginally superior results but also significantly longer training times. In conclusion, the preferred choice of the classifier might depend on the circumstances. On the one hand, the SVM might be the right choice if low computational complexity is preferred, e.g. for real-time systems. On the other hand, if classifier performance is of more importance and the long training time can be disregarded, then CNN might be the better choice.

As was recognized in the LOSO-CV variant, a high data variance is important. It could therefore be useful to include additional test subjects in order to better compensate for outliers such as test subject S_3. In addition, a similar group of people is currently covered, in which the activities do not differ greatly. Therefore, subjects from different age groups could also be included.

For future work, other ML or DL methods could also be taken into consideration. Given that the data are time series, network architectures that contain temporal components, such as recurrent neural networks (RNNs) or long short-term memory (LSTM) networks, could be tested. With regard to the SVM, further features could be investigated that originate from areas other than the time domain, such as Fourier coefficients. A combination of both approaches could also be investigated. In order to avoid the use of hand-crafted features, a CNN could be employed to identify relevant features. Subsequently, a SVM could be utilized to estimate the correct activity class based on the selected features. We can conclude that using one easy-to-use, non-intrusive IMU sensor is able to model dynamic movements and can be successfully used for the recognition of ADL using traditional ML methods such as the SVM, as well as DL methods such as CNNs.

Acknowledgements. The study is funded by the German Federal Ministry of Education and Research (Project No. 01ZZ2007).

Disclosure of Interests. The authors have no conflict of interest.

References

1. Aggarwal, C.C.: Neural Networks and Deep Learning - A Textbook. Springer (2018)
2. Augustinov, G., et al.: Transformer-based recognition of activities of daily living from wearable sensor data. In: Proceedings of the 7th International Workshop on Sensor-Based Activity Recognition and Artificial Intelligence, iWOAR 2022. Association for Computing Machinery, New York (2023). https://doi.org/10.1145/3558884.3558895
3. Bento, N., et al.: Comparing handcrafted features and deep neural representations for domain generalization in human activity recognition. Sensors (Basel) 22(19), 7324 (2022)
4. Bevilacqua, A., MacDonald, K., Rangarej, A., Widjaya, V., Caulfield, B., Kechadi, T.: Human activity recognition with convolutional neural networks. In: Brefeld, U., et al. (eds.) ECML PKDD 2018. LNCS (LNAI), vol. 11053, pp. 541–552. Springer, Cham (2019). https://doi.org/10.1007/978-3-030-10997-4_33
5. Ciortuz, G., Grzegorzek, M., Fudickar, S.: Effects of time-series data pre-processing on the transformer-based classification of activities from smart glasses. In: Proceedings of the 8th International Workshop on Sensor-Based Activity Recognition and Artificial Intelligence, iWOAR 2023. Association for Computing Machinery, New York (2023). https://doi.org/10.1145/3615834.3615858
6. Ciortuz, G., Pour, H.H., Fudickar, S.: Evaluating movement and device-specific deepconvlstm performance in wearable-based human activity recognition. In: Proceedings of the 17th International Joint Conference on Biomedical Engineering Systems and Technologies - Volume 2: HEALTHINF, pp. 746–753. INSTICC, SciTePress (2024). https://doi.org/10.5220/0012471300003657
7. Edemekong, P.F., Bomgaars, D., Sukumaran, S., Levy, S.B.: Activities of daily living (2019). https://digitalcollections.dordt.edu/faculty_work/1222
8. Fan, C., Gao, F.: Enhanced human activity recognition using wearable sensors via a hybrid feature selection method. Sensors 21(19), 6434 (2021). https://doi.org/10.3390/s21196434
9. Ferrari, A., Micucci, D., Mobilio, M., Napoletano, P.: Hand-crafted features vs residual networks for human activities recognition using accelerometer, pp. 153–156 (2019). https://doi.org/10.1109/ISCE.2019.8901021
10. Ferrari, A., Micucci, D., Mobilio, M., Napoletano, P.: Trends in human activity recognition using smartphones. J. Reliable Intell. Environ. 7(3), 189–213 (2021). https://doi.org/10.1007/s40860-021-00147-0
11. Fida, B., Bernabucci, I., Bibbo, D., Conforto, S., Schmid, M.: Varying behavior of different window sizes on the classification of static and dynamic physical activities from a single accelerometer. Med. Eng. Phys. 37(7), 705–711 (2015). https://doi.org/10.1016/j.medengphy.2015.04.005. https://www.sciencedirect.com/science/article/pii/S1350453315001009
12. Fudickar, S., et al.: Validation of the ambient tug chair with light barriers and force sensors in a clinical trial. Assist. Technol. 32(1), 1–8 (2018). https://doi.org/10.1080/10400435.2018.1446195
13. Hayat, A., Morgado-Dias, F., Bhuyan, B.P., Tomar, R.: Human activity recognition for elderly people using machine and deep learning approaches. Information 13(6) (2022). https://doi.org/10.3390/info13060275. https://www.mdpi.com/2078-2489/13/6/275
14. Hellmers, S., et al.: Towards an automated unsupervised mobility assessment for older people based on inertial tug measurements. Sensors 18(10) (2018). https://doi.org/10.3390/s18103310. https://www.mdpi.com/1424-8220/18/10/3310

15. Hellmers, S., et al.: Stair climb power measurements via inertial measurement units - towards an unsupervised assessment of strength in domestic environments. In: Proceedings of the 11th International Joint Conference on Biomedical Engineering Systems and Technologies. SCITEPRESS - Science and Technology Publications (2018). https://doi.org/10.5220/0006543900390047

16. Humotion: Smart run app - reliable running data with the push of a button (2018). https://smartracks.run/de/smartracks-run-app/

17. Kulsoom, F., Narejo, S., Mehmood, Z., Chaudhry, H., Butt, A., Bashir, A.: A review of machine learning-based human activity recognition for diverse applications. Neural Comput. Appl. **34** (2022). https://doi.org/10.1007/s00521-022-07665-9

18. Matthies, D.J., Haescher, M., Nanayakkara, S., Bieber, G.: Step detection for rollator users with smartwatches. In: Proceedings of the 2018 ACM Symposium on Spatial User Interaction, SUI 2018, pp. 163–167. Association for Computing Machinery, New York (2018). https://doi.org/10.1145/3267782.3267784

19. Moran, J., Ramirez-Campillo, R., Granacher, U.: Effects of jumping exercise on muscular power in older adults: a meta-analysis. Sports Med. **48**(12), 2843–2857 (2018). https://doi.org/10.1007/s40279-018-1002-5

20. Okemuo, A.J., Gallagher, D., Dairo, Y.M.: Effects of rebound exercises on balance and mobility of people with neurological disorders: a systematic review. PLoS ONE **18**(10), e0292312 (2023). https://doi.org/10.1371/journal.pone.0292312. http://dx.doi.org/10.1371/journal.pone.0292312

21. Osakwe, Z.T., Larson, E., Agrawal, M., Shang, J.: Assessment of activity of daily living among older adult patients in home healthcare and skilled nursing facilities: An integrative review. Home Healthcare Now **35**(5) (2017). https://journals.lww.com/homehealthcarenurseonline/fulltext/2017/05000/assessment_of_activity_of_daily_living_among_older.4.aspx

22. Pesenti, M., Invernizzi, G., Mazzella, J., Bocciolone, M., Pedrocchi, A., Gandolla, M.: IMU-based human activity recognition and payload classification for low-back exoskeletons. Sci. Rep. **13**(1), 1184 (2023). https://doi.org/10.1038/s41598-023-28195-x

23. Ronao, C.A., Cho, S.B.: Human activity recognition with smartphone sensors using deep learning neural networks. Expert Syst. Appl. **59**, 235–244 (2016). https://doi.org/10.1016/j.eswa.2016.04.032. https://www.sciencedirect.com/science/article/pii/S0957417416302056

24. Serpush, F., Menhaj, M.B., Masoumi, B., Karasfi, B.: Wearable sensor-based human activity recognition in the smart healthcare system. Comput. Intell. Neurosci. **2022** (2022). https://doi.org/10.1155/2022/1391906

25. Steven Eyobu, O., Han, D.S.: Feature representation and data augmentation for human activity classification based on wearable IMU sensor data using a deep LSTM neural network. Sensors **18**(9) (2018). https://doi.org/10.3390/s18092892. https://www.mdpi.com/1424-8220/18/9/2892

An Experimental Study on the Energy Efficiency of Feature Selection for Human Activity Recognition with Wrist-Worn Devices

Susanna Peretti, Chiara Contoli[✉], and Emanuele Lattanzi

Department of Pure and Applied Sciences, University of Urbino, Urbino, Italy
s.peretti@campus.uniurb.it, {chiara.contoli,emanuele.lattanzi}@uniurb.it

Abstract. Incorporating machine and deep learning methodologies into wearable devices has enhanced the capacity to accurately recognize human activity, thus enabling a range of applications including healthcare monitoring and fitness tracking. However, machine and deep learning can be costly in terms of the computational resources and energy consumption required. In this work, we study how a feature selection decision impacts the energy consumption of an ESP32 wearable device by evaluating the best trade-off between classification performance and energy expenditure. Experimental results, conducted on publicly available datasets, demonstrate that the best trade-off between energy consumption and accuracy is reached by selecting between 20 and 25 features, with an accuracy ranging between 73.56% and 87.44%, and an energy consumption between 2340.945 µJ and 3759.270 µJ.

Keywords: Human Activity Recognition · Feature Selection · Energy Efficiency · Wearables · Constrained Devices

1 Introduction

The field of sensor-based Human Activity Recognition (HAR) has emerged as a pivotal area of research within the domain of wearable computing and ubiquitous sensing. Its applications span a wide range of domains, including health monitoring and the development of smart environments [13,24]. Wrist-worn devices, such as smartwatches and fitness trackers, have become particularly popular due to their unobtrusive nature and their ability to collect data continuously. These devices frequently employ a multitude of sensors, including accelerometers, gyroscopes, and magnetometers, to capture a comprehensive array of signals that can be processed to infer user activities. Sensor-based activity recognition has yielded excellent results, mainly due to the application of machine learning (ML) techniques, both in shallow and deep approaches [33].

Nowadays, deep neural networks (DNNs) have become state-of-the-art in many machine learning applications, ranging from computer vision to speech

O. Konak et al. (Eds.): iWOAR 2024, LNCS 15357, pp. 40–54, 2025.
https://doi.org/10.1007/978-3-031-80856-2_3

recognition, by processing raw sensor data directly. However, the impressive performance of DNNs comes at the cost of significant computational resources required for both training and inference. A common approach to address these computational demands is to delegate the model inference to a cloud-based framework. On the other hand, maintaining inference tasks to wearable devices offers several compelling advantages: (i) it eliminates latency issues associated with cloud communication, thereby enhancing responsiveness; (ii) it enhances privacy and security by keeping data local to the device; and (iii) it can improve energy efficiency by balancing the energy demands of computation and communication [1,4]. However, the deployment of such devices is often constrained by their limited battery life, necessitating the development of energy-efficient solutions to prolong operational duration without compromising accuracy. In this context, several studies have demonstrated that concerning tiny devices, shallow tools are more energetically advantageous than deep approaches while maintaining comparable classification capabilities [3,16,17,23].

In shallow ML, representative features must be extracted from raw sensor data in a process known as feature selection to identify activities. The extraction can be performed in the time domain, frequency domain, or both to leverage the unique characteristics of each domain. The shallow approach envisages domain experts with specialized knowledge analyzing and selecting hand-crafted features, typically using heuristic algorithms [9]. Hand-crafted features often pertain to statistical information, regardless of the domain. Feature selection consists of discarding features that do not provide helpful information, i.e., irrelevant. Other discarded features are those that do not provide more information compared to currently selected ones, i.e., redundant. According to the literature [21,26], feature selection strategies can be classified into three categories, which are the most widely used: filter-based, wrapper-based, and embedded-based approaches. More recently, two other categories have been identified, i.e., hybrid and ensemble [36].

Existing literature in the area of feature selection mainly focuses on proposing new algorithms to improve the selection of the best feature subset [2,14,30,37]. Despite the high interest in the topic, feature computational complexity and resulting energy impact are often neglected. In [8], the authors propose a many-objective feature selection algorithm based on the computational complexity of features. However, the complexity of each feature is not determined, and they chose to assign a fixed, random cost value. Moreover, they did not consider the energy impact. Therefore, our work is motivated by the limited literature in exploring the computational complexity of each single feature and the evaluation of the energy consumption on constrained devices in the HAR context, leaving room for investigation. Momeni et al. consider features' computational complexity and try to estimate the energy consumption of the features on an ARM Cortex M3 hardware platforms [27]. However, the exploration was carried out for multimodal acute stress monitoring, which entails adopting, placing, and analyzing sensor data different from those used for HAR.

This paper extends our previous work [31] by thoroughly investigating the energy consumed by each feature during the feature selection process, measuring the actual consumption with a device rather than hypothesizing it, considering data collected via wearable devices such as smartwatches and smartphones. In this work, we consider activities of daily living, ranging from hand-based activities such as brushing teeth and preparing sandwiches to locomotion activities such as walking and running. The goal is to find the best trade-off between the energy consumption associated with feature selection and recognition accuracy. We used the Recursive Feature Elimination and Select From Model methods with RidgeCV regularization as feature selection algorithms.

To validate our approach, we consider three datasets to extract features in the time and frequency domains. One is a homemade dataset, *Ad-Hoc DB* [25], and the other two are the public *Watch_ HAR* [35] and the *RealWorld2016* [34]datasets. To consider only signals acquired from wrist-worn devices, we filtered traces collected in the *RealWorld2016* dataset with the sensor positioned at the wrist. To assess the recognition accuracy, we used a Random Forest classifier. On the one hand, this choice is motivated by the successful results yielded in HAR and, on the other, by the fact that these algorithms and classifiers are lighter than other deep-learning approaches. Such an approach greatly simplifies the deployment on a lower-power-constrained device because it allows us to avoid the adoption of optimization deployment strategies [10]. Results show that our approach effectively balances energy consumption and recognition accuracy, demonstrating the potential to save energy while preserving accuracy when machine learning models are deployed on wearable devices.

The rest of the paper is organized as follows: Sect. 2 reports related work on the impact associated with the feature selection process; in Sect. 3 we describe our proposed approach and discuss achieved results in Sect. 4. We then summarize the contribution of this work in Sect. 5.

2   Related Work

Feature selection is a critical phase of the HAR process, which deserves attention from the research community. This attention has increased in the last decade because of the high amount of data fostered by the pervasiveness of mobile and wearable devices that allow for constant monitoring of human activity and biosignals [29]. Indeed, this phase highly impacts the quality of the classification accuracy since it is supposed to select the most relevant features. It also impacts the computational burden since each feature is supposed to have its computational complexity, thus leading to a lighter or heavier impact on devices' resource consumption.

Karagiannaki *et al.* evaluated three feature selection methods: Feature Selection based on Feature Similarity, Relief-F, and Clustering with Node Centrality. These methods were provided by a library, which was subsequently evaluated in terms of execution time and energy consumption. The algorithms were evaluated in the HAR context, and they found that the extraction and selection of features are the most time-consuming operations and that Relief-F is the fastest in terms of maximum execution time, around 28 s. In contrast, the energy requirement of their framework is around 20.3 J. However, those results were obtained by implementing their architecture on a Samsung Galaxy Tab4, which differs from low-power wearable devices.

In [15], Ghasemzadeh *et al.* investigated the power optimization of wearable sensor nodes by performing instruction-level energy analysis of the feature selection phase. They used the TI MSP430 microcontroller to process real data collected from three subjects using wearable motion sensors. Specifically, they considered TI MSP430's 'mov' instruction to quantify the energy cost associated with each feature. To perform such a quantification, the authors leveraged the results of the work by Lane and Campbell [22], who assessed the energy consumption due to the execution of different types of the MSP430 processor instructions. However, Ghasemzadeh *et al.* considered only statistical features. Ding *et al.* focused on the reduction of energy consumption of wearable device-based HAR systems by exploring i) the use of hybrid, i.e., non-uniform, window techniques, ii) the use of a mutual information-based feature selection method, and iii) their proposed Random Forest methods [12]. They considered only time-domain features and, despite the focus on wearable devices, the experimental evaluation was performed on a XIAOMI 5 smartphone, which acts as a data collector from integrated sensors, and a Fujitsu SH771 laptop, which runs their proposed feature extraction and recognition algorithm. Moreover, the energy efficiency was evaluated in terms of computational time reduction, i.e., the time taken by the laptop to perform the recognition activity.

Another work exploring non-uniform window segmentation for energy-efficient HAR is the one of Bhat *et al.* [7]. The authors proposed a HAR framework that leverages textile-based stretch sensors and an accelerometer to capture raw data from 9 users. They considered features only from the frequency domain, i.e., Fast Fourier Transform and Discrete Wavelet Transform. They then used different classifiers, such as Support Vector Machine, Random Forest, Decision Tree, k-Nearest Neighbors, and their proposed neural network. The framework was implemented on the TI-CC2650 microcontroller, and the authors measured both the power and the energy consumed during the sensing, feature selection and classification, and communication via Bluetooth phase. However, the authors considered all the sets of selected features as if they were all equally relevant in their contribution to the activity recognition. Subsequently, Bhat *et al.* used a commercial analog front end to propose a fully integrated ultra-low power hardware accelerator for HAR that provides all steps from reading raw sensor data to activity classification. However, the feature selection was not the focus of the work.

Most of the literature does not consider the computational complexity of individual features, thus neglecting their varying complexity and, consequently, their different impact on energy consumption. Some works, such as the one by Barandas *et al.*, focused on providing tools that help users get an idea of the computational cost of feature extraction [6]. The authors developed a Python package named Time Series Feature Extraction Library (TSFEL), which provides a set of implemented feature extraction methods based on Numpy and SciPy. The proposed library allows users to analyze time series data and extract features in the temporal, statistical, and spectral domains. As output, it provides an estimation of the complexity of the feature. Moreover, the library is designed to allow users to write their feature extraction method and its corresponding domain so that other features can be added to those available by default in the library.

Compared to the existing literature, we consider simultaneously time and frequency domain features, and we evaluate the energy impact of each selected feature on a low-power device after considering the computational complexity of each feature.

3 Methodology

In this section, we provide background on the feature selection process, and we describe our proposed methodology to extract, select, and estimate the energy consumption of the features.

3.1 Background

The HAR process comprises four phases, typically: i) data gathering, ii) data pre-processing, iii) feature engineering, and iv) classification. Feature engineering consists of feature extraction and feature selection steps. Feature extraction is about analyzing the raw signal in the time, frequency, and time-frequency domains and subsequently extracting distinctive features. This step can be carried out manually by a so called domain expert, also with the help of optimization algorithms, or can be carried out automatically with the help of deep learning algorithms.

Feature selection is about discarding irrelevant and redundant features to select a subset of meaningful features. Filter-based, wrapper-based, and embedded-based approaches are the most widely used in this step. Filter methods leverage training data characteristics to identify feature importance and do not depend on the learning algorithm. Wrapper methods iteratively search for the relationship between optimal feature subset selection and feature relevance until a stopping criterion is met, and the search relies on the predictive performance of the specific learning algorithm. Dhal and Azad surveyed feature selection techniques and the corresponding area of ML applications [11], concluding that: i) the filter approach is much faster than the other two, but it is less accurate; ii) the wrapper approach is the most accurate, but it suffers high computational time, whereas the embedded approach overcomes the problems of the other two approaches; iii) results of feature selection methods vary depending on the used dataset and adopted ML approach.

3.2   Proposed Approach

Extracting relevant features from both time and frequency domains provides more benefits. Indeed, time domain features are commonly used because of their low computation cost. However, identifying complex dynamics and hidden patterns, such as repetitive movements or other periodic components, may require analyzing signals in the frequency domain to unveil those peculiarities that are not so easily discernible in time domain analysis. Therefore, we extract features from both domains. In particular, we extract statistical data, such as mean and standard deviation, and other relevant metrics, such as interquartile range, autoregressive coefficients, signal magnitude area, and root mean square from the time domain. We used the Fast Fourier Transform (FFT), a mathematical technique that decomposes the data into different frequency components, to extract features such as skewness, kurtosis, peaks, and energy in the frequency domain.

3.3   Feature Energy Characterization

In order to analyze the trade-off between the energy consumption of the considered features and the corresponding classification accuracy, we developed a sensor-based HAR application. The application comprises two distinct tasks. The first task is responsible for data collection from a triaxial accelerometer and gyroscope, while the second task is responsible for computing each feature on the gathered data. The software was compiled for the ESP32 platform and executed on the wearable device while the power-drawn trace was recorded to estimate the energy consumption. An example of a power trace is presented in Fig. 1.

In particular, the figure reports the power consumption when computing the FFT followed by the Kurtosis, standard deviation, and Skewness features. The energy bursts corresponding to each feature have been highlighted by dotted rectangles. It is noteworthy that the FFT exhibits a higher power level with respect to the computation of the feature. This is likely due to the fact that it has been implemented using the Espressif ESP32 library which involves the usage of the internal digital signal processor (DSP). Moreover, the periodic bursts corresponding to the reading of the sensor samples are also clearly visible. Notice that to make the bursts in the figure more visible, both the FFT and feature calculations were consecutively repeated ten times. The features considered in this work, together with the corresponding energy consumption, are listed in Table 1.

Notice that FFT appears to be the most expensive in terms of energy, reaching almost 1400 μJ, despite using a dedicated co-processor (DSP). Moreover, features involving simple operations such as multiplications, sums, and comparisons record a consumption lower than one μJ. An intermediate range is shown by features that involve more complex operations, such as sorts, exponentials, and square roots.

Starting from the characterization of the proposed features, we leverage both wrapper and embedded approaches as feature selection strategies. In particular, we use the Recursive Feature Elimination (LR-RFE) wrapper-based method that

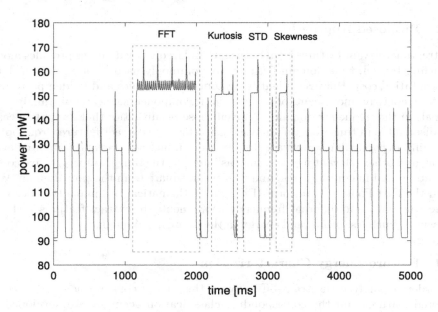

Fig. 1. Power consumption trace of the ESP32 collected during features computation.

Table 1. Characterization of the features energy consumption.

Feature	Formula	Energy [μJ]
Mean	$\frac{1}{n}\sum_{i=1}^{n} s_i$	0.21
Min	$min(s_1, s_2, ...s_n)$	0.19
Max	$max(s_1, s_2, ...s_n)$	0.19
Median	$median(s_1, s_2, ...s_n)$	152.66
Standard Deviation	$\sqrt{\frac{1}{n}\sum_{i=1}^{n}(s_i - \mu_s)^2}$	409.81
N Peaks	The number of signal peaks	0.15
Peak-to-Peak Amplitude	$max(s) - min(s)$	0.17
Interquartile Range	$perc(s, 75) - perc(s, 25)$	119.32
Autocorrelation	$\frac{1}{n}\sum_{i=1}^{n-k}(s_i - \bar{s}) * (s_{i+k} - \bar{s})$	0.17
Energy	$\frac{\sum_{i=1}^{n} s_i^2}{length(s_i)}$	0.15
Autoregressive coefficients	$\sum_{i=1}^{n} \alpha_i x(n - i) + \epsilon(n)$	0.15
Signal Magnitude Area	$\frac{1}{n}\sum_{i=1}^{n-1}(|x_i| + |y_i| + |z_i|)$	0.15
Root Mean Square	$\sqrt{\frac{1}{n}\sum_{i=1}^{n} s_i^2}$	385.47
FFT	$\sum_{n=0}^{N-1} x(n) \cdot e^{-j2\pi \frac{kn}{N}}$	1399.61
Spectral Mean	$\frac{\sum_{i=1}^{n} k|S_i|^2}{\sum_{i=1}^{n} |S_i|^2}$	0.15
Skewness	$\frac{\mathcal{E}[(s_i - \bar{s})^4]}{\mathcal{E}[(s_i - \bar{s})^2]^2}$	189.11
Kurtosis	$\mathcal{E}[(\frac{s_i - \bar{s}}{\sigma})^3]$	186.98
Growth factor	$\frac{max(|s|)}{\sqrt{mean(s^2)}}$	10.32

gradually reduces the number of features combined with logistic regression. This method considers all features and, subsequently, removes iteratively the least relevant ones. We also use the Select From Model with RidgeCV regularization (SFM-RidgeCV) embedded-based method, which involves a set of RidgeCV models. Each RidgeCV model has a different set of selected features and chooses the best feature subset based on cross-validated performance metrics. The method then leverages the optimal feature subset to train the final model.

4 Experimental Evaluation

In this section, we provide a thorough description of the experimental setup, and we present the results of several experiments.

4.1 Setup

Feature selection algorithms, model training, and testing have been executed on a personal computer equipped with an Intel Core i7-4712MQ × 8 processor and 8 GB of RAM using Python. The energy characterization of each feature was done by executing it on an ESP32 connected to an MPU6050 triaxial accelerometer and gyroscope [20].

To estimate the device's energy consumption, we measured the voltage drop across a (9.8Ω) sensing resistor placed in series with the device's power supply. The device was powered at 3.3V using an NGMO2 Rohde & Schwarz dual-channel power supply [32]. During the experiments, we sampled the monitored signals using a National Instruments NI-DAQmx PCI-6251 16-channel data acquisition board [28].

The solidness of our methodology has been evaluated using three representative datasets collected via wrist-worn devices have been evaluated, namely Watch_HAR, Ad-hoc DB, and RealWorld2016.

Watch_HAR [5,35]: in this dataset, 13 subjects (both male and female) wearing a smartwatch on their dominant hand performed activities (commonly executed at home or at work) in a laboratory environment. Data are collected from the accelerometers, gyroscopes, and magnetometers. Each subject, in its own style, carried out 16 activities for approximately 1 to 3 min: *brushing teeth, preparing sandwiches, reading a book, typing, using a phone, using remote control, walking freely, walking holding a tray, walking with a handbag, walking with hands in pockets, walking with objects underarm, washing face and hands, washing mug, washing plate, writing.* Note that we removed the walking activities from this dataset because we wanted to focus solely on the recognition of hand-based activities.

Ad-hoc DB [25]: we created this dataset specifically to study the recognition of *handwashing* and *handrubbing* activities performed during the day. Data are collected from the triaxial accelerometer and gyroscope of a smartwatch positioned on the wrist of the dominant hand of four participants during real-life activities. Each subject wore the smartwatch for several hours on different days and was asked to annotate the start and the end of each handwashing or hand-rubbing activity performed during the day. Together with the activities of interest, we also collected *Unknown Activities* (*UAs*) data by randomly sampling the sensors during the day. For each subject, we collected about 2 h spent washing hands, about 2 h and 30 min spent rubbing, and about 3 h of *UAs*.

RealWorld2016 [34]: the dataset includes movements from 15 different subjects, comprising 8 males and 7 females, engaged in various activities such as standing, lying down, sitting, jumping, climbing up, climbing down, walking, and running. Data for each activity were gathered using six sensors that measured acceleration, GPS, gyroscope, light, magnetic field, and sound levels. These sensors were positioned at various body locations, including the chest, forearm, head, shin, thigh, upper arm, and waist. Additionally, each movement was recorded with a video camera for further analysis. The subjects had an average age of 32 years, an average weight of 74 kg, and an average height of 171 cm, with each activity lasting approximately 10 min on average.

The signals of the three datasets have been divided into a 2.56 s time window. Choosing the time window size and the percentage of overlap is non-trivial. The choice motivation is manifold: on the one hand, according to the literature, in HAR tasks, different window lengths have been used, from 1 s up to 30 s [18,19]. On the other, in our preliminary exploration, we found that the best value for the datasets resulted in 2 s without overlap. Last but not least, using the FFT requires a power of 2 sample length to allow a more efficient computation. Therefore, we opted for 256 samples, which resulted in 2.56 s, giving a sampling frequency of 100 Hz.

The dataset contains accelerometer and gyroscope signals, each measuring movement along three axes (x, y, z). The Signal Magnitude Area (SMA) is computed across all three axes together as a single value for each sensor type. For the time domain, there are 12 features per 3 axes and 2 types of sensors (accelerometer and gyroscope), thus resulting in $12 \times 3 \times 2$ features. For the frequency domain, there are 8 features per axis, resulting in $8 \times 3 \times 2$ features. As result, the total number of features is 122 features.

4.2 Accuracy Results

By varying the number of features, the two selection methods, SFM-RidgeCV and LR-RFE, have been applied to the three datasets. The best set of selected features was then used to train and test the recognition accuracy of a Random Forest classifier.

Figure 2 shows the classification accuracy obtained with the SFM-RidgeCV and LR-RFE selection methods when varying the number of the selected features, expressed as a fraction of totals. Results are shown for Ad-hoc DB (blue line), Watch_HAR (orange line), and RealWorld2016 (green line) datasets. Each point of the plots is obtained by averaging 5 executions using different random seeds, and vertical bars represent the standard deviation.

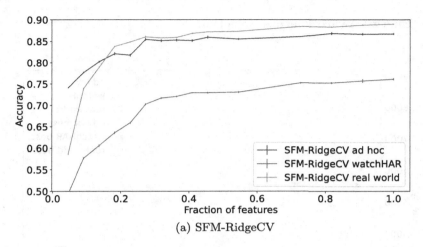

(a) SFM-RidgeCV

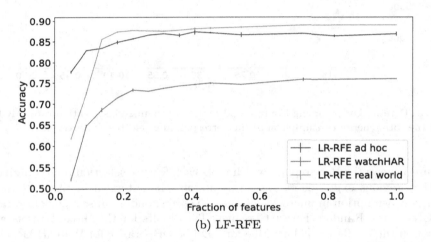

(b) LF-RFE

Fig. 2. Classification accuracy with respect to the number of selected features expressed as a fraction of totals.

The Ad-hoc DB dataset reaches a stable accuracy value close to the maximum using about 50% of the available features with both selection methods. Although the other datasets require a higher percentage of available features to get closer to the maximum accuracy, it is interesting to note that a high level of accuracy (i.e., greater or equal to 80%) is reached with less than 20% of available features for the Ad-hoc DB and RealWorld2016 datasets with both selection methods. This means that, depending on the application requirements, it is possible to save energy without sacrificing accuracy too much.

4.3 Energy-Aware Feature Selection

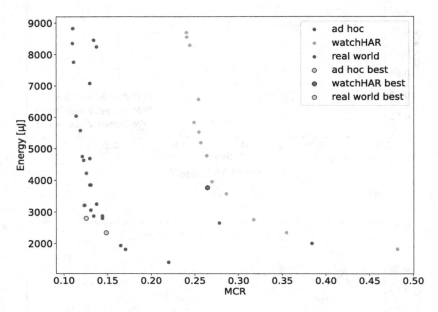

Fig. 3. Pareto plan reporting the trade-off between the miss-classification rate (MCR) and the total energy consumption of the corresponding selected features.

Figure 3 shows the Pareto plan, which plots each feature selection point obtained in the previous experiments. These points are characterized in terms of total energy consumption in micro joules and the corresponding misclassification rate (MCR) of the Random Forest Classifier. The results for the three datasets are shown in three different colors: blue for AD-hoc DB, orange for WatchHAR, and green for RealWorld2016.

For each dataset, the best trade-off point, which minimizes both energy consumption and MCR, is highlighted in specific colors: light blue for Ad-hoc DB, red for WatchHAR, and yellow for RealWorld2016. The optimal point for Watch-HAR includes 25 features, while the other two datasets count 20 features.

(a) Ad-hoc DB

(b) WatchHAR

(c) RealWorld2016

Fig. 4. Visual representation of the selected features in the Pareto optimal points by means of word clouds.

To better understand which features were selected at each optimal point and how they contribute to global energy consumption, we constructed the three word clouds corresponding to the three optimal points highlighted in the Pareto plot. Each cloud is a visual representation of the occurrence of each feature tag in the way that the words appear bigger the more often they are used. For instance, considering a feature named `gyroY_fft_npeaks`, which is the number of peaks calculated over the spectral representation of the y component of the gyroscope, it contributes to the word cloud by increasing both the `gyroY`, `fft` and `npeaks` counters.

Figure 4 shows the three resulting word clouds corresponding to the experiments conducted on top of the three reference datasets. It is interesting to note that the proposed method provides an optimal feature list in all three datasets that mainly contains features computed from the FFT despite its high energy cost. This demonstrates the fact that to have a good compromise between accuracy and energy consumption, it is still necessary to spend the energy needed to shift to the frequency domain instead of calculating features directly on top of the time series data. An additional observation derived from an analysis of the figure indicates that, in all three datasets, the signals derived from the accelerometer appear to be more significant than those derived from the gyroscope. Consequently, the computed features primarily originate from it.

5   Conclusion

High dimensional sensor data poses challenges in terms of pattern recognition and computational complexity for sensor-based human activity recognition, which also impact the system energy expenditure. This paper proposes a method to extract, select, and characterize the energy associated with each feature involved in activity recognition. The method aims to select the most informative features while considering their energy impact. We tested our methodology on three datasets, and the results show that it is possible to fine-tune feature selection to find the best compromise between accuracy and energy consumption. The analysis also highlights that a good compromise is reached when features are selected from the frequency domain, although this implies selecting features with a higher energy cost. Our proposed methodology is general enough to be applied in different classification scenarios, and it can help tune the energy impact of machine learning models deployed on wearable devices.

References

1. Abdel-Basset, M., Hawash, H., Chang, V., Chakrabortty, R.K., Ryan, M.: Deep learning for heterogeneous human activity recognition in complex IoT applications. IEEE Internet Things J. (2020). https://doi.org/10.1109/JIOT.2020.3038416
2. Ahadzadeh, B., Abdar, M., Safara, F., Khosravi, A., Menhaj, M.B., Suganthan, P.N.: SFE: a simple, fast and efficient feature selection algorithm for high-dimensional data. IEEE Trans. Evol. Comput. (2023)
3. Alam, F., Mehmood, R., Katib, I., Albeshri, A.: Analysis of eight data mining algorithms for smarter Internet of Things (IoT). Procedia Comput. Sci. **98**, 437–442 (2016)

4. Alessandrini, M., Biagetti, G., Crippa, P., Falaschetti, L., Turchetti, C.: Recurrent neural network for human activity recognition in embedded systems using PPG and accelerometer data. Electronics **10**(14), 1715 (2021)
5. Alevizaki, A., Trigoni, N.: watchHAR: A Smartwatch IMU dataset for Activities of Daily Living (2022). https://doi.org/10.5281/zenodo.7092553
6. Barandas, M., et al.: TSFEL: time series feature extraction library. SoftwareX **11**, 100456 (2020)
7. Bhat, G., Deb, R., Chaurasia, V.V., Shill, H., Ogras, U.Y.: Online human activity recognition using low-power wearable devices. In: 2018 IEEE/ACM International Conference on Computer-Aided Design (ICCAD), pp. 1–8. IEEE (2018)
8. Bidgoli, A.A., Ebrahimpour-Komleh, H., Rahnamayan, S.: A many-objective feature selection algorithm for multi-label classification based on computational complexity of features. In: 2019 14th International Conference on Computer Science & Education (ICCSE), pp. 85–91. IEEE (2019)
9. Chen, Z., Zhang, L., Cao, Z., Guo, J.: Distilling the knowledge from handcrafted features for human activity recognition. IEEE Trans. Ind. Inf. **14**(10), 4334–4342 (2018)
10. Contoli, C., Lattanzi, E.: A study on the application of tensorflow compression techniques to human activity recognition. IEEE Access (2023)
11. Dhal, P., Azad, C.: A comprehensive survey on feature selection in the various fields of machine learning. Appl. Intell. **52**(4), 4543–4581 (2022)
12. Ding, G., Tian, J., Wu, J., Zhao, Q., Xie, L.: Energy efficient human activity recognition using wearable sensors. In: 2018 IEEE Wireless Communications and Networking Conference Workshops (WCNCW), pp. 379–383. IEEE (2018)
13. Diraco, G., Rescio, G., Siciliano, P., Leone, A.: Review on human action recognition in smart living: sensing technology, multimodality, real-time processing, interoperability, and resource-constrained processing. Sensors **23**(11), 5281 (2023)
14. El-Hasnony, I.M., Barakat, S.I., Elhoseny, M., Mostafa, R.R.: Improved feature selection model for big data analytics. IEEE Access **8**, 66989–67004 (2020)
15. Ghasemzadeh, H., Amini, N., Saeedi, R., Sarrafzadeh, M.: Power-aware computing in wearable sensor networks: an optimal feature selection. IEEE Trans. Mob. Comput. **14**(4), 800–812 (2014)
16. Gupta, C., et al.: Protonn: compressed and accurate KNN for resource-scarce devices. In: International Conference on Machine Learning, pp. 1331–1340. PMLR (2017)
17. Haigh, K.Z., Mackay, A.M., Cook, M.R., Lin, L.G.: Machine Learning for Embedded Systems: A Case Study. BBN Technologies, Cambridge (2015)
18. Hassan, M.M., Uddin, M.Z., Mohamed, A., Almogren, A.: A robust human activity recognition system using smartphone sensors and deep learning. Futur. Gener. Comput. Syst. **81**, 307–313 (2018)
19. Hou, C.: A study on IMU-based human activity recognition using deep learning and traditional machine learning. In: 2020 5th International Conference on Computer and Communication Systems (ICCCS), pp. 225–234 (2020)
20. InvenSense Inc.: MPU-6050 product specification (2023). https://invensense.tdk.com/products/motion-tracking/6-axis/mpu-6050/. Accessed 14 June 2024
21. Kumar, V., Minz, S.: Feature selection. SmartCR **4**(3), 211–229 (2014)
22. Lane, N., Campbell, A.: The influence of microprocessor instructions on the energy consumption of wireless sensor networks. In: Third Workshop on Embedded Networked Sensors (EmNets 2006), vol. 34 (2006)

23. Lattanzi, E., Calisti, L.: Energy-aware tiny machine learning for sensor-based hand-washing recognition. In: Proceedings of the 2023 8th International Conference on Machine Learning Technologies, pp. 15–22 (2023)
24. Lattanzi, E., Calisti, L., Freschi, V.: Unstructured handwashing recognition using smartwatch to reduce contact transmission of pathogens. IEEE Access **10**, 83111–83124 (2022)
25. Lattanzi, E., Calisti, L., Freschi, V.: Unstructured handwashing recognition using smartwatch to reduce contact transmission of pathogens. IEEE Access **10**, 83111–83124 (2022). https://doi.org/10.1109/ACCESS.2022.3197279
26. Li, J., et al.: Feature selection: a data perspective. ACM Comput. Surv. (CSUR) **50**(6), 1–45 (2017)
27. Momeni, N., Valdés, A.A., Rodrigues, J., Sandi, C., Atienza, D.: CAFS: cost-aware features selection method for multimodal stress monitoring on wearable devices. IEEE Trans. Biomed. Eng. **69**(3), 1072–1084 (2021)
28. National.Instruments: PC-6251 datasheet (2020). http://www.ni.com/pdf/manuals/375213c.pdf. Accessed 14 June 2024
29. Nguyen, B., Coelho, Y., Bastos, T., Krishnan, S.: Trends in human activity recognition with focus on machine learning and power requirements. Mach. Learn. Appl. **5**, 100072 (2021)
30. Peng, H., Ying, C., Tan, S., Hu, B., Sun, Z.: An improved feature selection algorithm based on ant colony optimization. IEEE Access **6**, 69203–69209 (2018)
31. Peretti, S., Contoli, C., Lattanzi, E.: Complexity-aware features selection for wrist-worn human activity recognition. In: 2024 IEEE International Conference on Pervasive Computing and Communications Workshops and other Affiliated Events (PerCom Workshops), pp. 799–804. IEEE (2024)
32. Rohde&Schwarz: Ngmo2 datasheet (2020). https://www.rohde-schwarz.com/it/brochure-scheda-tecnica/ngmo2/. Accessed 14 June 2024
33. Suto, J., Oniga, S., Lung, C., Orha, I.: Comparison of offline and real-time human activity recognition results using machine learning techniques. Neural Comput. Appl. **32**, 15673–15686 (2020)
34. Sztyler, T., Stuckenschmidt, H.: On-body localization of wearable devices: an investigation of position-aware activity recognition. In: 2016 IEEE International Conference on Pervasive Computing and Communications (PerCom) (2016)
35. Trigoni.Zenodo, A.A.N.: Watchhar: a smartwatch IMU dataset for activities of daily living. (2022). http://dx.doi.org/10.5281/zenodo.7092553. Accessed 20 Oct 2023
36. Zebari, R., Abdulazeez, A., Zeebaree, D., Zebari, D., Saeed, J.: A comprehensive review of dimensionality reduction techniques for feature selection and feature extraction. J. Appl. Sci. Technol. Trends **1**(1), 56–70 (2020)
37. Zhou, H., Zhang, J., Zhou, Y., Guo, X., Ma, Y.: A feature selection algorithm of decision tree based on feature weight. Expert Syst. Appl. **164**, 113842 (2021)

Multi-modal Atmospheric Sensing to Augment Wearable IMU-Based Hand Washing Detection

Robin Burchard$^{(\boxtimes)}$ and Kristof Van Laerhoven

University of Siegen, 57076 Siegen, Germany
robin.burchard@uni-siegen.de
https://ubicomp.eti.uni-siegen.de/

Abstract. Hand washing is a crucial part of personal hygiene. Hand washing detection is a relevant topic for wearable sensing with applications in the medical and professional fields. Hand washing detection can be used to aid workers in complying with hygiene rules. Hand washing detection using body-worn IMU-based sensor systems has been shown to be a feasible approach, although, for some reported results, the specificity of the detection was low, leading to a high rate of false positives. In this work, we present a novel, open-source prototype device that additionally includes a humidity, temperature, and barometric sensor. We contribute a benchmark dataset of 10 participants and 43 hand-washing events and perform an evaluation of the sensors' benefits. Added to that, we outline the usefulness of the additional sensor in both the annotation pipeline and the machine learning models. By visual inspection, we show that especially the humidity sensor registers a strong increase in the relative humidity during a hand-washing activity. A machine learning analysis of our data shows that distinct features benefiting from such relative humidity patterns remain to be identified.

Keywords: Multi-modal · Hand washing detection · Human activity recognition · Data recording · Open source

1 Introduction

Hand washing is very relevant for our personal health because it effectively reduces the amount of bacteria, viruses, and other pathogens that we spread [4]. Added to protecting our own health, effective hand washing can also reduce the spread of illnesses to other human beings or animals. Many professional applications require food-safe or sterile environments, for which hand washing and e.g. alcohol-based hand sanitizers can be used. Automatically measuring the frequency, duration, and quality of hand washing therefore could be beneficial in a multitude of applications. There are also prospective applications in the field of mental health. Hand washing detection has for instance been proposed as a

O. Konak et al. (Eds.): iWOAR 2024, LNCS 15357, pp. 55–68, 2025.
https://doi.org/10.1007/978-3-031-80856-2_4

measure to aid in the treatment of people with Obsessive Compulsive Disorder (OCD) with washing compulsions [3,15,16].

Spotting hand washing in the real world and distinguishing it from everyday activities and activities of daily living (ADL) has been shown to be difficult and inaccurate using only data from wrist-worn IMU devices. However, additional cues from the environment such as Bluetooth beacons near sinks can be used to support the hand washing detection [5,12]. The current approaches for hand washing detection employ a multitude of sensors, although the most frequently used sensors are RGB(D)-cameras and inertial measurement units (IMUs). One category of sensors that has recently been incorporated in wearable devices remains under-explored, namely atmospheric sensors which allow the capturing of humidity, temperature, and air pressure.

Goals and Contributions
The goal of this work is to explore the use of additional sensing capabilities and their effect on the detection performance of hand washing detection using wearable devices. The contributions of our work are the following:

1. Description of the development and evaluation of an open-source, cost-effective sensor recording device
2. Evaluation and comparison of the impact of the added sensors for hand washing detection
3. Providing an expert-annotated and easy-to-extend dataset and code to reproduce our results and further develop the device and hand washing detection methods.

2   Related Work

In the following section, we discuss existing research work on hand washing detection and on the usage of atmospheric sensors in Human Activity Recognition (HAR) in particular. Although several recent smartwatches do contain cost-effective miniature sensors such as the Bosch BME280 that sense the humidity of the wearer's surroundings, the modality of humidity is not very prevalent in wearable studies. To the best of the authors' knowledge, there exists no previously published research that combines the use of wearable atmospheric sensors with the goal of hand washing detection. In this work, we focus only on body-worn sensors, as externally placed sensors (e.g. cameras) have several disadvantages for hand washing detection, such as the need to deploy them in sensitive environments such as users' bathrooms, and would need to cover all possible places where users could possibly wash their hands.

Hand Washing Detection
For hand washing detection, the most used sensors are inertial measurement unit (IMU) sensors, which contain inertial 3D sensors such as accelerometers and gyroscopes. While studies have shown that these sensors on their own can deliver adequate data to detect lab-recorded hand washing and hand washing steps [9–11,17,18], no large-scale in-the-wild study exists thus far that can detect

hand washing from IMU data alone with close-to-perfect precision and recall [3]. In-lab studies offer higher performance [20].

Hence, additional sensors or cues could offer a way to make the detection of hand washing more reliable. As an example of popular technology, the Apple Watch can detect hand washing by allegedly using a combination of IMU sensing and the microphone with a proprietary algorithm [7,8]. Zhuang et al. also employ an acoustic model [21] for hand washing detection. Added to that, some studies have used Bluetooth beacons as part of their detection framework [5,12]. However, this only makes sense in certain environments and contexts, in which hand washing should be detected. Similarly to external sensors, this limitation of beacons holds true for all kinds of external cues. Another approach is to utilize capacitive sensing and to make use of the fact that the metallic piping of water outlets is usually grounded. By measuring the changes in capacitive resistance, events can be detected when the user has touched the outlet or is in contact with the water stream coming out of it [19]. However, the assumption that the piping system of wash basins is grounded might not always hold, as these pipes are increasingly built out of plastic materials.

In general, high performances with F1-scores of over 0.9 can be reached [10,20] both in-lab and out-of-lab. However, differences in sensing modalities, environmental cues, and activities included in the datasets make direct comparisons between the existing datasets unfeasible.

Atmospheric Sensors in HAR
Although they are far from omnipresent in Human Activity Recognition (HAR), previous HAR research does use ambient environment sensors such as atmospheric sensors (temperature, pressure, and humidity sensors). For example, in works by De et al. and Bharti et al. [2,6], atmospheric sensors are utilized to enhance the recognition of complex activities of daily living. Similarly, the sensors are included in a work by Vepakomma et al. [14]. These works have in common that they aim to recognize multiple activities of daily living in a living environment ("at home"). By including the ambient environment sensors and additional Bluetooth beacons in their data, they add context to the otherwise harder-to-classify IMU sensor values. They also argue that this sensor type can be used to do on-body localization of wearable devices. For example, the ambient pressure measurement on ankle-worn devices is usually lower compared to wrist-worn devices.

In another research study by Barua et al. [1], the usefulness of temperature and humidity data is highlighted for the specific activity of using a bathroom, due to the additional context they provide. They find that bathrooms usually deliver higher humidity readings.

Compared to the aforementioned related work, our work similarly uses atmospheric sensors to add context to the IMU recording. However, we specifically show that the humidity and temperature do not only add context about the current location of the user or device but can also be actively employed to directly measure the specific activity of hand washing.

3 Recording and Evaluation of Example Hand Washing Data

To evaluate the addition of atmospheric sensors, we developed a prototype. We then recorded data using the prototype in a hand-washing detection scenario and analyzed the collected data using visual, statistical, and machine-learning methods.

3.1 Recording Device Setup

We used for our custom wrist-worn wearable prototype a Puck.js embedded units and attached additional atmospheric sensors. We then re-programmed this unit so that it can be used to digitally acquire the integrated IMU's sensor values and the additional atmospheric sensors' values. Since the Puck.js has a limited storage space, we immediately streamed all data to a nearby recording device via Bluetooth low energy (BLE) (Fig. 1).

Fig. 1. Overview of the wiring needed to attach the BME280 sensor board. The Puck.js provides power to the sensor which can be read via I^2C using the D1 and D2 pins.

Figure 2 shows our initial design. The Puck.js device is powered by a 3V cell battery. The battery life of a single 3V cell battery in our prototype is at least 6 h, as found per our experiments. In the future, a battery with a larger capacity could be attached as the power source to prolong the battery life and hence increase the maximum recording duration.

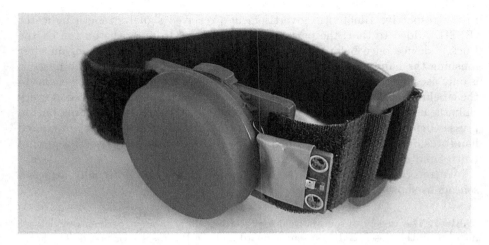

Fig. 2. Our prototype consists of a Puck.js with the attached BME280 sensor. A custom 3D-printed enclosure can be mounted on the wrist using the wristband.

3.2   Example Data Recording

To evaluate the usefulness of the addition of the different sensors, we recorded sample data from unscripted hand washes and background activities. We then visually inspected the recordings and trained machine learning classifiers with the collected and annotated data. Finally, we compared the models' performances on different sensor subsets to obtain the influence of each sensor's addition.

We recorded a total of $n = 10$ participants (8 m, 2 f) for 1 h per participant. The participants were recorded over multiple weeks, in which highly different external outside conditions were met. The recorded data include recording during sunny and warm days as well as rainy, moist, and cold days. During the 1 h recording period, each participant washed their hands for a set amount of 4 times. There were no instructions given about the order or duration of hand washing steps, in order not to influence the participants. To also include background data in the recording period, we also included some other activities. During the 1 h period, the participants were mostly working at their desks. Some recordings also include activities of daily living like cooking pasta and folding laundry. Additionally, we asked each participant to take a walk around the building they were in, which was either an office building or the building they lived in. The walk was constrained to include descending and ascending at least two flights of stairs. Other than this, no further constraints or activities were enforced, so that the data contain mostly realistic daily activities along with the four hand-washing instances.

To be able to annotate the recordings as accurately as possible, we placed a single Puck.js near designated hand-washing sinks to act as a dedicated BLE beacon. The signals from these beacons were recorded alongside all the sensor data by the wearable units. The proximity to the sink is expected to be correlated to the respective Bluetooth advertisement's received signal strength indicator (RSSI). Added to that, the participants were asked to press the button on the Puck.js device once before starting the hand wash and then once again after finishing the hand wash. This additional data from button presses and beacons is only used for the gathering of ground truth. We restricted the use of beacons to the labeling because to gather this data, beacons would have to be placed at every sink, the user would wash their hands at. Similarly, in the real application, button presses before and after each hand-wash would nullify the need for automated hand-washing detection, hence the button presses are also only used for ground truth annotation.

We recorded the sensor data from the integrated and externally attached sensors as shown in Table 1.

Table 1. The variety of sensors used for recording data in our experiment, which are included in the Bosch BME280 sensor board and the Puck.js sensor board. The latter collects all sensor readings to be forwarded via Bluetooth Low Energy.

sensor type	axes	device	sampling frequency
Accelerometer	3	Puck.js	52 Hz
Gyroscope	3	Puck.js	52 Hz
Humidity	1	BME280	1 Hz
Temperature	1	BME280	1 Hz
Atm. Pressure	1	BME280	1 Hz

The recorded data was then manually annotated in Label Studio [13]. For the annotation, the button presses and the proximity values to the Bluetooth beacons were visualized alongside the IMU sensor values and the values of the atmospheric sensors. This enabled us to accurately label the hand-washes.

In addition to recording sensor data, we also noted down the recording day's weather conditions for each recording, i.e. mean temperature, mean relative humidity, condition (rainy, sunny, cloudy), and mean air pressure. We include this meta-information in the dataset. Overall, we recorded on 6 different days, with rainy to sunny conditions, temperatures from 13 to 21°C, humidity between 63.5 and 89, and pressure in the range of 996.7 to 1007.7 hPa. However, since the data was recorded indoors, the outside weather conditions likely did not impact the results severely. Also, we found that the readings of the recorded atmospheric sensors are not well-calibrated, i.e. the absolute values are not always correct. In contrast, the relative values are reliable, showing similar changes to external sensors to which we compared them.

3.3   Evaluation of Collected Data

In total, we collected 43 instances of hand washing. In Fig. 3 we show the distribution of the hand-washing duration for all hand-washes contained in the recorded data. The mean (25.19 s), median (26.34 s), and the quartiles of the duration of a hand-washing instance are between 20 s and 30 s. However, the minimum (6.48 s) and the maximum (44.08 s) deviate from the mean. In total, the recorded data has a length of 10 h and 3.5 min. The contained hand washing has a total duration of 17.85 min. Thus, the collected dataset is highly imbalanced with the null class making up 97 % of the data. However, we argue that this is a desirable feature of our dataset, as hand washing is also scarce in the real world, where it only makes up a tiny percentage of a potential user's daily activities.

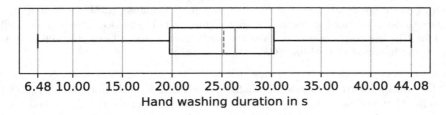

Fig. 3. Statistics for the duration in seconds of all 43 recorded hand washes. The box plot shows the median (red solid line), mean (green dashed line), quartiles (box extents), and minimum and maximum (whiskers). (Color figure online)

3.4   Visual Representation

To inspect the additional sensors' usefulness for our tasks, we created visual representations, which will be shown and discussed in this chapter.

One example of hand washing is displayed in Fig. 4, which shows the accelerometer values and the humidity change compared to the start of hand washing. In the plot, we can observe the participant walking to the sink, then starting to wash their hands, and then drying off their hands before finally walking again. The humidity level rises shortly after the hand washing is started by the participant, and begins to fall one the tap is turned off and the participant is drying off the hands.

The humidity change after starting to wash hands is shown in Fig. 5(a). As expected, the measured humidity begins to increase around the moment at which the participant starts their handwashing procedure. The signal then peaks some seconds after the start of the hand wash, depending on the duration of the hand wash. It can also be observed that after a hand wash, the sensor values only slowly decrease again until they reach the same level that they were at before starting the hand wash. During the hand wash, the humidity usually monotonously rises until the hand wash is finished and the participant starts to dry off their hands. Interestingly, the humidity already starts to rise before the hand wash is started, which is probably due to the room in which the sink is located having a slightly higher humidity in comparison to other rooms, which would align well with the findings in [1].

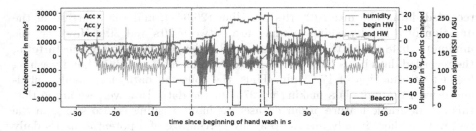

Fig. 4. Example accelerometer and humidity sensor plot of one hand washing (HW in legend) instance. We can observe the humidity rising once the participant starts washing their hands at time t = 0. Additionally, the signal RSSI received from a Bluetooth beacon placed at the sink is shown (navy blue). The Beacon signal was only used for labeling and is non-zero while the participant remained near the sink, e.g. to dry off the hands after washing. (Color figure online)

The temperature response of washing one's hands is displayed in Fig. 5(b). It seems that the hand-washing has no immediate effect on the measured temperature, as the temperature remains stable during the wash. However, before the hand wash, the temperature decreases and afterward it increases again. We assume that this is due to the bathroom/kitchen being colder than the other rooms the participants were in before hand washing. Therefore, although there seems to be no change during the hand washing, the temperature sensor might deliver context about the room in which a user might be staying.

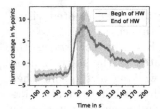 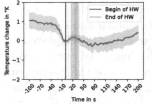 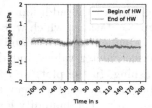

(a) Humidity: After the end of the hand washing, the humidity decreases. The decrease is not as sudden as the prior increase, which occurs around the start of the handwashing.

(b) Temperature: The readings tend to decrease slightly (note the Y axis scale) when entering the bathroom or kitchen, and rises after leaving it again.

(c) Air Pressure: The pressure sensor's readings stay relatively constant during the hand washing. The larger deviation after the hand washing comes from one participant who took a walk up the stairs of the building shortly after washing.

Fig. 5. Response of the (a) humidity, (b) temperature, and (c) pressure sensors to hand washing, averaged (in dark blue) over all recorded hand washes, with bootstrapped 95% confidence interval (in light blue). The start of the hand washing is marked with a green vertical line. The yellow vertical lines mark the respective ends of all the handwashing instances. (Color figure online)

As expected, the pressure sensor's reading stays almost perfectly constant before, during, and after washing one's hands. Therefore, we did not include a visual representation of it in this report. It follows that the pressure sensor readings are unlikely to have a large effect on hand washing detection accuracy. However, when the pressure sensor shows a high rate of change, we can also rule out hand washing as the user's current activity. In that sense, there is still an expected benefit of including it in the data, e.g. filtering out the "stairs" activity.

3.5 Machine Learning Experiments

After the visual inspection of the recorded data showed promising correlations between the newly added humidity sensor and the hand washing labels, we trained random forest classifiers on the data. The goal of the machine learning experiment was not to maximize the performance but rather to explore the importance of the multi-modal sensor setup. Specifically, each sensor's impact on the prediction performance of the trained classifier was to be evaluated.

Hence, we trained models using different sensor configurations in a small-scale ablation study and recorded the performance of the random forest classifier for each sensor set. The sensor subsets we used are listed in Table 2. The different sensor combinations are used to measure the impact of each sensor's addition or removal from the dataset.

Table 2. Sensor subsets used for training and evaluation. H stands for humidity, T for temperature and P for pressure.

sensors	abbreviation
Accelerometer	A
Acc + H. + T. + P	A+HTP
Accelerometer + Gyroscope	AG
Acc. + Gyro. + Humidity	AG+H
Acc. + Gyro + Temperature	AG+T
Acc + Gyro + Pressure	AG+P
Acc + Gyro + H. + T. + P.	ALL

We trained and evaluated the models on non-overlapping 2.5 s and 5 s-long sliding windows using the feature set in the enumeration below:

- mean
- standard deviation
- minimum
- maximum
- slope (last value - first value)
- median

- inter-quartile-range
- first quartile
- third quartile
- average crossings (times the signal crosses the mean)
- skewness
- kurtosis

We chose this window length in line with other hand-washing detection literature ([3]: 3 s, [5]: 6 s). The feature set was designed to represent the findings of the previously mentioned visual inspection of the data. We included the usual statistical features of mean, std, min, max, and interquartile ranges for each sensor axis. Additionally, we added the slope of all sensors. One could also go a step further and add features in the frequency domain, but for the basic evaluation of the recorded data, we did not include this type of feature in this work.

To receive an estimate of the participant-independent performance, we explored a leave-one-participant-out (LOPO/LOSO) cross-validation. Additionally, we used per-participant personalized models, to show the effect on single participants. For the personalized model, we trained and evaluated on a train-test split, using 33 % of the user's data for testing and the rest for training the model.

We used a seeded random number generator and repeated the experiment five times to reduce the randomness of the outcome.

4   Results

The resulting F1-scores of our machine learning experiments are displayed in Table 3 for both the LOSO-split and for the personalized machine learning.

We also included the maximal baseline performance of a dummy classifier to better relate the achieved F1 scores. The dummy classifier performance is chosen as the best-performing dummy classifier performance in any of the splits for the relevant task and window size. Hence we over-estimate the dummy performance and find an upper bound for the chance level.

The trained model's performance is significantly above the chance level, with an average F1 score of 69.15 % for the participant-independent task with 5 s windows, and an average F1 score of 85 % for the personalized task. This performance shows that the classifiers were able to detect hand washing from the recorded background activities with high precision and recall. On the other hand, the higher performance on the personalized task also shows that hand washing is highly user-dependent. This could be explained by user-specific rituals and patterns of hand-washing.

However, the results do not yield the expected result, that the addition of the atmospheric sensors boosts machine learning performance. Unlike the visual inspection proposed, the selected sensor subset did not have a measurable impact on the performance. For the participant-independent task, the "classic" combination of accelerometer and gyroscope reached the highest performance. In the personalized task, the atmospheric sensors in combination with the accelerometer yielded the highest performance, with a tiny lead.

5   Discussion

The results show that the addition of the atmospheric sensors can provide additional context. In the visual inspection (see Fig. 4 and Fig. 5(a)) of the collected data, it becomes apparent that the increase of humidity near the running tap can be measured reliably by the used sensors. This could be helpful in visual inspection and retrospective annotation of wearable sensor data where hand washing might occur. Thus, we would have expected, that the hand washing detection performance is best with all sensors or at least the humidity sensor included. There could be several reasons why this is not the case in our experiment, with the manually crafted features not taking advantage of this additional sensor's potential as the most likely explanation. This points to the need for more specific features for the slower and relative changes in humidity readings in particular.

Table 3. Resulting **F1 scores** of the machine learning experiments. No sensor set performed significantly better than the others. In the participant-independent task, the Accelerometer & Gyroscope performed best, while in the personalized task, the Accelerometer & Gyroscope together with Pressure, and Accelerometer & all atmospheric sensors took the lead. Note that these results also show that the dataset is more challenging than previous work, which sometimes reaches F1 scores over 0.9 (see Sect. 2).

sensors	window size	A	A+HTP	AG	AG+H	AG+T	AG+P	ALL	Chance
LOSO	2.5 s	0.663	0.636	**0.679**	0.675	0.673	0.676	0.667	0.111
	5 s	0.681	0.683	**0.704**	0.693	0.691	0.702	0.688	0.077
Personalized	2.5 s	0.819	0.846	0.844	0.830	0.848	**0.857**	0.849	0.188
	5 s	0.854	**0.860**	0.859	0.848	0.844	0.833	0.852	0.076

We also visualized the effect of hand washing on the temperature recorded by the sensors. The change of measured temperature in proximity to the running tap is found to be negligible, whilst the change of room is consistently picked up in the sensor data.

While we can think of other applications for the atmospheric pressure sensor, we do not see a large benefit in using it for hand washing detection. While the pressure sensor probably helps to filter out activities involving altitude changes, it likely does not provide additional discriminatory performance against hand washing for most activities.

In future work, more data and more background activities could be recorded using the same system, which can be replicated as it is open-source. A different machine learning paradigm, like end-to-end deep learning, could also be employed to more precisely capture the characteristic patterns of hand washing for the additional sensors.

Our developed prototype itself is easy to build and records the data reliably. One limitation of the prototype is its reliance on a nearby recording device. For our experiments, we used a laptop, that was carried around by a researcher following the respective participant everywhere. In the future, if we keep the prototype based on the Puck.js, a smartphone application can be used in a similar fashion. A smartphone with the application could be carried around by participants in their pockets, without creating additional disturbance.

Another limitation lies in the nature of the humidity sensor itself. Due to it measuring the humidity in the air, the sensor values only rise slowly, once the user starts washing their hands. They also decrease over a long period of time, inducing some lag that current features do not account for perfectly. The added sensor thus provides a limited benefit if we want to detect the exact onset or offset of the hand-washing activity, due to its slow adaptation. For offline analysis, time-shifting the humidity signal by an appropriate amount of milliseconds could be beneficial. For online analysis, no such workaround seems obvious. Therefore, the humidity sensor is only an addition to the much more frequently used IMU sensor and likely should not be seen as a replacement for the latter.

6   Conclusions

This work showcases an open-source implementation of a hand-washing detection system that uses sensing capabilities that go beyond the usual sensing modalities that are used in wearable-based Human Activity Recognition (HAR). The developed prototype and its software are evaluated in a feasibility study, recording the hand-washing behavior of 10 participants. By analyzing the recorded data visually, it is shown that the addition of some of the modalities, in particular humidity, can provide distinctive readings for improving the hand washing detection performance. Concrete evidence of a large effect on machine learning performance must be provided by further research on more data, and more specific features for these new modalities. Such features should e.g. better capture the observed pattern of rising humidity after most hand washing onsets.

Applications for hand washing detection, hand washing duration predictions, hand washing quality prediction, and similar problems are manifold and can be found in the domains of industry, healthcare, mental health, and more.

Based on our work, we argue that especially atmospheric sensors should be considered for wearable devices aimed at reliably detecting hand washing and distinguishing it from other activities. In general, while atmospheric sensors have been proposed to be used for HAR in the past, recent research has usually neglected them. We argue that there are still more potential applications of them to be explored in the future. The open question of extracting distinctive features that describe the relative humidity rise and drop before and after hand washing is the topic of such work in progress.

The firmware files for the Puck.js, the data recording script, the recorded data, as well as the code used to produce our results, can be found in our GitHub repository[1].

---

[1] https://github.com/kristofvl/wearPuck.

Acknowledgements. This project is funded by the Deutsche Forschungsgemeinschaft (DFG, German Research Foundation) - 425868829 and is part of Priority Program SPP2199 Scalable Interaction Paradigms for Pervasive Computing Environments.

Disclosure of Interests. The authors have no competing interests to declare that are relevant to the content of this article.

References

1. Barna, A., Masum, A.K.M., Hossain, M.E., Bahadur, E.H., Alam, M.S.: A study on human activity recognition using gyroscope, accelerometer, temperature and humidity data. In: 2019 International Conference on Electrical, Computer and Communication Engineering (ECCE), pp. 1–6. IEEE, Cox'sBazar, Bangladesh (2019). https://doi.org/10.1109/ECACE.2019.8679226. https://ieeexplore.ieee.org/document/8679226/
2. Bharti, P., De, D., Chellappan, S., Das, S.K.: HuMAn: complex activity recognition with multi-modal multi-positional body sensing. IEEE Trans. Mob. Comput. **18**(4), 857–870 (2019). https://doi.org/10.1109/TMC.2018.2841905. https://ieeexplore.ieee.org/document/8374816/
3. Burchard, R., Scholl, P.M., Lieb, R., Van Laerhoven, K., Wahl, K.: WashSpot: real-time spotting and detection of enacted compulsive hand washing with wearable devices. In: Proceedings of the 2022 ACM International Joint Conference on Pervasive and Ubiquitous Computing, pp. 483–487. ACM, Cambridge United Kingdom (2022). https://doi.org/10.1145/3544793.3563428. https://dl.acm.org/doi/10.1145/3544793.3563428
4. Burton, M., Cobb, E., Donachie, P., Judah, G., Curtis, V., Schmidt, W.P.: The effect of handwashing with water or soap on bacterial contamination of hands. Int. J. Environ. Res. Public Health **8**(1), 97–104 (2011). https://doi.org/10.3390/ijerph8010097. http://www.mdpi.com/1660-4601/8/1/97
5. Cao, Y., Li, F., Chen, H., Liu, X., Yang, S., Wang, Y.: Leveraging wearables for assisting the elderly with dementia in handwashing. IEEE Trans. Mob. Comput. **22**(11), 6554–6570 (2023). https://doi.org/10.1109/TMC.2022.3193615. https://ieeexplore.ieee.org/document/9839489. Conference Name: IEEE Transactions on Mobile Computing
6. De, D., Bharti, P., Das, S.K., Chellappan, S.: Multimodal wearable sensing for fine-grained activity recognition in healthcare. IEEE Internet Comput. **19**(5), 26–35 (2015). https://doi.org/10.1109/MIC.2015.72. http://ieeexplore.ieee.org/document/7155432/
7. Hayes, D.: Apple Watch Can Now Tell If You're Washing Your Hands (2020). https://deadline.com/2020/06/apple-watch-can-tell-if-you-are-washing-your-hands-coronavirus-1202966657/
8. Inc., A.: Set up Handwashing on Apple Watch (2024). https://support.apple.com/en-my/guide/watch/apdc9b9f04a8/watchos
9. Ivanovs, M., Kadikis, R., Lulla, M., Rutkovskis, A., Elsts, A.: Automated Quality Assessment of Hand Washing Using Deep Learning (2020). http://arxiv.org/abs/2011.11383. arXiv:2011.11383 [cs]
10. Lattanzi, E., Calisti, L., Freschi, V.: Unstructured handwashing recognition using smartwatch to reduce contact transmission of pathogens. IEEE Access **10**, 83111–83124 (2022). https://doi.org/10.1109/ACCESS.2022.3197279. Conference Name: IEEE Access

11. Li, H., et al.: Wristwash: towards automatic handwashing assessment using a wrist-worn device. In: Proceedings of the 2018 ACM International Symposium on Wearable Computers, ISWC 2018, pp. 132–139. Association for Computing Machinery, New York (2018). https://doi.org/10.1145/3267242.3267247. https://dl.acm.org/doi/10.1145/3267242.3267247

12. Mondol, M.A.S., Stankovic, J.A.: Harmony: a hand wash monitoring and reminder system using smart watches. In: Proceedings of the 12th EAI International Conference on Mobile and Ubiquitous Systems: Computing, Networking and Services. ACM, Coimbra, Portugal (2015). https://doi.org/10.4108/eai.22-7-2015.2260042. http://eudl.eu/doi/10.4108/eai.22-7-2015.2260042

13. Tkachenko, M., Malyuk, M., Holmanyuk, A., Liubimov, N.: Label Studio: Data Labeling Software (2020). https://github.com/heartexlabs/label-studio

14. Vepakomma, P., De, D., Das, S.K., Bhansali, S.: A-Wristocracy: deep learning on wrist-worn sensing for recognition of user complex activities. In: 2015 IEEE 12th International Conference on Wearable and Implantable Body Sensor Networks (BSN), pp. 1–6. IEEE, Cambridge, MA, USA (2015). https://doi.org/10.1109/BSN.2015.7299406. http://ieeexplore.ieee.org/document/7299406/

15. Wahl, K., Scholl, P.M., Miché, M., Wirth, S., Burchard, R., Lieb, R.: Real-time detection of obsessive-compulsive hand washing with wearables: Research procedure, usefulness and discriminative performance. J. Obsessive-Compulsive Related Disorders **39**, 100845 (2023). https://doi.org/10.1016/j.jocrd.2023.100845. https://linkinghub.elsevier.com/retrieve/pii/S2211364923000660

16. Wahl, K., et al.: On the automatic detection of enacted compulsive hand washing using commercially available wearable devices. Comput. Biol. Med. **143**, 105280 (2022). https://doi.org/10.1016/j.compbiomed.2022.105280. https://linkinghub.elsevier.com/retrieve/pii/S0010482522000725

17. Wang, C., Sarsenbayeva, Z., Chen, X., Dingler, T., Goncalves, J., Kostakos, V.: Accurate measurement of handwash quality using sensor armbands: instrument validation study. JMIR Mhealth Uhealth **8**(3), e17001 (2020). https://doi.org/10.2196/17001. http://mhealth.jmir.org/2020/3/e17001/

18. Wang, F., Wu, X., Wang, X., Chi, J., Shi, J., Huang, D.: You Can Wash Better: Daily Handwashing Assessment with Smartwatches (2021). http://arxiv.org/abs/2112.06657, [cs, eess]

19. Wolling, F., Laerhoven, K.V., Bilal, J., Scholl, P.M., Völker, B.: WetTouch: touching ground in the wearable detection of hand-washing using capacitive sensing. In: 2022 IEEE International Conference on Pervasive Computing and Communications Workshops and other Affiliated Events (PerCom Workshops), pp. 769–774 (2022). https://doi.org/10.1109/PerComWorkshops53856.2022.9767345

20. Zhang, Y., Xue, T., Liu, Z., Chen, W., Vanrumste, B.: Detecting hand washing activity among activities of daily living and classification of WHO hand washing techniques using wearable devices and machine learning algorithms. Healthcare Technol. Lett. **8**(6), 148–158 (2021). https://doi.org/10.1049/htl2.12018. https://onlinelibrary.wiley.com/doi/abs/10.1049/htl2.12018

21. Zhuang, H., Xu, L., Nishiyama, Y., Sezaki, K.: Detecting hand hygienic behaviors in-the-wild using a microphone and motion sensor on a smartwatch. In: Distributed, Ambient and Pervasive Interactions: 11th International Conference, DAPI 2023, Held as Part of the 25th HCI International Conference, HCII 2023, Copenhagen, Denmark, 23–28 July 2023, Proceedings, Part II, pp. 470–483. Springer, Heidelberg (2023). https://doi.org/10.1007/978-3-031-34609-5_34

Equimetrics - Applying HAR Principles to Equestrian Activities

Jonas Pöhler$^{(\boxtimes)}$ and Kristof Van Laerhoven

University of Siegen, 57076 Siegen, Germany
jonas.poehler@uni-siegen.de

Abstract. This paper presents the Equimetrics data capture system. The primary objective is to apply HAR principles to enhance the understanding and optimization of equestrian performance. By integrating data from strategically placed sensors on the rider's body and the horse's limbs, the system provides a comprehensive view of their interactions. Preliminary data collection has demonstrated the system's ability to accurately classify various equestrian activities, such as walking, trotting, cantering, and jumping, while also detecting subtle changes in rider posture and horse movement. The system leverages open-source hardware and software to offer a cost-effective alternative to traditional motion capture technologies, making it accessible for researchers and trainers. The Equimetrics system represents a significant advancement in equestrian performance analysis, providing objective, data-driven insights that can be used to enhance training and competition outcomes. The system has been made available at [1].

Keywords: Activity Recognition · Equestrian Activities · Transformer

1 Introduction

The field of human activity recognition (HAR) has seen significant advancements in recent years, with researchers exploring the application of various sensor technologies and algorithms to recognize and classify human movements and behaviors [9,10,13,20]. One emerging area of interest is the application of these techniques to the domain of equestrian activities, where the complex interplay between rider and horse movements presents a unique challenge.

The Equimetrics sensor system is a novel approach to capturing and analyzing the motion of both the rider and the horse during equestrian activities. This system utilizes a network of wearable inertial sensors to collect real-time data on the movements and interactions of the rider and horse, with the goal of applying human activity recognition principles to better understand and optimize equestrian performance [2,10,13,20].

The use of wearable inertial sensors, such as accelerometers and gyroscopes, has been a common approach in human activity recognition research, as they can provide detailed information on the movements and orientations of the we

O. Konak et al. (Eds.): iWOAR 2024, LNCS 15357, pp. 69–78, 2025.
https://doi.org/10.1007/978-3-031-80856-2_5

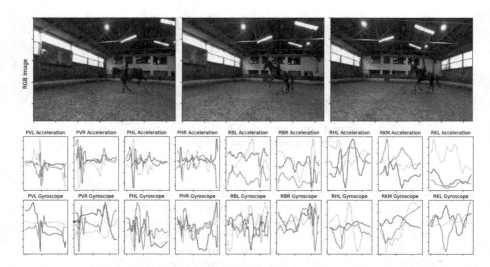

Fig. 1. Exemplary captured data from the Equimetrics system during horse jumping, as recorded from 130 Hz Inertial Measurement Units that were positioned at the horses' ankles and the rider's wrist, ankle, waist, and head, all synchronized with external camera footage.

arer's body [2,12]. These sensors can be strategically placed on the rider's body and the horse's limbs and torso to capture the complex biomechanics involved in equestrian activities (Fig. 1).

This approach has been successful in recognizing human daily activities and sport activities, with researchers developing algorithms to classify motion patterns and detect transitions between different activities. Similarly, the Equimetrics system aims to leverage these techniques to identify and differentiate between various equestrian activities, such as walking, trotting, cantering, and jumping, as well as to detect and analyze subtle changes in the rider's posture and the horse's movements that may be indicative of fatigue, strain, or other performance-relevant factors [3,4,6,7,10,20].

By combining the data from the rider and horse sensors, the Equimetrics system can provide a comprehensive view of the equestrian interaction, enabling a deeper understanding of the factors that contribute to successful performance. This aligns with research on human and animal motion tracking using inertial sensors, which has highlighted the potential of such systems to provide valuable insights into the health and wellbeing of both humans and animals [15].

One key challenge in applying human activity recognition to equestrian activities is the need to address the complex interactions between the rider and the horse. While previous research has primarily focused on single-person scenarios, the Equimetrics system must be able to recognize and differentiate between the movements and behaviors of both the rider and the horse, as well as their coordinated interactions. To address this, the system may incorporate additional sensors or computer vision techniques, as demonstrated in the DEEM system, which combined RFID and computer vision data to recognize exercises performed by multiple individuals in a gym environment [13]. Another important consideration is the potential for variations in equestrian activities due to factors such as horse breed, size, and temperament, as well as the skill level and riding style of the rider. The Equimetrics system must be able to adapt to these individual differences and provide accurate activity recognition across a diverse range of equestrian scenarios. Up until now these observations where only made through manual observation or with expensive and complex motion capture systems [8,16,19].

Previously, the analysis of equestrian activities was largely reliant on subjective assessments of ideal movements by experienced trainers, based on their intuition and expertise. In contrast, the Equimetrics sensor system enables a more objective, data-driven approach to analyzing equestrian movements and training quality, by capturing and classifying the motion data from both the rider and the horse using wearable sensors.

2   Related Work

The application of human activity recognition principles to equestrian activities is a relatively new area of research, but there are several relevant studies that provide a foundation for the Equimetrics system.

One such study, "A framework for the recognition of horse gaits through wearable devices" [4], developed a system for recognizing horse gaits using a smartphone and smartwatch. The researchers placed sensors on the horse's saddle and the rider's wrist, and used machine learning algorithms to classify different horse gaits.

Similarly, the "Smartwatch Application for Horse Gaits Activity Recognition" study also explored the use of wearable sensors to recognize horse gaits, with a focus on the effects of sliding window size and sampling frequency on the accuracy of the system.

These studies demonstrate the potential of wearable sensor technology to capture and analyze the complex movements involved in equestrian activities, and provide a starting point for the Equimetrics system [3].

Additionally, the "Stochastic Recognition of Physical Activity and Healthcare Using Tri-Axial Inertial Wearable Sensors" study highlights the broader applications of human activity recognition in the healthcare and remote monitoring domains, which could be relevant to the Equimetrics system's goal of optimizing equestrian performance and monitoring the health and wellbeing of both the rider and the horse.

In many of the studies done in literature [4,16], the focus has been on using wearable sensors to recognize equine gaits and movements. However, the Equimetrics system aims to go beyond this by also considering the interactions between the rider and the horse, and how these interactions can be used to improve equestrian performance and overall well-being.

One study that touches on this aspect is the "Time-Series-Based Feature Selection and Clustering for Equine Activity Recognition Using Accelerometer Data" paper, which proposed a data-efficient algorithm for recognizing equine activities that considers both the horse and rider movements [19]. The researchers used a combination of feature selection and clustering techniques to develop a model that required only a small amount of labeled data, suggesting the potential for more nuanced activity recognition in the equestrian domain.

In the realm of human activity recognition IMU sensors are often used to classify motion patterns and detect transitions between different activities [19]. Especially for sport activities there is a lot of literature.

Human activity recognition research has explored the potential of wearable inertial sensors to track and analyze complex movements, with applications in healthcare, sports, and other domains [11,12,14,18]. These studies have demonstrated the ability of these sensors to capture detailed information on the orientation and motion of the wearer's body, and to use machine learning algorithms to classify different activities and detect transitions between them.

3   Equimetrics Sensor System

IMU Sensor placement:

- Horses Ankle
- Riders Wrist
- Riders Ankle
- Riders Waist
- Riders Head

Fig. 2. The positions for the 10 IMU sensors in the Equimetrics sensor system.

The Equimetrics sensor system consists of a network of 10 inertial measurement unit (IMU) sensors strategically placed on both the rider and the horse to capture comprehensive motion data from both sources. The sensors are installed on the rider's torso, head, arms, and legs, as well as on the horse's legs (see Fig. 2), enabling a holistic view of the equestrian interaction. The sensor data is transmitted wirelessly to a central processing unit, which stores the information and is then able to recognize and classify the rider's and the horse's activities in later stages of the analysis.

Each sensor node in the system comprises a MPU-6050 NEMS with a 3-axis gyroscope and a 3-axis accelerometer, as well as an ESP32 microcontroller used to stream the data via Wi-Fi using a UDP data transfer protocol. In addition to the IMU sensors, the Equimetrics system also incorporates a video camera that tracks the rider's movements using the PIXEM camera system. This visual data enables a close observation of the rider's activities and can be used for labeling purposes, as well as for more detailed movement analysis with the OpenPose framework.

The central processing unit captures the 3D motion data from all the sensors at a high sampling rate of 130 Hz. The accelerometer has a data range of $\pm16\,g$, while the gyroscope has a range of ±2000 dps. The collected data is then preprocessed to ensure consistency across the sensor data, including sensor alignment, calibration, and resampling.

The Equimetrics system offers a cost-effective alternative to traditional motion capture technologies by leveraging open-source hardware and software. The hardware designs as well as the software are published openly, making the Equimetrics system accessible and affordable for researchers and equestrian trainers (published at anonymized). This open approach enables the creation of a multimodal dataset, combining motion data from the sensor network and visual data from the video cameras, to support the comprehensive analysis of equestrian activities.

Drawing on the insights and approaches from previous studies on human activity recognition and equestrian activity analysis, the Equimetrics system utilizes a combination of feature engineering and advanced machine learning techniques to recognize and classify the complex equestrian activities captured by the sensor network.

4   Preliminary Data Capture Results

To validate the capabilities of the Equimetrics sensor system, preliminary data collection and analysis was conducted on a small sample of riders and horses. The dataset consits of 45 min of data from two horses where the horses perform all the basic gaits as well as jumping over small obstacles.

The data from the inertial sensors and the video cameras was synchronized and annotated to create a labeled dataset for activity recognition.

The preliminary data capture demonstrated that the sensors maintained consistent synchronization and stability throughout the data collection period.

5   Automatic Analysis

The high-frequency sensor data from the Equimetrics system offers substantial opportunities for automated analysis of equestrian activities. An initial step in the data analysis could involve leveraging the data from the four limb sensors on the horse to detect the precise timing of each hoof's contact with the ground. This could be achieved by fusing the accelerometer and gyroscope data from these

Fig. 3. Possible visualizations of the Equimetrics system. Left: Highlighting the hoof-on and hoof-off events. Right: The extracted movements enables the computation of activity maps for the rider.

sensors and converting it to quaternion representations, which would enable the identification of the individual hoof placement events. This detailed information on the horse's gait and movement patterns could provide valuable insights into the horse's performance and health, and could be used to optimize the rider's techniques and the overall equestrian interaction [17]. The results presented in Fig. 3 demonstrate the effectiveness of the sensor data analysis for detecting the precise timing of hoof-on and hoof-off events. This was validated through comparison with annotated video data, which confirmed a high level of precision, with an average precision of 8.98 milliseconds. This performance aligns with the findings reported in the existing literature and represents a modest improvement over the results reported by Tjissen et al. The ability to accurately detect individual hoof placement events from the sensor data provides valuable insights into the horse's gait patterns and movement characteristics, which can be used to optimize the rider's techniques and assess the horse's overall performance and health. Furthermore, the combination of the rider and horse sensor data could enable the recognition of more complex equestrian activities, such as specific dressage movements, jumping techniques, or even the detection of rider falls or other safety-critical events. To discern the distinct movements of the horse's limbs and the rider's limbs individually is crucial. In equestrian activities, the

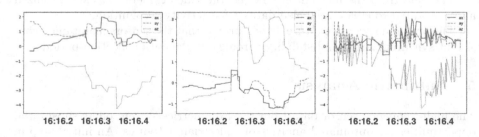

Fig. 4. Illustration for the extraction of the principal movement of the rider's leg by subtraction of the horse's movement

sensor data from the rider captures a combination of the horse's movements and the rider's own movements. It is now possible to extract the rider's independent movement by subtracting the horse's movement from the combined data. The sensor placed on the rider's hips is particularly useful for this purpose, as it represents the point of greatest stability between the rider and the horse, resulting in the least amount of the rider's own movement and the highest overlap with the horse's movement. The data shown in Fig. 4 represents the rider's leg movement with the horse's movement filtered out. This allows for a detailed assessment of the rider's independent limb movement, which can then be used to calculate a comprehensive movement magnitude index (MMI) that precisely quantifies and rates the specific characteristics of the rider's movements, as depicted in Fig. 3. The MMI allows for the characterization of the rider's movement quality by quantifying the rider's ability to suppress unwanted motion. Additionally, it can be used to analyze the temporal relationship between the rider's movements and the horse's responses.

6   Activity Recognition and Classification

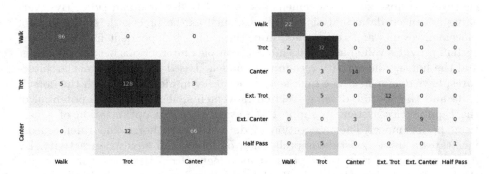

Fig. 5. The confusion matrices for the simple (left) as well as for the complex (right) classifiers.

For the activity recognition component, a set of standardized equestrian test movements published by the Fédération Équestre Nationale (FN) was used as the basis for the analysis. This test protocol involved a combination of basic gaits, such as walk, trot, and canter, performed by the horses. The collected sensor data was then used to train two distinct Transformer-based human activity recognition models [5]. The first model focused on recognizing the specific gait of the horse, while the second model aimed to identify the dressage-related tasks being performed, such as specific movements and maneuvers. The test protocol consisted of 6 distinct movement tasks, some of which were executed in both directions to capture the horses' responses in different orientations. Due to the relatively short duration of certain tasks, 5-second data windows were utilized for the analysis to ensure the capture of the key movement characteristics. The Transformer models were trained on data from two different horses, each performing the test protocol twice, to increase the diversity of the training dataset and improve the models' generalization capabilities. The resulting F1 scores demonstrated a high level of accuracy, with 0.9324 for correctly identifying the horse's gait and 0.7601 for recognizing the specific dressage movements, indicating the effectiveness of the Equimetrics system in capturing and classifying equestrian activities.

The confusion matrices (see Fig. 5) for both classifiers demonstrate that the classification of the horse's gaits is reliable. However, in the case of the more complex dressage movements, the Half Pass movement exhibits a lower classification accuracy. This is likely due to the unique diagonal movement of the horse during the Half Pass, which differs from the other tested movements. Additionally, the limited number of samples for this specific movement may have contributed to the decreased classification performance.

7   Discussion

The Equimetrics sensor system has shown promising results in its ability to capture and analyze the movement patterns of both horse and rider. By leveraging advanced data analysis techniques, such as the precise detection of hoof placement events and the extraction of the rider's independent movement, the system provides valuable insights into the complex interactions between the rider and the horse. The activity recognition models, based on Transformer architectures, have demonstrated a high level of accuracy in identifying both the horse's gaits and the specific dressage-related movements, showcasing the potential of the Equimetrics system to support the evaluation and optimization of equestrian performance. The integration of data from the horse and rider sensors facilitates a more holistic comprehension of the overall equestrian activity. By distinguishing the rider's independent movements from the horse's movements, the system can offer valuable feedback to the rider regarding their technique and coordination, thereby enabling the optimization of the rider-horse interaction. However, some limitations are associated with these preliminary findings, as the small number of horse-rider pairs examined constrains the generalizability of the results to a broader range of riders and horses. Further empirical investigations and structured data collection are necessary to address this limitation and expand the scope of the study. Evaluating the Equimetrics system with a larger and more diverse sample of horse-rider pairs would help validate the robustness of the activity recognition models and provide deeper insights into the nuances of equestrian performance. Additionally, longitudinal studies that track the progress of riders over time could shed light on the system's ability to facilitate long-term skill development and adaptation. Exploring these avenues would strengthen the evidence supporting the Equimetrics system as a valuable tool for enhancing equestrian training and competition.

Acknowledgements. This project is funded by the Deutsche Forschungsgemeinschaft (DFG, German Research Foundation) - 425868829 and is part of Priority Program SPP2199 Scalable Interaction Paradigms for Pervasive Computing Environments.

Disclosure of Interests. The authors have no competing interests to declare that are relevant to the content of this article.

References

1. limlug/equimetrics: Version 0.1 (2024). https://doi.org/10.5281/ZENODO. 13367775. https://zenodo.org/doi/10.5281/zenodo.13367775
2. Bruno, B., Mastrogiovanni, F., Sgorbissa, A.: Wearable inertial sensors: applications, challenges, and public test benches. IEEE Robot. Autom. Mag. **22**(3), 116–124 (2015). https://doi.org/10.1109/mra.2015.2448279
3. Casella, E., Khamesi, A.R., Silvestri, S.: Smartwatch application for horse gaits activity recognition (2019). https://doi.org/10.1109/smartcomp.2019.00080
4. Casella, E., Khamesi, A.R., Silvestri, S.: A framework for the recognition of horse gaits through wearable devices. Pervasive Mob. Comput. **67**, 101213–101213 (2020). https://doi.org/10.1016/j.pmcj.2020.101213
5. Dirgová Luptáková, I., Kubovčík, M., Pospíchal, J.: Wearable sensor-based human activity recognition with transformer model. Sensors **22**(5) (2022). https://doi.org/10.3390/s22051911. https://www.mdpi.com/1424-8220/22/5/1911
6. Echterhoff, J.M., Haladjian, J., Brügge, B.: Gait and jump classification in modern equestrian sports (2018). https://doi.org/10.1145/3267242.3267267
7. Eerdekens, A., et al.: Horse jumping and dressage training activity detection using accelerometer data. Animals **11**(10), 2904–2904 (2021). https://doi.org/10.3390/ani11102904
8. Eerdekens, A., et al.: Resampling and data augmentation for equines' behaviour classification based on wearable sensor accelerometer data using a convolutional neural network (2020). https://doi.org/10.1109/coins49042.2020.9191639
9. Guo, J., Mu, Y., Xiong, M., Liu, Y., Gu, J.: Activity feature solving based on TF-IDF for activity recognition in smart homes. Complexity **2019**, 1–10 (2019). https://doi.org/10.1155/2019/5245373
10. Hsu, Y., Yang, S.C., Chang, H.C., Lai, H.C.: Human daily and sport activity recognition using a wearable inertial sensor network. IEEE Access **6**, 31715–31728 (2018). https://doi.org/10.1109/access.2018.2839766
11. Kyritsis, A.I., Deriaz, M., Konstantas, D.: Considerations for the design of an activity recognition system using inertial sensors (2018). https://doi.org/10.1109/healthcom.2018.8531145
12. Lima, W.S., Souto, E., El-Khatib, K., Jalali, R., Gama, J.: Human activity recognition using inertial sensors in a smartphone: an overview. Sensors **19**(14), 3213–3213 (2019). https://doi.org/10.3390/s19143213
13. Liu, Z., Liu, X., Li, K.: Deeper exercise monitoring for smart gym using fused RFID and CV data (2020). https://doi.org/10.1109/infocom41043.2020.9155360
14. López-Nava, I.H., Muñoz-Meléndez, A.: Wearable inertial sensors for human motion analysis: a review (2016). https://doi.org/10.1109/jsen.2016.2609392
15. Marin, F.: Human and animal motion tracking using inertial sensors. Sensors **20**(21), 6074–6074 (2020). https://doi.org/10.3390/s20216074

16. Nankervis, K., Hodgins, D., Marlin, D.: Comparison between a sensor (3D accelerometer) and proreflex motion capture systems to measure stride frequency of horses on a treadmill. Comp. Exerc. Physiol. **5**(3–4), 107–107 (2008). https://doi.org/10.1017/s1478061508017027
17. Tijssen, M., et al.: Automatic hoof-on and -off detection in horses using hoof-mounted inertial measurement unit sensors. PloS One **15**(6), e0233266–e0233266 (2020). https://doi.org/10.1371/journal.pone.0233266
18. de Villa, S.G., Casillas-Pérez, D., Martín, A.J., Domínguez, J.J.G.: Inertial sensors for human motion analysis: a comprehensive review. IEEE Trans. Instrum. Measur. **72**, 1–39 (2023). https://doi.org/10.1109/tim.2023.3276528
19. Waele, T.D., et al.: Time-series-based feature selection and clustering for equine activity recognition using accelerometers. IEEE Sens. J. **23**(11), 11855–11868 (2023). https://doi.org/10.1109/jsen.2023.3265811
20. Zhu, C., Sheng, W.: Recognizing human daily activity using a single inertial sensor (2010). https://doi.org/10.1109/wcica.2010.5555072

Applications in Vision-Based Recognition

Leveraging Vision Language Models for Facial Expression Recognition in Driving Environment

Ibtissam Saadi[1,3]([envelope])[ID], Abdenour Hadid[2][ID], Douglas W. Cunningham[1][ID], Abdelmalik Taleb-Ahmed[3][ID], and Yassin El Hillali[3][ID]

[1] Faculty 1 MINT, Brandenburg University of Technology BTU Cottbus-Senftenberg, Cottbus, Germany
ibtissam.saadi@b-tu.de
[2] Sorbonne Center for Artificial Intelligence, Sorbonne University Abu Dhabi, Abu Dhabi, UAE
[3] Laboratory of IEMN, CNRS, Centrale Lille, UMR 8520, Univ. Polytechnique Hauts-de-France, Valenciennes, France

Abstract. We are witnessing an increasing interest in vision-language models (VLMs) as reflected in the impressive results across a large spectrum of tasks. In this context, we introduce in this paper a novel architecture that exploits the capabilities of VLMs for facial expression recognition in driving environment to enhance road safety. We present an approach called CLIVP-FER, which uses the Contrastive Language-Image Pretraining (CLIP) and combines both visual and textual data to overcome the environmental challenges and ambiguities in facial expression interpretation. In addition, we apply average pooling to improve the accuracy and the computational efficiency. The proposed approach is thoroughly evaluated on a benchmark driving dataset called KMU-FED. The experiments showed superior performance compared to state-of-the-art methods, achieving an average accuracy of 97.36%. Cross-database evaluation is also provided showing good generalization abilities. The ablation study gives more insights into the performance of our proposed architecture. The obtained results are interesting and confirm the capabilities of vision-language models in vision tasks, demonstrating their promising applications in efficient driver assistance and intervention systems. We are making the code of this work publicly available for research purposes at https://github.com/Ibtissam-SAADI/CLIVP-FER.

Keywords: Facial Expression Recognition · Driver's Emotions · Vision Language Models · Contrastive Language-Image Pretraining

1 Introduction

Road safety is a major concern for the automotive industry. Human error is a significant contributor to road accidents, resulting in various safety issues. Technological advancements have led to the development of systems aimed at enhancing

O. Konak et al. (Eds.): iWOAR 2024, LNCS 15357, pp. 81–93, 2025.
https://doi.org/10.1007/978-3-031-80856-2_6

the driving experience and reducing accident rates. Specifically, facial expression recognition (FER) systems are increasingly being integrated into autonomous vehicles and advanced driver assistance systems (ADAS), as illustrated in Fig. 1. These systems are crucial for detecting emotional states in driving environment [12,16].

(a) Camera installed in a car.   (b) FER for a driver.

Fig. 1. Example of driver's facial expression recognition using a camera installed inside a car. The figure is only for illustration and is partially generated using OpenAI's ChatGPT-4.

In this context, numerous studies have investigated methodologies for recognizing drivers' facial expressions, ranging from using handcrafted features to deep learning such as [4,6,13,15,22]. These systems typically depend mainly on visual data to analyze facial cues and infer emotions. However, several factors may significantly affect the accuracy of these systems, including variable lighting conditions and uncooperative users. Moreover, an over-reliance on visual data can restrict the contextual interpretation of emotions, possibly leading to errors in prediction. Additionally, some models are not suitable for driving environment due to the high computational cost.

On the other hand, very recent works have explored the use of vision-language models for facial expression recognition yielding very interesting results [2,9,11,25]. For instance, authors in [9] proposed a Contrastive Language-Image Pretraining (CLIP)-based framework for dynamic and static facial expression recognition, incorporating fine-grained text descriptors for each expression. Similarly, Zhao and Patras [25] focused on dynamic facial expression recognition, incorporating temporal modeling and learnable context to capture fine-grained temporal features. Foteinopoulou and Patras [2] addressed zero-shot classification challenges in dynamic facial expression recognition by using sample-level text descriptions for natural language supervision. A quantitative assessment of

GPT-4V's performance in General Emotion Recognition (GER) tasks is provided in [11]. These few recent works showed interesting results and proved the usefulness of vision language models in facial expression recognition.

Inspired by the methods above, we propose a novel architecture that exploits the capabilities of the vision-language models for facial expression recognition in a driving environment. In fact, while the existing VLM-based approaches have shown promising results, they do not deal with driving environments and may struggle to achieve high accuracy in real-world scenarios due to their dependence on complex textual descriptors and the high computational costs involved. We propose an elegant approach that uses the Contrastive Language-Image Pretraining [14] and combines both visual and textual data to overcome the environmental challenges and ambiguities in facial expression interpretation in a driving environment. In addition, we apply average pooling to the features extracted by CLIP to reduce the dimensionality and highlight the salient information, thereby reducing the computational cost and improving the performance of the classifier. The contributions of our work are described as follows:

- We introduce CLIVP-FER, an innovative approach for extracting features from both images and text using the CLIP model, along with Multilayer Perceptron (MLP) classifier for accurate classification. This method effectively leverages multimodal data to provide a detailed understanding of the driver's facial expressions.
- Our methodology harnesses the CLIP model solely as a feature extractor, without additional training. This strategy enables us to leverage the strengths of a pre-trained model, significantly reducing computational costs.
- We apply average pooling to the features extracted by CLIP to reduce dimensionality of the features and highlight salient information, thereby improving the performance of the classifier.
- We conduct a comprehensive evaluation of the proposed approach, which includes assessing its generalization capabilities, speed efficiency, and performing an ablation study.
- We compare our approach to the state-of-the-art and existing methods on benchmark dataset of a driving environment, resulting in significant performance improvements.

The rest of this paper is structured as follows: Sect. 2 provides a review of existing works related to facial expression recognition. Section 3 describes our proposed approach, detailing the different steps from data pre-processing to feature extraction with CLIP to emotion classification. Section 4 discusses the experimental data and setup. Section 5 presents the obtained results and compares them to state-of-the-art. To better gain insights into our proposed architecture, cross-database evaluation, and ablation study are also provided in this section. Finally, Sect. 6 summarises our findings, draws some conclusions, and suggests possible directions for future research.

2   Related Work

Several studies have investigated the challenging task of identifying driver's emotions, primarily focusing on physiological signals and facial expression cues. In the realm of physiological signals, Wang *et al.* employed electroencephalography (EEG) signals and proposed an end-to-end Convolutional Neural Networks (CNN) model in order to improve the cross-subject emotion recognition accuracy [21]. By doing this, the authors achieved a good performance in determining human emotions. In another work, using a back-propagation network and Dempster-Shafer evidence approach, Wang *et al.* employed multiple-electrocardiogram (ECG) feature fusion including time-frequency domain, waveform, and non-linear features to recognize driver's emotion [20]. In contrast, various other approaches have focused on visual data for facial expression inference. For instance, Chen *et al.* introduced a modified ResNet18 network with an enhanced feature attention (EFA) module to extract rich features from facial expression images [1]. They employed a joint discriminative correlation alignment (JDCA) loss to align feature distributions between single-driver (SD) and two-driver (TD) images while leveraging label information for driver facial expression recognition. In [18], the authors used transfer learning with pre-trained CNN architectures such as AlexNet, SqueezeNet, and VGG19 to perform facial emotion recognition. The models were evaluated on various benchmark datasets with real-time in-vehicle challenges. Results indicated that the pre-trained VGG19 model generally outperforms AlexNet and SqueezeNet.

In [5], a novel facial expression recognition method designed for real-time embedded systems is proposed. The method utilizes a DLib detector [7] to detect the face landmarks and extract geometric features. The extracted features are then employed using a hierarchical Weighted Random Forest classifier to accurately classify the facial expressions, claiming interesting results.

To analyze driver's behavior, a pre-trained VGG16 model was used in [8] to extract features and perform classification of emotions under the challenges of multi-pose and varying illumination conditions, achieving interesting results. In the same context, a real-time framework for stress detection was presented in [23]. It consists of three modules, face detection using MTCNN, a connected convolutional network (CCNN) that combines low-level and high-level features for the facial expression module, and a module for stress detection. The proposed framework achieved a performance comparable to that of a state-of-the-art one.

Among the most recent and appealing works on facial expression recognition are those exploiting vision-language models [2,9,11,19,25]. These works showed interesting results and proved the usefulness of vision language models in facial expression recognition. However, their efficiency in real-world driving environments is not yet proven. To the best of our knowledge, our present paper is the first work focusing on exploring the capabilities of the vision-language models for facial expression recognition in driving environments. A comprehensive survey on driver's emotion recognition can be found here [16].

3   Proposed Approach

Our proposed architecture, called CLIVP-FER, is illustrated in Fig. 2. The inputs of the system consist of a face image and a tokenized text descriptor. Feature extraction is independently conducted on each input utilizing CLIP [14] encoder. Subsequently, a two-stage average pooling layer (AvgPool1d) is applied to the image features and to the concatenated image-text features, in order to enhance the feature saliency and decrease the dimensionality. These refined features are then fed into a Multilayer Perceptron (MLP) classifier for determining the facial expression of the driver.

3.1   Data Preprocessing

For the visual data, and to enhance the model's robustness and prevent overfitting, a series of transformations are applied to the input images, including random horizontal flip and random rotation, hence introducing variability that simulates different orientations and perspectives seen in real-world scenarios. Additionally, resizing and normalization are applied to the images.

The textual data in our study consists of descriptive captions for each class, detailing the corresponding facial expressions. These captions are generated by the advanced language model, ChatGPT-4, rather than using standard class names. For example, for the 'Happy' class, the caption is: 'A facial expression characterized by wide, bright eyes, raised cheeks, a broad smile revealing teeth, and relaxed eyebrows'. This strategy, inspired by the work presented in [25], allows for a more detailed and nuanced representation of facial expressions. The preprocessing of these captions involves tokenization and embedding using CLIP to convert the tokens into feature vectors that can be processed alongside the visual data.

3.2   Extracting and Refining Features Using CLIP and Average Pooling

We use CLIP, a multimodal neural network trained on a large number of text-image pairs, to extract the features. CLIP has been designed with two distinct encoders: a visual encoder, E_{visual}, and a text encoder, E_{text}, which operate independently to handle their respective data modalities. For our purposes, we select the pre-trained ViT-B/32 CLIP variant, which employs a Vision Transformer (ViT) architecture. The ViT-B/32 is especially useful since it is able to generate highly expressive and contextual features for both text and images, which is critical for capturing the nuances of facial expressions, especially in scenarios where visual data might be partially occluded or unclear. During feature extraction, CLIP encoders process the preprocessed images and text without additional training. Let V denote the preprocessed image, and T the preprocessed text. The feature extraction is defined as follows:

$$f_{\text{v}} = E_{\text{visual}}(V) \tag{1}$$

$$f_{\text{t}} = E_{\text{text}}(T) \tag{2}$$

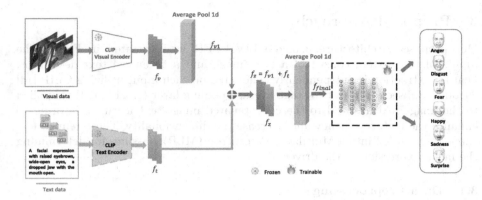

Fig. 2. The figure illustrates our proposed CLIVP-FER architecture. The visual inputs are processed with Contrastive Language-Image Pretraining(CLIP) [14] encoder into a vector f_v. The textual inputs are processed into a vector f_t. The visual feature vector f_v is then processed through an average pooling layer to produce f_{v1}, which is subsequently combined with f_t to form f_z. This combined vector is further processed by an additional average pooling layer, resulting in the final feature vector f_{final}, used to classify the facial expressions by a Multilayer Perceptron (MLP). The figure highlights the frozen (non-trainable) and trainable components.

where f_v and f_t are the image and text feature vectors, respectively.

The resulting image feature vector undergoes average pooling, which condenses information, reduces dimensionality, and discards noise:

$$f_{v1} = \text{AvgPool1d}(f_v) \tag{3}$$

The process of average pooling is directly applied to the high-level features extracted by CLIP's vision transformer-based visual encoder. This contrasts with applying pooling layer to features extracted by CNN and leverages the advanced representations provided by the transformer architecture. Subsequently, a second average pooling operation is performed on the combined image-text features set. This two-stage pooling process ensures focusing on the most relevant features for classification:

$$f_z = \text{Concat}(f_{v1}, f_t) \tag{4}$$

$$f_{final} = \text{AvgPool1d}(f_z) \tag{5}$$

Finally, the condensed feature set f_{final} is used to train our classifier.

3.3 Emotion Classification

We utilize a specialized MLP classifier with a hidden layer that is specifically designed for categorizing emotions. This classifier is trained to accurately interpret the extracted set of final features, f_{final}, by CLIP. The structure of the classifier is as follows: The initial fully connected layer, known as `fc1`, transforms the input vector into a hidden representation that consists of 512 dimensions. This transformation is achieved using the equation:

$$h = \text{ReLU}(W_1 f_{\text{final}} + b_1) \tag{6}$$

Here, the weights and bias of `fc1` are denoted as W_1 and b_1, respectively. The Rectified Linear Unit activation function, ReLU, is applied in this process. To enhance generalization and prevent overfitting, a dropout layer is implemented with a rate of 0.5 on this hidden representation. The final layer, referred to as `fc2`, maps the hidden representation to the output space that corresponds to the number of emotion categories. This mapping is achieved using the equation:

$$o = W_2 h + b_2 \tag{7}$$

In this equation, W_2 and b_2 represent the weights and bias of `fc2`, respectively. The output denoted as o, represents the raw scores for each emotion category.

4   Experimental Data and Setup

We carried out a comprehensive evaluation of the proposed architecture using a publicly available benchmark dataset of a driving environment namely: KMU-FED (Keimyung University Facial Expression of Drivers) [5]. Example images from this dataset are shown in Fig. 3. Additionally, we considered two other datasets (FER 2013 [3], and RAF-DB [10].) for cross-database analysis to assess the generalization of our approach.

Fig. 3. Examples of images from KMU-FED dataset. As can be noticed, the problem of facial expression recognition in driving environment has some different challenges (in terms of lighting and user's cooperation) compared to "conventional" facial expression recognition.

The KMU-FED dataset [5] provides an exceptional context for evaluating the effectiveness of our method in real-life driving scenarios, especially due to its emphasis on driver-specific facial expressions. It comprises 1106 images of 12 subjects, each displaying the six basic emotions: anger, disgust, fear, happiness, sadness, and surprise. The images were captured in real driving conditions using near-infrared cameras. These cameras were subject to varying lighting conditions and partial occlusion. To ensure statistically consistent experimentation, we used a 10-fold cross-validation approach to split the dataset, following most state-of-the-art methods, as the dataset does not have an official train and test split.

We implemented our approach using the open-source PyTorch framework on an NVIDIA Quadro RTX 5000 GPU with 16 GB RAM. Facial image pre-processing involved the use of Multi-task Cascaded Convolutional Networks (MTCNN) [24] to detect and crop the faces in the KMU-FED dataset, all images in this dataset were resized to 224×224 pixels. During the training phase, we set a batch size of 64, a learning rate of 0.003, and a weight decay of 1e-4. We employed the Adaptive Moment Estimation (Adam) optimizer, cross-entropy loss function, and trained for 40 epochs. Early stopping was implemented when no accuracy improvement was obtained after 10 epochs.

5   Experimental Results and Analysis

This section describes the obtained results using our proposed approach on the KMU-FED dataset along with a comparative analysis against some state-of-the-art methods. In addition, a cross-database evaluation is given assessing the generalization ability and speed efficiency of our approach. Finally, an ablation study is presented giving more insights into the performance of our proposed architecture.

5.1   Obtained Results

Table 1 shows the obtained result using our CLIVP-FER model and a comparison against some recent and state-of-the-art methods on the KMU-FED dataset. The table clearly indicates that our approach yields an impressive performance of 97.36% outperforming all other methods. It shows a gain of 2.66% over the hierarchical WRF method, 2.26% over the LMRF method, and 3.09% over the pre-trained VGG16 method. The confusion matrix in Fig. 4 confirms the accuracy of our model, with high accuracy for 'Happy' and 'Surprised', and some confusion between 'Angry' and 'Sad', as well as between 'Fear' and 'Sadness', which can be attributed to the subtle visual similarities of these emotional states. Despite these few cases of misclassification, the result confirms CLIVP-FER's ability to accurately interpret complex emotions, demonstrating its potential for real-world applications.

5.2   Cross-Database Evaluation

In order to thoroughly investigate the generalisability and speed efficiency of our proposed CLIVP-FER approach, we performed a cross-database analysis by training our model on the KMU-FED dataset and evaluating it on the FER2013 and RAF-DB datasets.

As shown in Table 2, various performance metrics, including accuracy, precision, recall and F1 score, are reported to measure the model's ability to correctly

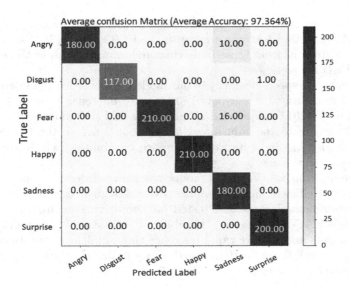

Fig. 4. Confusion matrix of our CLIVP-FER model on the KMU-FED dataset.

Table 1. Obtained results using our CLIVP-FER model, compared with state-of-the-art methods on the KMU-FED dataset.

Methods	Accuracy
Hierarchical WRF (2018) [5]	94.70%
LMRF (2020) [6]	95.10%
Pre-trained-VGG16 (2021) [8]	94.27%
Modified SqueezeNet (2022) [17]	83.40%
CLIVP-FER (Our method)	**97.36%**

identify facial expressions. Precision and recall, although closely related to accuracy, provide more detailed information about the performance of the model. Precision indicates how many of the positive outcomes predicted by the model were actually positive, and recall indicates how many of the actual positive outcomes were correctly predicted by the model. The F1 score, a combination of precision and recall, indicates a well-balanced model that is both accurate and sensitive.

When trained on the KMU-FED dataset (i.e. which corresponds to a driving environment), the model achieves an accuracy of 0.89 on FER2013 (non-driving environment) and 0.92 on RAF-DB (non-driving environment). For a fair comparison, given the fact that our model was trained on 6 classes, we tested the model on the same number of classes, excluding the seventh class (Neutral) from both test datasets. The model is still shown to be quite accurate, with a slight drop in performance when tested on unbalanced samples, which is due to the balanced nature of its training set. This decrease in accuracy can also be attributed to the fact that certain features present in the FER2013 and RAF-DB datasets are somehow different from those in driving environment, such as those found in the KMU-FED dataset.

To evaluate the speed efficiency of our model, we recorded the inference time across the two datasets, we achieved an average inference time of 2.6 ms per image on the FER2013 dataset and 2.7 ms on the RAF-DB dataset. These results not only demonstrate the robustness of our model across the two emotional datasets but also highlight its rapid inference capabilities, which are essential for real-time applications.

In summary, our CLIVP-FER model has shown interesting generalization capabilities and efficient inference times, even though it is trained solely on a driving environment dataset and tested on non-driving environment (i.e. the FER2013 and RAF-DB datasets). Its ability to maintain high accuracy across different datasets and achieve rapid inference times indicates its robustness and potential for practical applications, particularly in driving contexts where accurate facial expression recognition is crucial.

Table 2. Cross-database performance evaluation of our proposed CLIVP-FER model. KMU-FED dataset corresponds to a driving environment while FER2013 and RAF-DB datasets correspond to a non-driving environment. The training is conducted on KMU-FED and the testing is on FER2013 and RAF-DB datasets.

Datasets	KMU-FED	
	FER2013 [3]	RAF-DB [10]
Accuracy	0.89	0.92
Precision	0.92	0.85
Recall	0.87	0.87
F1-score	0.88	0.85

5.3   Ablation Study

In order to determine the impact of different image- and text-derived features on the overall performance of our CLIVP-FER model, an ablation study is conducted. The results of this ablation study are detailed in Table 3. Using only CLIP image features, the model yields in quite low performance, achieving an average accuracy of 0.63, a precision of 0.62, a recall of 0.60 and an F1 score of 0.62. Incorporating textual features in addition to the image features significantly improves the model's performance, as evidenced by a better average accuracy of 0.84, highlighting the benefits of the fusion (image and text). The gains in precision (0.88) and recall (0.81) further highlight the model's refined ability to accurately classify expressions and reliably identify the majority of classes. Our proposed approach, taking advantage of a concatenated set of image and text features combined with average pooling layer, achieves excellent performance (accuracy: 0.97, precision: 0.98, recall: 0.97 and F1 score: 0.97). These results highlight the importance of integrating multimodal features into the model and demonstrate the importance of each component of the system.

Table 3. Evaluating the impact of CLIVP-FER model's components on the KMU-FED dataset. The first row shows the results of using only image features. The second row shows the results of combining image and text features. The last row demonstrates the performance of our model utilizing both visual and textual features, along with an average pooling layer.

Methods	Accuracy	Precision	Recall	F1-score
Visual	0.63	0.62	0.60	0.62
Visual+Text	0.84	0.88	0.81	0.81
Visual+Text+AvgPool	**0.97**	**0.98**	**0.97**	**0.97**

6 Conclusion and Future Work

In this paper, we introduced CLIPV-FER, a novel approach that utilizes the CLIP vision-language model to recognize facial expressions in driving scenarios. Our approach concatenates the features extracted by a pre-trained CLIP variant from images and text descriptions, leading to a more comprehensive representation of facial expression recognition. The feature set is further refined by applying average pooling, enabling the classifier to train with more focus and pertinent information while minimizing the dimensionality of the features. We assessed the performance of our approach on a benchmarking dataset of a driving environment and conducted a cross-database evaluation that demonstrated good generalization ability and speed efficiency of our approach. The experimental results showed significant performance enhancement, highlighting the effectiveness of our approach in recognizing facial expressions in a driving environment.

This work is by no means complete. First, the findings should be further validated using other driving datasets, despite the current scarcity of such datasets. Another direction for future research is to investigate how the model performs with video data, which would capture the temporal changes in facial expressions. Additionally, exploring the integration of other modalities such as data from wearable sensors, could enhance the model's performance. Of interest is also the exploration of a multi-camera system in the driving scenario, which would be beneficial for capturing and handling various head poses.

Acknowledgements. We wish to convey our deep appreciation to the EUNICE Alliance for the financial support. Abdenour Hadid is funded by TotalEnergies collaboration agreement with Sorbonne University Abu Dhabi.

References

1. Chen, X., Du, J., Deng, F., Zhao, F.: Transferable driver facial expression recognition based on joint discriminative correlation alignment network with enhanced feature attention. IET Intell. Transport Syst. **17**(12), 2444–2457 (2023)
2. Foteinopoulou, N.M., Patras, I.: EmoCLIP: a vision-language method for zero-shot video facial expression recognition. arXiv preprint arXiv:2310.16640 (2023)
3. Goodfellow, I.J., et al.: Challenges in representation learning: a report on three machine learning contests. In: Neural Information Processing: 20th International Conference, ICONIP 2013, Part III, Daegu, Korea, 3–7 November 2013, pp. 117–124. Springer (2013)
4. Jain, D.K., Dutta, A.K., Verdú, E., Alsubai, S., Sait, A.R.W.: An automated hyperparameter tuned deep learning model enabled facial emotion recognition for autonomous vehicle drivers. Image Vis. Comput. **133**, 104659 (2023)
5. Jeong, M., Ko, B.C.: Driver's facial expression recognition in real-time for safe driving. Sensors **18**(12), 4270 (2018)
6. Jeong, M., Nam, J., Ko, B.C.: Lightweight multilayer random forests for monitoring driver emotional status. IEEE Access **8**, 60344–60354 (2020)
7. King, D.E.: Dlib-ml: a machine learning toolkit. J. Mach. Learn. Res. **10**, 1755–1758 (2009)
8. Leone, A., Caroppo, A., Manni, A., Siciliano, P.: Vision-based road rage detection framework in automotive safety applications. Sensors **21**(9), 2942 (2021)
9. Li, H., Niu, H., Zhu, Z., Zhao, F.: CLIPER: a unified vision-language framework for in-the-wild facial expression recognition. arXiv preprint arXiv:2303.00193 (2023)
10. Li, S., Deng, W., Du, J.: Reliable crowdsourcing and deep locality-preserving learning for expression recognition in the wild. In: Proceedings of the IEEE Conference on Computer Vision and Pattern Recognition, pp. 2852–2861. IEEE (2017)
11. Lian, Z., et al.: GPT-4v with emotion: a zero-shot benchmark for generalized emotion recognition. Inf. Fusion **108**, 102367 (2024)
12. Paradies, M.: Is human error the cause of 94% of vehicle accidents? Would automation stop these crashes? (2022). https://www.taproot.com/is-human-error-the-cause-of-vehicle-accidents/. Accessed 04 Dec 2023
13. Patil, M., Veni, S.: Driver emotion recognition for enhancement of human machine interface in vehicles. In: 2019 International Conference on Communication and Signal Processing (ICCSP), pp. 0420–0424. IEEE (2019)
14. Radford, A., et al.: Learning transferable visual models from natural language supervision. In: International Conference on Machine Learning, pp. 8748–8763. PMLR (2021)
15. Saadi, I., Cunningham, D.W., Abdelmalik, T.A., Hadid, A., El Hillali, Y.: Driver's facial expression recognition using global context vision transformer. In: 2023 IEEE International Conference on Computer Vision and Machine Intelligence (CVMI), pp. 1–8. IEEE, Gwalior (2023). https://doi.org/10.1109/CVMI59935.2023.10464794
16. Saadi, I., Cunningham, D.W., Taleb-Ahmed, A., Hadid, A., El Hillali, Y.: Driver's facial expression recognition: a comprehensive survey. Expert Syst. Appl. **242**, 122784 (2024)
17. Sahoo, G.K., Das, S.K., Singh, P.: Deep learning-based facial emotion recognition for driver healthcare. In: 2022 National Conference on Communications (NCC), pp. 154–159. IEEE, Mumbai (2022)

18. Sahoo, G.K., Das, S.K., Singh, P.: Performance comparison of facial emotion recognition: a transfer learning-based driver assistance framework for in-vehicle applications. Circuits Syst. Signal Process. 1–28 (2023)
19. Tao, Z., et al.: A3lign-DFER: pioneering comprehensive dynamic affective alignment for dynamic facial expression recognition with CLIP. arXiv preprint arXiv:2403.04294 (2024)
20. Wang, X., Guo, Y., Ban, J., Xu, Q., Bai, C., Liu, S.: Driver emotion recognition of multiple-ECG feature fusion based on BP network and d-s evidence. IET Intell. Transp. Syst. **14**(8), 815–824 (2020)
21. Wang, Z., Chen, M., Feng, G.: Study on driver cross-subject emotion recognition based on raw multi-channels EEG data. Electronics **12**(11), 2359 (2023)
22. Zaman, K., Sun, Z., Shah, S.M., Shoaib, M., Pei, L., Hussain, A.: Driver emotions recognition based on improved faster R-CNN and neural architectural search network. Symmetry **14**(4), 687 (2022)
23. Zhang, J., Mei, X., Liu, H., Yuan, S., Qian, T.: Detecting negative emotional stress based on facial expression in real time. In: 2019 IEEE 4th International Conference on Signal and Image Processing (ICSIP), pp. 430–434. IEEE (2019)
24. Zhang, K., Zhang, Z., Li, Z., Qiao, Y.: Joint face detection and alignment using multitask cascaded convolutional networks. IEEE Signal Process. Lett. **23**(10), 1499–1503 (2016)
25. Zhao, Z., Patras, I.: Prompting visual-language models for dynamic facial expression recognition. arXiv preprint arXiv:2308.13382 (2023)

Analyzing Exercise Repetitions: YOLOv8-Enhanced Dynamic Time Warping Approach on InfiniteRep Dataset

Michal Slupczynski[1]($\boxtimes$) (ID), Aleksandra Nekhviadovich[1] (ID), Nghia Duong-Trung[2] (ID), and Stefan Decker[1] (ID)

[1] Information Systems and Databases, RWTH Aachen University, Aachen, Germany
slupczynski@dbis.rwth-aachen.de
[2] Educational Technology Lab, German Research Center for Artificial Intelligence (DFKI), Berlin, Germany
https://dbis.rwth-aachen.de,
https://www.dfki.de/web/forschung/forschungsbereiche/educational-technology-lab

Abstract. This paper presents a novel approach to exercise repetition analysis using the YOLOv8-pose model and Dynamic Time Warping (DTW) techniques applied to the InfiniteRep dataset. Our research addresses the challenges of accurate pose estimation and tracking in dynamic camera environments and with varying occlusions in synthetic datasets. By integrating YOLOv8's pose detection capabilities with the temporal analysis strength of DTW, we propose a method that significantly improves the detection and classification of exercise repetitions across diverse conditions. We demonstrate the effectiveness of this approach through rigorous experiments that test various scenarios, including changes in camera angles and exercise complexity. Our results indicate notable improvements in the accuracy and robustness of exercise recognition, suggesting promising applications in sports science and personal fitness coaching.

Keywords: Synthetic Dataset · InfiniteRep · Pose Tracking · Exercise Repetition Detection · Dynamic Time Warping (DTW) · YOLO · Fitness

1 Introduction and Motivation

Human action recognition is pivotal in various applications within multimedia computing, including intelligent surveillance, virtual reality, and human-computer interaction [1,10]. In sports and fitness, artificial intelligence (AI) assists humans in decision-making and problem-solving [17]. Garbett et al. conducted an intensive comparison and user evaluation of six AI fitness instructor applications [4]. This technology can track an individual's movements, analyze their performance data, and provide suggestions for improvement.

© The Author(s), under exclusive license to Springer Nature Switzerland AG 2025
O. Konak et al. (Eds.): iWOAR 2024, LNCS 15357, pp. 94–110, 2025.
https://doi.org/10.1007/978-3-031-80856-2_7

This is especially important for activities that require the learning of complex motor movements. Despite progress in computer vision for action recognition [3,6], the complexity and variability of human movements, combined with challenging datasets for pose tracking, limit the accuracy and efficiency of current models. However, many state-of-the-art models struggle to accurately recognize and track human poses with dynamic camera movements [20,21]. Additionally, the use of synthetic datasets poses another challenge. These datasets are often created by rendering images from parameterized 3D human models, involving complex processes like shaping, posing, dressing, and texturing. While these rendered images provide precise annotations, they can mislead pose estimation models due to their artificial nature.

1.1 Research Questions and Contributions

To guide our investigation and address the challenges identified in pose estimation and exercise repetition analysis, we formulated the following research questions:

RQ 1 Are there specific exercise types or movement patterns within the InfiniteRep dataset that are more susceptible to inaccuracies in pose estimation using YOLOv8 default model?

RQ 2 Are there strategies to mitigate camera angle, position variations, and body occlusions to maintain effectiveness in detecting exercise repetitions?

RQ 3 How can missing values and occlusions be effectively handled in pose estimation for exercise repetition analysis?

This paper presents a novel approach for exercise repetition analysis utilizing the YOLOv8-pose model [16] and Dynamic Time Warping (DTW) techniques [7, 11,12,15] applied to the InfiniteRep dataset. Our research tackles the challenges of accurate pose estimation and tracking in dynamic camera environments and under varying occlusions within synthetic datasets. By integrating YOLOv8's pose detection capabilities with the temporal analysis strengths of DTW, we propose a method that significantly enhances the detection and classification of exercise repetitions across various conditions.

We present several contributions as follows.

Application to InfiniteRep Dataset. This dataset encompasses substantial environmental variations and comprehensive annotations, making it an invaluable resource for evaluating the proposed methods. This emphasis addresses gaps in current research, which frequently depends on less diverse and richly annotated datasets.

Integration of YOLOv8 and DTW. This combination improves the accuracy and robustness of exercise repetition detection and classification, especially in dynamic camera environments and under varying occlusions, surpassing existing methods that typically manage these tasks independently.

These methods are critical for maintaining the accuracy of pose tracking under challenging conditions, addressing a common issue where occlusions and non-detections can significantly degrade performance.

Real-Time and Post-Workout Analysis Algorithms. This study proposes two distinct algorithms for exercise repetition detection: one for real-time (during-workout) analysis and another for post-workout analysis. The real-time algorithm delivers immediate feedback and correction, essential for sports coaching and physical therapy applications. In contrast, the post-workout algorithm enables a comprehensive review and detailed analysis after the exercise session, enhancing utility for various user needs.

Rule Creation Interface. A web-based application has been developed, enabling teachers and students to create and perform exercise routines. This interface leverages the motion detection and feedback mechanisms described in this paper, making advanced techniques accessible for practical use. The interactive rule creation tool allows users to define specific feedback rules, enhancing the educational and training value of the system.

2   Related Work on InfiniteRep Dataset

The InfiniteRep dataset[1] [20] is an open-source synthetic dataset designed for fitness and physical therapy applications. It features videos of diverse avatars performing multiple repetitions of common exercises, capturing significant variations in environment, lighting conditions, avatar demographics, and movement trajectories. This variability ensures that each repetition mimics real human performance differences. Key features of the InfiniteRep dataset include a comprehensive collection of 1,000 videos, distributed across 10 distinct exercises, each represented by 100 videos. The exercises covered in this dataset are pushups, alternating bicep curls, delt flys, squats, bird dogs, supermans, bicycle crunches, leg raises, front raises, and overhead presses. The dataset provides extensive annotations and metadata, including bounding boxes, segmentation masks, keypoints, joint angles, repetition counts, avatar characteristics, and camera settings.

Such detailed annotations are particularly valuable for various computer vision and machine learning tasks, enhancing the dataset's utility for research and application development. Regarding format and accessibility, the videos are provided in a 224×224 RGB format at 24 frames per second (fps).

To date, limited research has been conducted using the InfiniteRep dataset. We identified two notable studies in existing literature: Chang et al. [2] implemented a Spatio-Temporal Graph Convolutional Network (ST-GCN) for human action recognition to assess users' fitness statuses, utilizing skeleton data as input to model inter-skeleton connections. This approach was validated using the InfiniteRep dataset, demonstrating high accuracy.

---

[1] https://marketplace.infinity.ai/pages/infiniterep-dataset.

Conversely, Pande et al. [9] developed Fitwave, a fitness application designed to monitor and correct users' exercise postures. They employed transfer learning techniques on a pre-trained MobileNet architecture, refining their model using the InfiniteRep dataset with a focus on three exercises: arm raises, bicep curls, and squats. Despite advances in computer vision, the complexity of human movements and the variability in pose tracking datasets present significant challenges. Current models often fail to accurately track human poses in dynamic environments, particularly when using synthetic datasets. Integrating YOLOv8 for pose estimation with DTW for temporal sequence analysis offers a promising solution, significantly improving the detection and classification of exercise repetitions.

3   Technical Background

In this section, we introduce the underlying algorithms used in our application. First, we examine the YOLOv8 algorithm and its application in pose detection. Following this, we describe two algorithms designed for post- and during-workout repetition detection.

3.1   YOLOv8-Pose

The YOLO (You Only Look Once) architecture [16] became a key object detection algorithm by framing the problem as a single regression task, directly predicting bounding boxes and class probabilities from full images in a single evaluation. This approach contrasted with previous methods that required region proposal networks or sliding windows, thereby significantly reducing computation time and enabling real-time performance. Subsequent versions, YOLOv1 through YOLOv10, introduced various improvements, such as batch normalization, anchor boxes, multi-scale training, and feature pyramid networks, which collectively enhanced the models' speed and accuracy [5,18,19]. YOLOv8-Pose, the latest pose estimation framework from the YOLO models, builds on these advancements and focuses on pose estimation, a complex task that involves detecting keypoints on human bodies and mapping their spatial relationships. This model incorporates several key innovations:

Enhanced Backbone Network: YOLOv8 employs an enhanced backbone network that leverages advancements in convolutional neural network (CNN) architectures, such as deeper networks with more efficient layers, to capture more intricate features from input images.

Keypoint Detection. Figure 1 illustrates the YOLOv8 joint detection output, enhanced for exercise repetition analysis. Each keypoint corresponding to a body joint is marked and labeled with a unique identifier for precise tracking. The keypoints include the nose (1), eyes (2, 3), ears (4, 5), shoulders (6, 7), elbows (8, 9), wrists (10, 11), hips (12, 13), knees (14, 15), and ankles (16, 17).

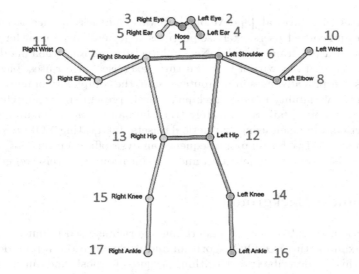

Fig. 1. Keypoint ID description.

Multi-Scale Feature Extraction: By integrating feature pyramid networks (FPN) and path aggregation networks (PAN), YOLOv8-Pose effectively extracts and utilizes features at multiple scales. This multi-scale approach is crucial for accurately detecting keypoints across a range of human poses and body sizes.

Keypoint Localization Segment Head: The pose estimation segment head in YOLOv8-Pose is designed to predict keypoints with high precision. It uses specialized loss functions and optimization techniques to ensure accurate localization of human joints and key body parts.

Real-Time Inference: Adhering to the YOLO philosophy, YOLOv8-Pose is optimized for real-time inference, making it suitable for applications requiring immediate feedback, such as motion capture, interactive fitness applications, and real-time video analytics. YOLOv8-Pose's application domains are diverse, spanning sports analytics, physical therapy, augmented reality, and human-computer interaction. Its ability to provide real-time, accurate pose estimation enables new interactive technologies and enhances user experiences. However, challenges persist, particularly when dealing with complex scenes, varying lighting conditions, and occlusions. The performance of YOLOv8-Pose is highly dependent on the quality and diversity of its training data. For instance, models pre-trained on standard datasets may struggle with domain-specific datasets like InfiniteRep, which includes various environmental variations such as occlusions.

Pose Detection Accuracy. In some frames, YOLO fails to detect the person, resulting in no skeletal data. In other frames, certain joints are not detected correctly, causing their coordinates to be recorded as zeros. Consequently, those joints are marked as $[0.0, 0.0]$ in the skeletal data instead of having a valid position.

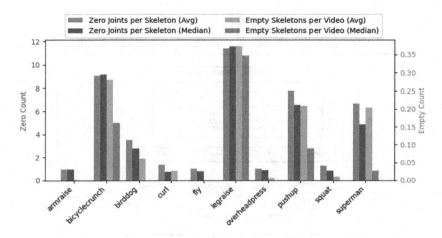

Fig. 2. YOLOv8l applied to InfiniteRep exercises: Comparison of average and median percentage of empty skeletons and zero joints *(higher is worse)*.

As illustrated in Fig. 2, when applied to the InfiteRep dataset, YOLOv8 is not ideal for estimating poses in exercises where the person is lying on the floor rather than standing, such as Bicycle Crunches, Bird Dogs, Leg Raises, Pushups, and Supermans. However, YOLOv8 performs better at estimating poses in exercises where the person is standing, such as Front Arm Raises (with dumbbells), Alternating Bicep Curls (with dumbbells), Delt Flys (with dumbbells), Overhead Press, and Squats. Simultaneously, the occlusion percentage in some videos is so high that YOLOv8 cannot be expected to detect anything. Analyzing the average occlusion percentage per video reveals that, for arm raises, the maximum average occlusion percentage is 22.64%, whereas for bicycle crunches it reaches 97.82%. Additionally, for a standing person, occlusion often affects the legs. This is problematic for exercises that involve leg movements, such as squats.

3.2 The Post-workout and During-Workout Algorithms

We employed slightly different algorithms for the post-workout and during-workout exercise repetition detection. The during-workout algorithm is designed for real-time analysis, where the learner performs actions in front of the camera.

The algorithm incrementally processes the data, continuously updating window parameters to detect exercise repetitions as they occur. This enables immediate feedback and correction. In contrast, the post-workout algorithm operates offline on uploaded videos, analyzing the entire sequence at once. It identifies multiple best matches and evaluates them against dynamic criteria, making it suitable for detailed post-exercise review and analysis without the need for immediate feedback. This distinction allows the during-workout algorithm to provide instant guidance, while the post-workout algorithm comprehensively evaluates the entire workout session.

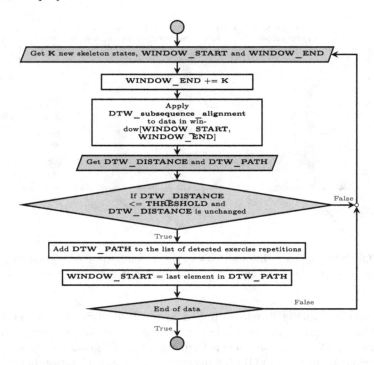

Fig. 3. Flowchart for DTW-based during-workout algorithm.

During-Workout Algorithm Continuous Analysis. The during-workout algorithm (see Fig. 3) operates using a data stream, continuously analyzing the learner's movements in real-time. Initially, the window's start is set to 0, and the end is advanced with each new frame received. When K new skeleton states are collected, the DTW alignment begins. The algorithm retrieves the DTW distance and path within this window. It detects an exercise repetition if the DTW distance is below a specified threshold and remains unchanged for I iterations or S seconds. The start of the window is then updated to the last frame of this detected repetition, allowing the process to continue.

If the DTW distance criterion is not met, the algorithm updates the window parameters and repeats the alignment and evaluation steps, ensuring continuous and immediate feedback for the learner.

Post-workout - Batch Processing. The post-workout algorithm (see Fig. 4) starts by applying Dynamic Time Warping (DTW) subsequence alignment to compare the learner's trajectory with an expert's trajectory. This algorithm generates a list of the K best matches. The algorithm then selects the best unchecked match, denoted as M, and checks if M's DTW distance is below a predefined threshold and within a factor T of the maximum DTW distance from the last checked match.

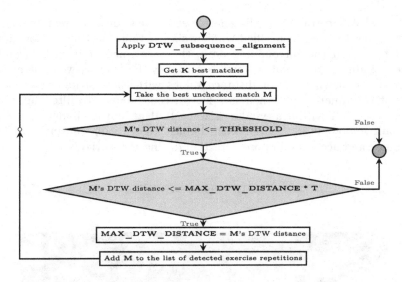

Fig. 4. Flowchart for DTW-based post-workout algorithm

If M meets these criteria, it is added to the list of detected exercise repetitions, and the maximum DTW distance is updated to M's distance. If not, M and all remaining unchecked matches are discarded. This process continues until all relevant matches have been evaluated, ensuring a comprehensive post-workout analysis of the exercise repetitions.

Replacing YOLO Non-detection Frames. For post-workout analysis, to address missing values caused by YOLO model non-detection, we interpolate unknown values by identifying the nearest known values before (see Fig. 5) and after the gap (see Fig. 6). Unknown angles or distances are replaced with values that transition from the nearest known value before the gap to the nearest known value after it. Similarly, zero joint coordinates are replaced with coordinates that gradually change from the nearest known value before the gap to the nearest known value after it.

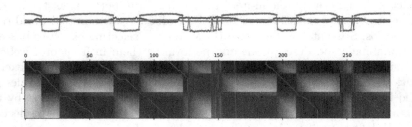

Fig. 5. DTW trajectories before filtering out outliers

Since DTW sub-trajectory alignment is sensitive to outliers, we filter them by examining data within a specified window size. If values in this window deviate significantly from the surrounding data, they are considered outliers and are replaced gradually to maintain data consistency. For during-workout analysis, we replace unknown angle or distance values with the last known angle; and zero joint coordinates with their last known coordinates. To filter outliers, we examine the data within a window size of 1. If an outlier is detected within this small window, it is replaced with the last known value, ensuring real-time consistency and accuracy in pose detection during the workout.

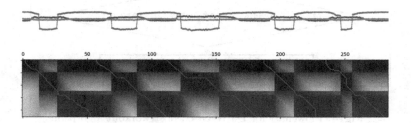

Fig. 6. DTW trajectories after filtering out outliers

4   Rule Creation Interface Description

A web-based application was built to enable learners and teachers to apply the proposed algorithm in practice. The user interface is designed to streamline the creation and performance of exercise routines, leveraging the described motion detection and feedback mechanisms. The back-end architecture of this system follows a multimodal sensor-based cloud pipeline [13,14]. The UI design for defining feedback rules focused on using angles to detect motion differences [8], ensuring consistency regardless of body shape. Expert feedback led to incorporating relative distances between body parts for more detailed feedback. Preliminary interviews with sports trainers and students provided useful insights, but a small sample size limited the statistical significance of the findings. Nonetheless, this feedback played a crucial role in iterating the design to better meet the needs of the users and ensure the effectiveness of the feedback system in real-world training scenarios. Students interact with the system by selecting exercises based on their thumbnails and descriptions and performing them in front of a webcam. The system then uses YOLOv8 to extract their skeleton data, match exercise repetitions, and provide immediate and summative feedback based on rules predefined by the teachers. Teachers initiate the exercise creation process by providing an expert recording of the exercise. From this recording, they select key poses and define specific rules for the algorithm to check, ensuring that learners perform the exercises accurately.

The underlying algorithm interpolates between the key poses defined in the exercise, identifying the closest match to apply the relevant rules to the learner's motion. The rule creation interface for teachers (see Fig. 7) allows for versatile input of feedback guidelines.

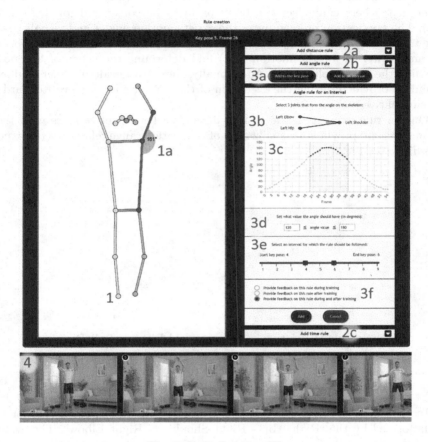

Fig. 7. Rule Creation UI.

Teachers can view a list of key poses (**4**) and select any key pose to see the corresponding extracted skeleton on the left side of the UI (**1**). For each key pose or interval between key poses, teachers can define various rules (**2**): distance rules (**2a**) specify the required distance between certain body joints (e.g., the distance between the left and right hand must be at least 1.5 times the distance between the shoulders). To do this, two distances are selected. For visualization purposes and to assist the user, the first distance is used to calculate a unit of measurement. The unit of measurement is 1/10 the first distance. The second distance is calculated using this unit of measurement. Then a chart shows the change of these two distances over time.

Angle rules (**2b**) set intervals for the angles between body joints (e.g., the angle between the arm and hip at the shoulder joint must be at least 120°); and time rules (**2c**) determine the timing requirements for holding or transitioning between key poses. Teachers can choose to apply these rules to a single key pose or across an interval between selected key poses (**3a**). By clicking on the skeleton, teachers can select the body parts to be considered for angle rules (**1a**). The application pre-computes the expert motion angles and visualizes the target motion range, simplifying the rule-creation process. Teachers then specify the angle interval for the motion (**3d**) and determine the range of key poses to which the rule applies (**3e**). Additionally, they can decide whether feedback should be provided during the execution of the learner's motion or afterward in the summative section (**3f**).

Once a rule is created, the system displays a list of active rules with their parameters and provides a visualization of the motion range relative to the expert recording (see Fig. 8).

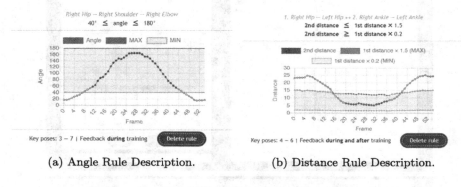

(a) Angle Rule Description.   (b) Distance Rule Description.

Fig. 8. Rule Description UI.

In the depicted angle rule example (see Fig. 8a), we can see a rule for the angle formed by the "Right Hip - Right Shoulder - Right Elbow". The system shows the acceptable angle range as 40° to 180°. A graph illustrates the recorded angle over time, with the x-axis for frame number and the y-axis for angle in degrees. The blue line represents the actual angle, while the red and orange lines mark the maximum (180°) and minimum (40°) allowable angles, with the allowed range highlighted in light orange. Points within the specified interval between key poses, where the rule must be followed, are filled in blue, and points outside this interval are filled in white. Additionally, the interface specifies that this rule applies to specific key poses and provides feedback during training. This allows teachers to review and adjust rules as necessary, ensuring that the exercises are both precise and effective. Overall, this structured and interactive UI ensures that teachers can create detailed and accurate exercises while students receive precise real-time feedback, enhancing their learning experience.

5   Experimental Results

We evaluated the effectiveness of our proposed method by analyzing the detection and classification accuracy of exercise repetitions using both the YOLOv8 pose model and DTW techniques. For our evaluation, we considered a detected repetition to be a true positive (TP) if the left and right boundaries differed by no more than 30% of the length of the repetition from the corresponding boundaries in the InfiniteRep dataset. We specifically used accuracy as our primary metric for evaluation, defined as Accuracy $= $ TP$/N$, where TP is the number of true positives, and N is the total number of repetitions.

We analyzed 30 videos for each exercise, focusing on various angles and distances. Specifically, we identified the top 10 angles and distances for front arm raises. The optimal angles and relative distances are summarized in Table 1.

Table 1. 10 Best angles and rel. dist. for "Front Arm Raises (With Dumbbells)"

	Accuracy	IDs of joints	ID decoding	
Angles				
1	0.9029	(10, 11, 12)	Angle: Left Wrist - Right Wrist - Left Hip	
2	0.8854	(6, 9, 11)	Angle: Left Shoulder - Right Elbow - Right Wrist	
3	0.8769	(12, 9, 17)	Angle: Left Hip - Right Elbow - Right Ankle	
4	0.8739	(9, 10, 1)	Angle: Right Elbow - Left Wrist - Nose	
5	0.8724	(7, 8, 10)	Angle: Right Shoulder - Left Elbow - Left Wrist	
6	0.8719	(10, 6, 13)	Angle: Left Wrist - Left Shoulder - Right Hip	
7	0.8717	(12, 9, 15)	Angle: Left Hip - Right Elbow - Right Knee	
8	0.8704	(7, 10, 8)	Angle: Right Shoulder - Left Wrist - Left Elbow	
9	0.8629	(10, 8, 15)	Angle: Left Wrist - Left Elbow - Right Knee	
10	0.8585	(11, 9, 1)	Angle: Right Wrist - Right Elbow - Nose	
Relative Distances (1st distance and 2nd distance – used to calculate a unit of measurement)				
1	0.9505	(6, 11) | (9, 13)	Dist.: Left Shoulder - Right Wrist	Rel. to: Right Elbow - Right Hip
2	0.9472	(11, 1) | (9, 12)	Dist.: Right Wrist - Nose	Rel. to: Right Elbow - Left Hip
3	0.9418	(11, 1) | (9, 13)	Dist.: Right Wrist - Nose	Rel. to: Right Elbow - Right Hip
4	0.9406	(7, 11) | (9, 13)	Dist.: Right Shoulder - Right Wrist	Rel. to: Right Elbow - Right Hip
5	0.9317	(11, 1) | (11, 15)	Dist.: Right Wrist - Nose	Rel. to: Right Wrist - Right Knee
6	0.9291	(9, 1) | (9, 13)	Dist.: Right Elbow - Nose	Rel. to: Right Elbow - Right Hip
7	0.9277	(8, 1) | (9, 13)	Dist.: Left Elbow - Nose	Rel. to: Right Elbow - Right Hip
8	0.9241	(6, 9) | (9, 13)	Dist.: Left Shoulder - Right Elbow	Rel. to: Right Elbow - Right Hip
9	0.9238	(7, 14) | (9, 13)	Dist.: Right Shoulder - Left Knee	Rel. to: Right Elbow - Right Hip
10	0.9228	(11, 17) | (6, 1)	Dist.: Right Wrist - Right Ankle	Rel. to: Left Shoulder - Nose

The results suggest that our method can effectively be used for detecting and classifying exercise repetitions. Accuracy metrics reveal that certain angles and relative distances are more reliable for correct repetition detection in dynamic camera environments and with varying occlusions. For instance, the angle formed by between the Left Wrist - Right Wrist - Left Hip achieved the highest accuracy of 0.9029, showcasing the algorithm's robustness in correctly identifying front arm raises. Additionally, the best relative distances, such as Left Shoulder -

Right Wrist relative to Right Elbow - Right Hip 0.9505, offer further context for enhancing detection accuracy.

Findings indicate that specific joint configurations are essential for accurate recognition of exercise movements. Analyzing the joint angles, such as Wrist-Elbow-Shoulder, shows that these angles can be affected by the person's orientation relative to the camera. For more accurate results, selecting joints that are not directly involved in the movement seems advantageous. For instance, when lifting arms, using the left and right wrist along with the nose, hip, or knee can improve detection accuracy (see Table 1).

Additionally, we compared the accuracy of after-workout and during-workout algorithms, utilizing combinations of the best angles and distances, in detecting exercise repetitions using the InfiniteRep dataset (see Fig. 9). The evaluation included both ideal dataset data and data obtained with YOLOv8 models. The highest accuracy is achieved with the after-workout algorithm on ideal data, followed by the during-workout algorithm on ideal data. Accuracy decreases significantly when using YOLOv8 pose detection, especially for exercises performed on the floor, such as Bicycle Crunches, Bird Dogs, Leg Raises, Pushups, and Supermans, highlighting YOLOv8's limitations in scenarios where body parts of the trainees were occluded, e.g. due to them laying on the ground.

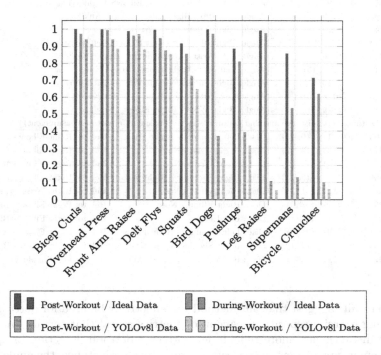

Fig. 9. Highest Accuracy Comparison Across Exercises Using Post- and During-Workout Algorithms with Ideal and YOLOv8l Pose Detection

6   Limitations

The design and implementation of our psychomotor learning application exhibit several limitations that may impact the system's effectiveness and applicability in diverse contexts. The manual rule creation process in the application is susceptible to expert error, and users may struggle to determine which expert rules to trust.

While the application's approach to analyzing angles and relative distances is designed to be non-discriminatory regarding body shape, it does not account for the user's flexibility or fitness level. Another limitation of our contribution is the lack of comparison of YOLOv8 with existing human pose models used in kinematic analysis, such as MediaPipe[2], OpenPose[3], or other available open source models. This comparison would be crucial for validating the system's performance against established benchmarks and could help address the limitations of YOLOv8. Additionally, while our method is not directly comparable with other studies utilizing the InfiniteRep dataset, as those typically focus on detecting exercise types without tracking the exact number of repetitions or their timing, applying our algorithm to other datasets would make such a comparison feasible. As mentioned, the default YOLOv8 models present challenges in detecting poses for users who are lying down or are heavily occluded. Furthermore, YOLOv8 does not detect finer skeleton details such as fingers or toes, which could be beneficial for certain exercises requiring detailed analysis. Finally, the UI evaluation was conducted with a small sample size, limiting the statistical significance of the findings. Further studies with a larger participant pool are necessary to draw more robust conclusions and to drive a thorough UI design process.

7   Future Work

Future work could validate our approach across multiple heterogeneous datasets to understand its generalizability in various real-world scenarios. Given that our algorithm's performance on the InfiniteRep dataset isn't directly comparable with other studies, further evaluations on additional datasets and against other algorithms are necessary to establish broader applicability and effectiveness.

Additionally, introducing a rating system for exercises and fitness experts could enhance trust in the exercise creation process, mitigating potential errors in manual rule creation. To better accommodate users' varying fitness and flexibility levels, future iterations could incorporate detailed difficulty or expertise levels into exercises.

The system could be extended to support group training sessions, where real-time feedback is provided to multiple users simultaneously. This could be particularly useful for sports teams or fitness classes, where individual and group performance can be monitored and adjusted on the fly.

---

[2] https://github.com/google-ai-edge/mediapipe.
[3] https://github.com/CMU-Perceptual-Computing-Lab/openpose.

Integrating biomechanical models with pose estimation could improve accuracy by considering joint constraints and physical properties. This would imply implementing a model that assesses the risk of injury based on detected pose and movement patterns. Such a system could alert users to potential risks and suggest safer alternatives or modifications to exercises based on their form and physical condition.

Developing personalized feedback models that adapt to individual performance histories could tailor workouts to specific needs and goals. An adaptive feedback model could not only provide feedback but also adapt their coaching style based on the user's emotional state and motivation levels.

Evaluating user progress over time would provide valuable data to refine the algorithms, enhancing their predictive capabilities and adapting to long-term trends in user performance.

A critical area for future work involves comparing our pose estimation approach with existing kinematic analysis models like MediaPipe, OpenPose, or other open source models. This comparison could reveal areas for improvement or potential alternatives that might outperform YOLOv8 in certain scenarios. Moreover, addressing the limitations of YOLOv8, such as its difficulty in detecting poses for individuals lying down or occluded, as well as its inability to detect finer details like fingers or toes, is essential. Future work could also explore placing cameras on ceilings, fine-tuning YOLOv8, or exploring other pose detection models like MediaPipe to overcome these challenges.

Finally, a thorough UI evaluation with a larger and more diverse sample size is needed to gather statistically significant data. This feedback would inform a potential redesign, ensuring the interface is user-friendly and effective for a wider audience.

8   Summary and Conclusions

In this paper, we introduced an approach to exercise repetition analysis by integrating the YOLOv8-pose model with DTW techniques, specifically applied to the InfiniteRep dataset. This combination enhances the detection and classification of exercise repetitions, especially in dynamic environments and under varying occlusions, addressing the limitations of current state-of-the-art models.

We found that floor exercises like Bicycle Crunches, Bird Dogs, Leg Raises, Pushups, and Supermans are more susceptible to pose estimation inaccuracies using the YOLOv8 default model.

These exercises result in significant occlusions and complex body orientations, posing challenges for accurate keypoint detection and tracking (see **RQ1**).

Our method leverages the detailed annotations and environmental variations of the InfiniteRep dataset, including diverse lighting conditions, mirroring duplication, avatar demographics, and movement trajectories. We handled missing values and occlusions by proposing robust methods for interpolating unknown values and filtering outliers to improve accuracy (see **RQ2**). By developing during-workout and post-workout analysis algorithms, we offer solutions for immediate feedback during exercises and detailed reviews post-exercise, ensuring broad applicability from sports coaching to physical therapy. Zero joint coordinates can be substituted with their last known coordinates to maintain data continuity (see **RQ3**). For post-workout analysis, interpolation estimates missing values by identifying the nearest known values before and after gaps, creating a seamless transition.

For real-time analysis, continuously replacing unknown values with the most recent known values ensures consistency and accuracy, while filtering techniques identify and correct outliers in real-time. These approaches enhance the detection and classification of exercise repetitions under challenging conditions.

Our web-based application enhances practical utility by providing an interactive platform for creating exercise routines and performance assessments. This tool, with a rule creation interface, allows educators and trainers to tailor feedback and ensure precision in exercise execution. Our evaluation demonstrates the robustness and versatility of our approach across various exercises in the InfiniteRep dataset.

The experimental results highlight significant improvements in exercise recognition accuracy and robustness, suggesting promising applications in sports science and personal fitness coaching. This research advances the state-of-the-art in exercise repetition analysis and provides practical tools and methods for real-world settings. Integrating advanced pose estimation with temporal analysis opens new avenues for enhancing human motion analysis, significantly contributing to sports science.

Acknowledgements. This research was funded by the German Federal Ministry of Education and Research (BMBF) through the project "Multimodales Immersives Lernen mit künstlicher Intelligenz für Psychomotorische Fähigkeiten" ("MILKI-PSY" (https://milki-psy.de/)) (grant no. 16DHB4015). We extend our gratitude to the BMBF for their generous support and investment in this research.

References

1. Beddiar, D.R., Nini, B., Sabokrou, M., Hadid, A.: Vision-based human activity recognition: a survey. Multimed. Tools Appl. **79**(41), 30509–30555 (2020)
2. Chang, J.W., Liu, H.R.: Applying 5PKC-Based skeleton partition strategy into spatio-temporal graph convolution networks for fitness action recognition. In: Hung, J.C., Chang, J.W., Pei, Y. (eds.) Innovative Computing Vol 2 - Emerging Topics in Future Internet. pp. 728–737. Springer, Singapore (2023)
3. Gammulle, H., Ahmedt-Aristizabal, D., Denman, S., Tychsen-Smith, L., Petersson, L., Fookes, C.: Continuous human action recognition for human-machine interaction: a review. ACM Comput. Surv. **55**(13s), 1–38 (2023)
4. Garbett, A., Degutyte, Z., Hodge, J., Astell, A.: Towards understanding people's experiences of ai computer vision fitness instructor apps. In: Designing Interactive Systems Conference 2021, pp. 1619–1637. ACM, Virtual Event, USA (2021). https://doi.org/10.1145/3461778.3462094

5. Hussain, M.: YOLO-v1 to YOLO-v8, the rise of yolo and its complementary nature toward digital manufacturing and industrial defect detection. Machines **11**(7), 677 (2023)
6. Morshed, M.G., Sultana, T., Alam, A., Lee, Y.K.: Human action recognition: a taxonomy-based survey, updates, and opportunities. Sensors **23**(4), 2182 (2023)
7. Müller, M.: Dynamic time warping. Information retrieval for music and motion, pp. 69–84 (2007)
8. Paaßen, B., Baumgartner, T., Geisen, M., Riedl, N., Kravčík, M.: Few-shot keypose detection for learning of psychomotor skills (2022)
9. Pande, V., Mokashi, A., Patil, S., Singh, A., Jadhav, N.: Fitwave: a posture correction system based on machine learning. In: Vasant, P., Weber, G.W., Marmolejo-Saucedo, J.A., Munapo, E., Thomas, J.J. (eds.) ICO 2022. LNNS, vol. 569, pp. 410–418. Springer, Cham (2023). https://doi.org/10.1007/978-3-031-19958-5_38
10. Pareek, P., Thakkar, A.: A survey on video-based human action recognition: recent updates, datasets, challenges, and applications. Artif. Intell. Rev. **54**(3), 2259–2322 (2021)
11. Schneider, P., Memmesheimer, R., Kramer, I., Paulus, D.: Gesture recognition in rgb videos using human body keypoints and dynamic time warping. In: RoboCup 2019: Robot World Cup XXIII 23, pp. 281–293. Springer (2019)
12. Senin, P.: Dynamic time warping algorithm review. Info. Comput. Sci. Dept. Univ. Hawaii Manoa Honolulu USA **855**(1–23), 40 (2008)
13. Slupczynski, M.P., Klamma, R.: MILKI-PSY Cloud: MLOps-based multimodal sensor stream processing pipeline for learning analytics in psychomotor education. MILeS 2022 : Multimodal Immersive Learning Systems 2022: proceedings of the Second International Workshop on Multimodal Immersive Learning Systems (MILeS 2022) at the Seventeenth European Conference on Technology Enhanced Learning (EC-TEL 2022), Toulouse, France, pp. 8–14 (2022). https://doi.org/10.18154/RWTH-2022-09814
14. Slupczynski, M.P., Sanusi, K.A.M., Majonica, D., Klemke, R., Decker, S.J.: Implementing cloud-based feedback to facilitate scalable psychomotor skills acquisition (2023). https://doi.org/10.18154/RWTH-2023-09769
15. Tchane Djogdom, G.V., Otis, M.J.D., Meziane, R.: Dynamic time warping–based feature selection method for foot gesture cobot operation mode selection. Int. J. Adv. Manuf. Technol. **126**(9), 4521–4541 (2023)
16. Terven, J., Córdova-Esparza, D.M., Romero-González, J.A.: A comprehensive review of yolo architectures in computer vision: from yolov1 to yolov8 and YOLO-NAS. Mach. Learn. Knowl. Extract. **5**(4), 1680–1716 (2023)
17. Venkatachalam, P., Ray, S.: How do context-aware artificial intelligence algorithms used in fitness recommender systems? A literature review and research agenda. Int. J. Inf. Manage. Data Insights **2**(2), 100139 (2022)
18. Wang, A., et al.: YOLOv10: real-time end-to-end object detection. arXiv preprint arXiv:2405.14458 (2024)
19. Wang, C.Y., Yeh, I.H., Liao, H.Y.M.: YOLOv9: learning what you want to learn using programmable gradient information. arXiv preprint arXiv:2402.13616 (2024)
20. Weitz, A., Colucci, L., Primas, S., Bent, B.: InfiniteForm: a synthetic, minimal bias dataset for fitness applications. arXiv preprint arXiv:2110.01330 (2021)
21. Xiu, Y., Yang, J., Cao, X., Tzionas, D., Black, M.J.: ECON: explicit clothed humans optimized via normal integration. In: Proceedings of the IEEE/CVF Conference on Computer Vision and Pattern Recognition, pp. 512–523 (2023)

Supporting Thermal Imaging for Activity and Health Recognition by a Constant Temperature Device

Gerald Bieber[1]([⊠])(iD), Erik Endlicher[1]([⊠])(iD), Christopher Wald[2]([⊠])(iD),
Peter Gross[1]([⊠])(iD), and Bastian Kubsch[1]([⊠])(iD)

[1] Fraunhofer IGD, Joachim-Jungius-Straße 11, 18059 Rostock, Germany
{gerald.bieber,erik.endlicher,peter.gross,
bastian.kubsch}@igd-r.fraunhofer.de
[2] Fraunhofer IGP, Albert-Einstein-Straße 30, 18059 Rostock, Germany
christopher.wald@igp.fraunhofer.de

Abstract. The contactless detection of vital parameters in humans and animals is crucial for ensuring health. While sensors that touch the body or are invasive can already accurately capture parameters such as body temperature, heart rate, or respiratory rate, contactless systems are still under development. An interesting technological approach involves the use of thermal cameras for capturing vital data, as they can operate unobtrusively even in complete darkness and from a greater distance. Unfortunately, the section of measurements affects the recorded temperature; the absolute temperature is imprecise, and calibration is very complex and should be redone periodically. This paper presents a simple yet effective solution for enhancing thermal imaging. The solution is a temperature-controlled Peltier element with a feedback loop that provides an exact reference point in the desired temperature range. This might improve the detection of fever and infections and support further vital data recognition in humans and animals or condition monitoring in machines using thermal cameras.

Keywords: thermal camera · non contact · vital data recognition · condition monitoring

1 Introduction

In recent years, technological advancements have paved the way for novel approaches to physiological monitoring, and thermal cameras have emerged as a promising tool in this domain. Unlike conventional methods, thermal cameras offer a non-contact and non-intrusive means of capturing physiological data, making them an attractive option for inflammation, fever, or continuous heart rate monitoring.

© The Author(s), under exclusive license to Springer Nature Switzerland AG 2025
O. Konak et al. (Eds.): iWOAR 2024, LNCS 15357, pp. 111–123, 2025.
https://doi.org/10.1007/978-3-031-80856-2_8

Fig. 1. Contactless vital data assessment by thermal images.

Furthermore, the integration of thermal cameras in health monitoring systems (Fig. 1) aligns with the growing trend of wearable and ambient technology. This not only enhances user convenience but also opens avenues for continuous monitoring in various environments, including home settings, workplaces, and even during physical activities. The ubiquitous nature of thermal cameras makes them a versatile tool for capturing physiological signals without disrupting daily routines, offering a new paradigm in personalized healthcare.

Contactless determined vital data represent the health and fitness of humans and animals. Together with other medical data, this data provides information about the need for medication or further medical assistance. Temperature monitoring of the skin and body also helps to detect stress in the workplace and can reduce workload and enable a lifetime of healthy working. Furthermore, the recognition of vital data also makes it possible to enhance communication with other people at a distance. Communication is also improved with AI-based machines, as they are better able to assess the inner states of the person they are talking to and can therefore respond to them in particular.

Traditional approaches to vital data detection often involve cumbersome devices, uncomfortable sensors, or invasive procedures, limiting their widespread adoption and compliance among individuals.

The motivation behind exploring through thermal cameras lies in the potential to enhance how we monitor health. This approach could provide a seamless and unobtrusive method for individuals to track the health in real-time, facilitating early detection of anomalies and enabling timely intervention.

Even the resolution of thermal cameras and the relatively accuracy between each pixel (px) might be sufficient, the disadvantage is the absolute error of temperature assessment caused by the camera and the sections of measurement.

In this paper, we delve into the exploration of vital data detection using thermal cameras, aiming to bridge the gap between thermal camera technology and health monitoring. By presenting a calibration device that is easy to build and use, we show that a reference temperature spot beside the region of interest can be applied. This calibration device is mobile and allows an easy estimation of the absolute temperature of the object.

1.1 Physical Concept

All objects with a temperature above absolute zero $(-273.15\,^{\circ}\text{C})$ emit infrared radiation. The intensity and wavelength of this radiation depend on the object's temperature. This leads to the Stefan-Boltzmann Law that describes the total power radiated per unit surface area of a black body (an idealized object that absorbs all incident electromagnetic radiation) as a function of its temperature.

$$P = \sigma \cdot A \cdot T^4$$

P is the total power radiated,
σ is the Stefan-Boltzmann constant $(5.67 \times 10^{-8} \text{ W m}^{-2} \text{ K}^{-4})$,
A is the surface area of the object, and
T is the absolute temperature of the object in Kelvin.

This law implies that as the temperature of an object increases, the amount of infrared radiation it emits also increases significantly. Interestingly, as the temperature of an object increases, the peak wavelength of its emitted radiation decreases. This means that hotter objects emit radiation with shorter wavelengths, while cooler objects emit radiation with longer wavelengths. The cause lies in the circumstance that the energy of electromagnetic waves is directly related to their frequency. This relationship is described by the equation:

$$E = h \cdot f$$

where E is the energy, h is Planck's constant, and f is the frequency of the wave. Regarding the temperature, the Wien's Displacement Law is representing this as:

$$\lambda_{\text{max}} \cdot T = \text{constant}$$

where:
λ_{max} is the peak wavelength of radiation,
T is the absolute temperature of the object.

This law indicates that the peak wavelength (λ_{max}) of the emitted radiation from a black body is inversely proportional to its absolute temperature (T). As the temperature (T) increases, the peak wavelength of the emitted radiation decreases [5]. Prisms refract electromagnetic waves and split them according to their wavelength. An array of photosensitive sensors can detect the intensity of the different rays and generate an overall image. This principle is fundamental to the operation of thermal cameras, as they capture and interpret these infrared emissions to create thermal images, allowing us to visualize temperature variations across surfaces and objects.

1.2   Application Fields

Thermal cameras find applications in various fields due to their ability to capture infrared radiation and visualize temperature differences. Relevant applications can be found in the fields of physical and chemical reactions, agriculture, welding processes, building insulation, etc. Some notable applications include medical applications. Here, thermal cameras are used to detect inflammation, assess blood flow and monitor body temperature. They are also used in thermography to detect breast cancer. In addition, a thermal body scan can detect Covid infections [1]. Since thermal imaging cameras have become cheaper, they have become attractive for many purposes.

2   Related Work

Most thermal cameras in the market are calibrated and set to factory standards. However, over time, the calibration drifts due to the aging of the electronic components. Furthermore, the measuring section often varies. The measured temperature differs because of the surrounding temperature, moisture, distance between object and camera, and of course by the quality of the camera-sensor. The general calibration method is described in [9]. For an accurate calibration, a controlled environment with an almost ideal black body is applied. All achieved data is used to create a measurement model tailored to each camera's unique lens, filter, and temperature range [11]. High quality thermal cameras come along with a calibration certificate and it is recommended to recalibrate the camera each year. The accuracy of black bodies is usually in the range of 0.1–0.3 C. Other methods for calibration provide a trade of between effort, price and quality [16]. A rough calibration method is to use edge points like cold or boiling water (0 or 100°) but the surface of water is hard to measure. Unfortunately, the relationship between temperature and infrared energy is nonlinear, and a reference point close to the temperature region of interest is needed.

The camera based technologies are using the visible skin and body surface for heart beat detection. Hereby, the RGB camera is sensing the chromatic changes of the skin color that occur each heat beat. This technology, which is also used by the CareCam [8] in the working environment by standard webcams, is known as remote plethyphotogrammetry (rPPG). Thermal imaging cameras, on the other hand, use the temperature differences in the skin that occur during the heartbeat. But not only heart rate is relevant, Fig. 2 shows the blood flow in a cow's skin and illustrates the position of the arteries and vessels.

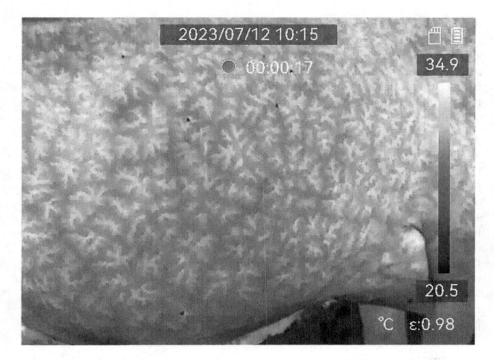

Fig. 2. The high resolution shows the blood flow of a cow, which can be recognized as a star pattern (by Mirjam Lechner).

2.1 Sensor Technology

Distance
Most IR-based fever thermometers only measure within half a meter. However, thermal imaging cameras can have an unlimited range (and are even used in remote sensing from satellites), but their accuracy is affected by the sequence of measurements. Cooled thermal cameras (e.g. used by the police) can detect people at a distance of 15 km [7].

Resolution
Due to the different areas of application, there are single-point and array sensors. Infrared (IR) thermometers, also used and known as ear thermometer, forehead, or temporal artery thermometers, usually consist of an infrared sensor to measure the temperature of the skin surface. Sensor arrays range from simple 8X8 sensor arrays (e.g. grid-eye [15]) to high-performance and high-resolution sensors (e.g. HD thermal videos). Plug-in modules for smartphones are typically available with $\frac{1}{4}$ of the VGA resolution.

NETD
But the resolution is not the only parameter of interest. Quantization, or thermal sensitivity, describes the smallest temperature difference that a camera can

detect. This sensitivity is referred to as Noise Equivalent Temperature Difference (NETD) and is measured in Kelvins (mK). The lower the number, the more sensitive the detector [18]. Obviously, thermal camera sensors consist of temperature sensitive semiconductors. Like any semiconductor, the electrical circuit suffers from thermal noise. Therefore, high performance thermal cameras are cooled to reduce the thermal noise. These type of cameras are extremely cost extensive and mainly used in area of research.

Absolute Temperature
While NETD describes the relative error between the pixel values, the absolute temperature error indicates how well the value corresponds to the actual temperature. The thermal imaging camera measures the thermal radiation from an object, so the radiation emitted can vary due to different surface properties. A shiny, golden surface reflects the thermal radiation in such a way that sometimes the temperature of other reflected objects is measured. For some materials that are transparent, such as a person's glasses, the thermal radiation is blocked and the eye/eye temperature cannot be measured. Furthermore, the angle of the view of sight is influencing the obtained temperature [17], the distance in the air [12], the presence of wind [3], and the influence of sunlight. This results to a total thermal error, depending on the thermal camera device, of approximately 3 °C [14].

Body Temperature
Determining the core body temperature with a thermal camera is always an indirect method and therefore prone to error. The result is influenced by various factors, as only the surface temperature is measured and this value is used to determine the core body temperature. The conversion of the surface temperature into the core body temperature is influenced by various factors such as the ambient temperature, physical activity and individual fluctuations. It is likely that the areas with the best blood flow are the most suitable for temperature estimation [10]. Interestingly, in farm animals the regions around the eyes (e.g. cows, 3) and the forehead in humans are particularly suitable.

As the absolute temperature accuracy of thermal imaging cameras from a distance may not be very precise, fever detection can be performed during group observations to identify outliers with a significantly higher temperature than the standard objects.

Further Vital Data Recognition
Respiration detection
With a thermal imaging camera, it is possible to indirectly detect and measure a person's respiration by recognizing temperature differences based on the body's heat radiation. When a person exhales, warmer air escapes from the respiratory tract, leading to a temperature difference compared to the surrounding environment [2]. Therefore, a low absolute temperature error is not necessary if a high NETD is provided.

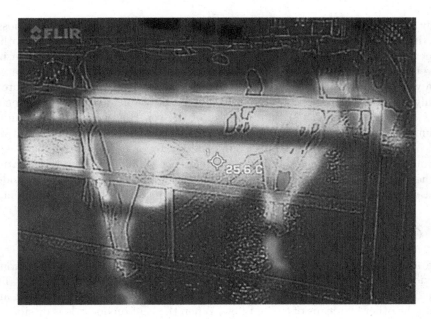

Fig. 3. Thermal image of a cow.

Heart Rate Detection
A thermal camera can indirectly estimate the heart rate by detecting subtle changes in the blood flow and variations in body temperature. When the heart pumps blood, it distributes warm blood throughout the body. Each heart beat, the skin and other body areas are supplied by the blood that is enriched with oxygen, heat, nutrients and other ingredients. By monitoring specific regions of interest on the face or other exposed body parts, a normal webcam can track volume or color variations over time [8]. Temperature variations also provide patterns that can be analyzed to estimate the heart rate indirectly. The temperature differences are very tiny and require a high resolution with a low noise recording [6]. It is obvious that heart rate can be detected by thermal cameras. [13] gives a good overview of the current work and technologies in this field. In [4] the authors used a 640 × 480 pixel camera with NETD = 30 mK and stated that heart rate and heart rate variability detection is possible and valid.

3   Challenges on Thermal Imaging

The literature analysis shows that although thermal imaging cameras are good at depicting the temperature difference within an image, the absolute temperature determination can sometimes be very faulty. This is due to the ability to measure the absolute temperature as well as the influences of the measuring distance, humidity, air speed and other influencing parameters. Furthermore, shiny surfaces may interfere the measurements. Hereby, reflections are possible that lead to inaccurate readings. The thermal radiation emitted by other objects in the environment can bounce off the surfaces being viewed, causing false temperature readings. If the resolution is too low, one pixel covers a larger area with possibly inhomogeneous temperature structures. If the temperature is highly relevant, the region of interest (roi) must be scanned with a resolution at least 4 times higher (2 * 2) than the size of the roi. However, super-resolution techniques, often based on deep learning, are used to convert low-resolution thermal images into higher-resolution counterparts. To accomodate the challenges, it would therefore be desirable to have a reference signal of known temperature in the field of view of a thermal image. This reference signal could be provided by a device that has a constant temperature independent of the environment.

4   Constant Temperature Device

The aim was to design a simple, easy-to-use but accurate device that would provide the desired reference temperature when taking a thermal image. The core of this device is a Peltier element, which cools one side of the element and heats the other by means of current flow. When the heat on one side is dissipated, for example with a cooling plate, the other side of the Peltier element can reach the desired temperature. If a thermometer is attached to the Peltier element with a thermal paste, the desired temperature can be set and achieved using a relay and a control circuit.

If the desired temperature is not yet reached, the Peltier element is heated; if the temperature is exceeded, the Peltier element is cooled. The arrangement (Fig. 4) therefore corresponded to a three-point controller (cool, heat, leave in state).

5   Implementation and Setup

For the purpose of a constant temperature device, we choose the following hardware elements. An arduino uno as the digital control circuit, a Peltier element (TEC1-12706, 15 V 6.4 A 65 W (L × B × H) 40 × 40 × 3.8 mm), a resistor of 6 Ω to limit the intake current, a relay (Debo SRD-05VDC-SL-C 2 Channel, 10 A) to switch the current or reverse the current direction, a heat sink (Kalolary Aluminium Heatsink 40 * 40 * 20 mm) and a thermometer (BMP280, DS18B20) attached directly to the Peltier element with conductive paste (Fig. 6).

6   Evaluation of Designed System

The prototype was used at a test set for the temperature measurement of cows. The camera was approx. 4 m away to the object, but the temperature reference device was directly close to the object (see Fig. 5). Within the field of view of the thermal camera, both the object and the reference device was clearly visible.

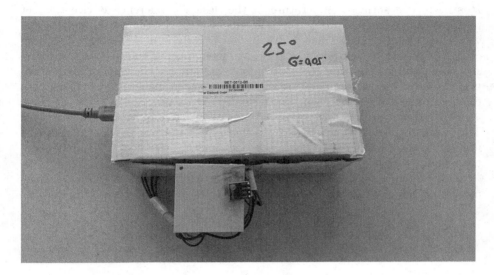

Fig. 4. First prototype of the temperature reference device.

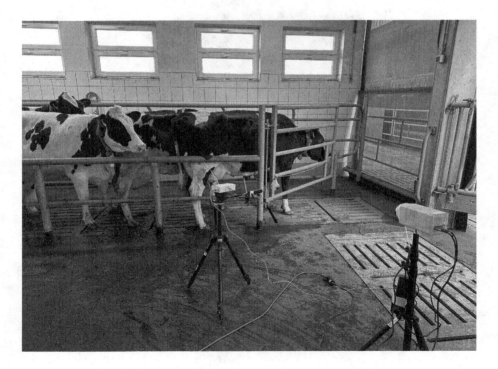

Fig. 5. Temperature assessment using a prototype device.

Results. The surface temperature of the designed reference device was set to 25 °C. The temperature of the reference system fluctuated around the set value, so that the mean value was achieved exactly, but a standard deviation of 0.05 °C could be measured. He measurement results showed that no over-shooting occurred and that the control loop was stable. The camera images displayed almost the set temperature of the reference system without calibration; the determined offset was then transferred to all pixels.

For the tests, we also used a thermal camera with a resolution of 640 × 480 px. The width of the field of view was 1.2 m that represents 5 px per centimeter. The used reference surface of the peltier element had the size of 4 × 4 cm, therefore the reference-surface was recorded with 400 px.

This amount of pixel was sufficient for our calibration procedure. Furthermore, the reference devices needed some time to reach it's reference temperature.

Fig. 6. Dust and dirt protected prototype.

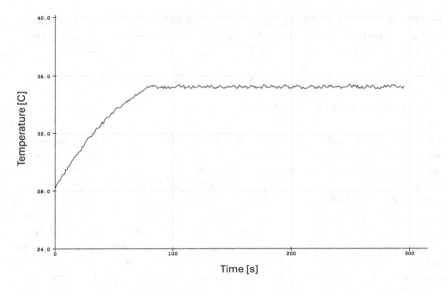

Fig. 7. Heating up the reference device to a constant value (here: 34°).

In Fig. 7, the calibration time was approx. one minute, depending on the environment temperature and the required reference temperature. The time delay can be easily changed in the set up by other resistors and power supply.

7 Discussion

The evaluation showed that a reference temperature is supporting a reliable and accurate measurement. On the other side, the introduced reference system is only used and designed to measure close to the reference temperature. It would be nice to retrieve a full range calibration, but this needs additional efforts and doesn't cover the error of the sections of measurement. Furthermore, we could see that the reference device produced a fluctuating temperature output. This reason is a three point controlling circuit that is currently not optimized. Here, an enhancement can be done in future. The performed evaluation was close of a simple proof-of-concept test. We suggest to perform an extensive evaluation that determines the influences or advantages of various measurement sections, e.g. high humidity, sun reflections etc. With the presented device, even very cheap thermal cameras can provide accurate thermal images and can be used for fever detection or other purposes. Some thermal camera do not provide a radimetric output but only a temperature representation as a gray image. With the know reference temperature, the absolute temperature can be estimated. In the tests, we could figure out, that the physical dimensions of the reference area should fit to the camera resolution. Therefore, a very small reference-area (far distance images) may provide insufficient pixel counts for a reliable reference information.

Possible solution might be an optical zoom or bigger reference surfaces. In the application field of vital data analysis of animals, a cow might carry a reference temperature as a tag or within the barn some reference points can be set up easily.

8   Conclusion and Outlook

Thermal imaging cameras impress with their ability to capture important data without contact and in complete darkness. Due to the ambient temperature, humidity, and distance to the object being measured, thermal imaging cameras provide inaccurate absolute values. The error is typically in the range of two degrees Celsius, which is not sufficient for many absolute measurement requirements. In this paper, we present a reference temperature system that is easy to build, easy to set up, and inexpensive, and that allows the improvement of the measurement of body temperature, fever, infection, etc. to be improved by absolute values. This system consists of a Peltier element that can maintain a constant, predetermined temperature through a control loop. This reference system is held in the field of view of the camera so that the absolute deviation can be determined and calculated. We anticipate that our concept of temperature difference can also be used as an ear tag for cows and for various measurements to determine animal health. In addition, very inexpensive thermosensor arrays can be improved as reference systems, making widespread monitoring plausible in the future. Further work will focus on the 3D propagation of thermal radiation to gain a broader understanding of the applicability of thermography.

Acknowledgements. This work was funded by the Fraunhofer Innovation Grant Program, Germany, and the Federal Ministry of Economic Affairs and Climate Action.

Disclosure of Interests. The authors have no competing interests to declare that are relevant to the content of this article.

References

1. Brzezinski, R.Y., et al.: Automated processing of thermal imaging to detect COVID-19. Sci. Rep. **11**(1), 17489 (2021). https://doi.org/10.1038/s41598-021-96900-9
2. Chauvin, R., et al.: Contact-free respiration rate monitoring using a pan-tilt thermal camera for stationary bike telerehabilitation sessions. IEEE Syst. J. **10**(3), 1046–1055 (2014). https://doi.org/10.1109/JSYST.2014.2336372
3. Church, J.S., et al.: Influence of environmental factors on infrared eye temperature measurements in cattle. Res. Vet. Sci. **96**(1), 220–226 (2014). https://doi.org/10.1016/j.rvsc.2013.11.006
4. Di Credico, A., et al.: Estimation of heart rate variability parameters by machine learning approaches applied to facial infrared thermal imaging. Front. Cardiovas. Med. **9**, 893374 (2022). https://doi.org/10.3389/fcvm.2022.893374

5. Fisenko, A., Ivashov, S.: Determination of the true temperature of emitted radiation bodies from generalized Wien's displacement law. J. Phys. D Appl. Phys. **32**(22), 2882 (1999). https://doi.org/10.1088/0022-3727/32/22/309
6. Garbey, M., Sun, N., Merla, A., Pavlidis, I.: Contact-free measurement of cardiac pulse based on the analysis of thermal imagery. IEEE Trans. Biomed. Eng. **54**(8), 1418–1426 (2007). https://doi.org/10.1109/TBME.2007.891930
7. GmbH, I.: Datasheet imageir® 8300 z. Website (2024). https://www.infratec.de/thermografie/waermebildkameras/imageir-8300-z/. Accessed 24 June 2024
8. Kraft, D., Van Laerhoven, K., Bieber, G.: CareCam: concept of a new tool for corporate health management. In: The 14th PErvasive Technologies Related to Assistive Environments Conference, pp. 585–593 (2021)
9. Lane, B., Whitenton, E.P., et al.: Calibration and measurement procedures for a high magnification thermal camera. Report no. NISTIR8098 (National Institute of Standards and Technology, Gaithersburg, MD) (2015)
10. Lin, J.W., Lu, M.H., Lin, Y.H.: A thermal camera based continuous body temperature measurement system. In: Proceedings of the IEEE/CVF International Conference on Computer Vision Workshops (2019). https://doi.org/10.1109/ICCVW.2019.00208
11. LLC, T.F.: Thermal camera calibration (2023). https://www.flir.eu/discover/professional-tools/how-do-you-calibrate-a-thermal-imaging-camera/. Accessed 14 June 2024
12. Minkina, W., Klecha, D.: Atmospheric transmission coefficient modelling in the infrared for thermovision measurements. J. Sens. Sens. Syst. **5**(1), 17–23 (2016). https://doi.org/10.5194/jsss-5-17-2016
13. Morton, M.L., Helminen, E.C., Felver, J.C.: A systematic review of mindfulness interventions on psychophysiological responses to acute stress. Mindfulness **11**, 2039–2054 (2020)
14. Petrie, P.R., Wang, Y., Liu, S., Lam, S., Whitty, M.A., Skewes, M.A.: The accuracy and utility of a low cost thermal camera and smartphone-based system to assess grapevine water status. Biosyst. Eng. **179**, 126–139 (2019). https://doi.org/10.1016/j.biosystemseng.2019
15. Shetty, A.D., Shubha, B., Suryanarayana, K., et al.: Detection and tracking of a human using the infrared thermopile array sensor-"grid-eye". In: 2017 International Conference on Intelligent Computing, Instrumentation and Control Technologies (ICICICT), pp. 1490–1495. IEEE (2017). https://doi.org/10.1109/ICICICT1.2017.8342790]
16. Swamidoss, I.N., Amro, A.B., Sayadi, S.: Systematic approach for thermal imaging camera calibration for machine vision applications. Optik **247**, 168039 (2021). https://doi.org/10.1016/j.ijleo.2021.168039
17. Tian, X., Fang, L., Liu, W.: The influencing factors and an error correction method of the use of infrared thermography in human facial skin temperature. Build. Environ. **244**, 110736 (2023). https://doi.org/10.1016/j.buildenv.2023.110736
18. Villa, E., Arteaga-Marrero, N., Ruiz-Alzola, J.: Performance assessment of low-cost thermal cameras for medical applications. Sensors **20**(5), 1321 (2020). https://doi.org/10.3390/s20051321

Estimation of Psychosocial Work Environment Exposures Through Video Object Detection
Proof of Concept Using CCTV Footage

Claus D. Hansen[1]([⊠])(iD), Thuy Hai Le[2], and David Campos[2](iD)

[1] Department of Sociology and Social Work, Aalborg University, Aalborg, Denmark
clausdh@socsci.aau.dk
[2] Department of Computer Science, Aalborg University, Aalborg, Denmark
dgcc@cs.aau.dk

Abstract. This paper examines the use of computer vision algorithms to estimate aspects of the psychosocial work environment using CCTV footage. We present a proof of concept for a methodology that detects and tracks people in video footage and estimates interactions between customers and employees by estimating their poses and calculating the duration of their encounters. We propose a pipeline that combines existing object detection and tracking algorithms (YOLOv8 and DeepSORT) with pose estimation algorithms (BlazePose) to estimate the number of customers and employees in the footage as well as the duration of their encounters. We use a simple rule-based approach to classify the interactions as positive, neutral or negative based on three different criteria: distance, duration and pose. The proposed methodology is tested on a small dataset of CCTV footage. While the data is quite limited in particular with respect to the quality of the footage, we have chosen this case as it represents a typical setting where the method could be applied. The results show that the object detection and tracking part of the pipeline has a reasonable performance on the dataset with a high degree of recall and reasonable accuracy. At this stage, the pose estimation is still limited to fully detect the type of interactions due to difficulties in tracking employees in the footage. We conclude that the method is a promising alternative to self-reported measures of the psychosocial work environment and could be used in future studies to obtain external observations of the work environment.

Keywords: CCTV · quantitative job demands · computer vision · human interactions

1 Introduction

The use of Closed Circuit Television (CCTV) in public and private settings has increased substantially over the last 20 years. Its use is often associated with the prevention of crimes and aggressive behaviour, apprehension of criminals and raising the general perception of safety in public spaces. However, there are a number of other widespread uses of CCTV as well such as the estimation of traffic flows, automatic number plate recognition and the monitoring of wildlife and weather conditions. Surveillance of people in shops and supermarkets are routinely used in order to prevent crimes and apprehend criminals that expose personnel for threats and assaults [20].

As theft can sometimes lead to violence and threats against employees, the use of CCTV can also be seen as a preventive measure against workplace violence and threats, creating a safer atmosphere for employees. This has been most explicitly researched in the transport sector where CCTV as well as body cams has been used to prevent violence as well as other types of aggressive behaviour towards personnel [19]. Fortunately, threats and violence are rare events in the retail sector. Arbejdstilsynet (The Danish Working Environment Authority) bi-annually carries out surveillance on the work environment in Denmark through the survey NOA-L [2]. In 2021, 6.3% of the employees in the retail sector reported that they had been exposed to threats of violence in the work environment, a majority of these events were reported to be from external sources i.e. customers. A much smaller proportion of employees reported that they had been exposed to actual violent events at their workplace.

Despite the widespread use of CCTV in the retail sector, the majority of the actual footage is never used for anything at all. The footage is being recorded and stored for the purpose of preventing in particular theft, i.e. primarily for the benefit of the company. However, the data could also be used for other purposes: it could for instance be used to advice customers on not to visit the shop at certain times of the day because the shop is too crowded which could be beneficial for the customers but also for the employees. Choosing not to use the data for these purposes could be seen as a missed opportunity to improve the work environment for the employees and the shopping experience for the customers. In this paper, we argue for the use of CCTV footage to estimate aspects of the psychosocial work environment and present a proof of concept demonstrating how this can be achieved using a combination of existing object detection and computer vision algorithms.

The psychosocial work environment is an important factor for employees health and well-being [27]. The global burden of work related accidents and diseases is substantial and is estimated to be 4% of the global GDP and 2.7% in Denmark [28]. Although work accidents and occupational diseases related to e.g. exposures to harmful substances and physical work environment factors are more common, the psychosocial work environment is becoming an increasingly important factor for employees health and well-being as the labour markets of highly developed countries such as Denmark are becoming more and more service oriented. For this reason, reducing adverse working conditions is important for society due to the costs associated with this, e.g. prolonged sick leave and early retirement. At the same time a safe and healthy work environment is associated with increased productivity and reduced turnover which are important goals for companies. From the perspective of the individual, psychosocial work environment factors are important for a number of reasons not least because being outside the labour market has profound negative effects on the quality of life and longevity. Being able to estimate aspects of the psychosocial work environment using CCTV footage thus constitutes a way of using information that is already being collected for other purposes in a way that is beneficial for society and for the individual employees without incurring additional ethical problems that are not already present in the current limited use of CCTV footage for crime prevention.

The contribution of this paper is thus to provide a proof of concept that demonstrates how the use of object detection algorithms can be extended to estimate important aspects of the psychosocial work environment using CCTV footage. The contribution of this paper can thus be summarised as follows:

– Our paper proposes an implementation of object detection algorithms as a way of estimating quantitative job demands in the psychosocial work environment using CCTV footage.
– We propose a set of metrics that can serve as proxy measures for important aspects of the psychosocial work environment.
– The methodology is tested on a dataset of CCTV footage establishing the feasibility of our approach (Fig. 1).

Fig. 1. Example footage of an interaction between employee and customer in CCTV footage

We have structured the paper as follows:

Section 2 reviews related work on computer vision algorithms for detecting and tracking people in video footage, as well as recognising human activities using such footage. We also review how psychosocial work environment factors have been measured in previous studies and how the use of CCTV footage could provide a way of estimating some of these factors.

Section 3 introduces the concepts and notation used in the paper.

Section 4 describes the overall system architecture and methodology used to analyse the CCTV footage. The approach used combines several existing computer vision algorithms to detect and track people in the footage as well as to estimate the interactions between customers and employees.

Section 5 presents the results of our experiments based on CCTV footage demonstrating the feasibility of our proposed method.

Section 6 discusses the results and points to future work that needs to be carried out in order to validate the method further. We discuss the limitations of the method and how they can be addressed in future work.

2   Related Work

2.1   Object Detection, Tracking and Human Activity Recognition

Object Detection. *Object detection* in images and video footage is a core task in computer vision [38]. Early approaches, like Histogram of Oriented Gradients (HOG) [8] and Haar cascades [31], relied on 'hand-crafted' features. Modern methods, however, use deep learning to automatically learn features from data. One of the most influential algorithms is You Only Look Once (YOLO) [23], which detects objects in real-time by dividing the image into a grid and predicting bounding boxes and class probabilities within each cell. Although YOLO is not the most precise, its speed makes it suitable for real-time applications or applications running on devices with limited computational resources.

In CCTV footage analysis, object detection helps identifying harmful objects and individuals [25]. Challenges include detecting small objects and dealing with low-quality footage, which might require fine-tuning or training the models on domain-specific data [38]. Existing solutions should be able to detect persons in the footage which is the basic requirement for estimating the psychosocial work environment factors.

Multi-object Tracking. *Multi-object tracking* (MOT) extends object detection by tracking objects across frames [16]. Approaches vary between online and offline tracking, with online tracking being crucial for real-time applications such as autonomous vehicles and CCTV footage analysis [1]. One prominent algorithm is Simple Online and Realtime Tracking (SORT) [5], which uses a Kalman filter to predict object trajectories based on bounding box movements. SORT is efficient but struggles with occlusions and non-linear movements. Deep-SORT [34] enhances SORT by integrating deep learning for appearance-based feature extraction, significantly improving tracking accuracy by reducing identity switches.

In crowded environments like shops, precise tracking of individuals is critical [26]. Combining object detection with tracking algorithms helps estimate core aspects of the psychosocial work environment, such as the number of customers and employees and the duration of their interactions. Object tracking, however, is not sufficient for analysing interactions taking place between customers and employees in the footage. For this purpose, we need to be able to assess the nature of the activities that the people are carrying out in the footage which can be done using human activity recognition algorithms.

Human Activity Recognition. One type of *human activity recognition* (HAR) involves identifying actions from video footage [3]. Deep learning algorithms like CNNs are commonly used, with applications focusing on daily activities rather than workplace settings. Notable HAR algorithms include OpenPose [7], which estimates poses with up to 135 key-points using Part Affinity Fields, and MediaPipe Pose [9], based on BlazePose [4], which uses 33 key-points and is optimized for real-time mobile applications.

Examples of HAR applications include Ruiz-Santaquiteria et al. [24], which combines object detection and pose estimation to identify handguns, and Paudel et al. [22], which estimates the ergonomic risk of workers' poses. These applications demonstrate the potential of pose estimation for recognizing specific human activities in video footage including the identification of interactions related to the psychosocial work environment.

Despite the availability of algorithms for object detection and tracking, no existing solution address the specific task of estimating psychosocial work environment factors from CCTV footage. Our approach combines object detection, tracking, and pose estimation to recognize and classify interactions between customers and employees, providing a novel method for estimating psychosocial work environment factors.

2.2   Workload Estimation and Psychosocial Work Environment Factors

Self-reported Estimation of Psychosocial Work Environment Factors. The job demands-control model by Karasek [13] is widely used to estimate the psychosocial work environment, focusing on job demands and job control. High job demands are linked to negative health outcomes like cardiovascular disease and depression [27]. Most research relies on self-reported data, making it vulnerable to biases and subjective evalutations [18]. Theorell and Hasselhorn [30] suggest supplementing self-reports with objective measures like expert ratings or job exposure matrices. Our paper contributes by proposing a computational approach to analyse CCTV footage, offering an alternative to traditional self-reported measures.

Observational Estimation of Psychosocial Work Environment Factors.
Few studies use person-independent measures for psychosocial work environment
factors. Waldenstrom et al. [32] used expert ratings for social support, Bosma et
al. [6] used expert ratings to estimate both levels of skill discretion as well as job
control, while Griffin et al. [11] used external observers to rate skill utilization
and job barriers. These methods are costly and time-consuming, limiting their
scalability. Imputed approaches estimate job demands based on average levels
in occupational groups, but face validity issues, especially for small groups [17].

Greiner et al. [10] used observational data to estimate work barriers and time
pressure, showing a link to blood pressure. However, this method is not scalable for larger populations. Routine CCTV monitoring in shops offer a unique
opportunity to obtain external observations of the psychosocial work environment factors. Using CCTV footage is cost-effective and scalable, unlike expert
ratings.

Fig. 2. Bounding box example with predictions (x, y, w, h) and class label. Photo:
Colourbox.com

3   Concepts and Notation

In the following, we will introduce some notation and concepts that form the
foundation of the methodology used in this paper.

3.1 Object-Detection and Multi-object Tracking Using Bounding Boxes

Bounding boxes are a common way of representing objects in images and video footage (see Fig. 2). A bounding box is a rectangle that encloses an object in the image or frame. The bounding box is defined by a tuple of four numbers (x, y, w, h) where x and y are the coordinates of the center of the bounding box and w and h are the width and height of the bounding box respectively. The bounding box is used to represent the position of the object detected in the frame and is used as input to algorithms that subsequently track the object across frames such as DeepSort. Bounding box regression involves predicting the boundaries of the rectangle that encloses an object in the image as well as the class of the object and the confidence with which the predicting has been made. In Fig. 2, the bounding box is used to represent the current position of the object in the frame as well as the predicted class of the object and the confidence with which the prediction has been made.

Multi-object tracking is a technique for tracking multiple objects in video footage. The technique is based on object detection algorithms that are able to detect objects in individual frames and track the objects across frames. The tracking is based on the movement of the bounding boxes of the objects in the frames and is used to estimate the trajectories of the objects in the video footage.

3.2 Human Activity Recognition Using Landmark Pose Detection

Landmark pose detection is a technique for estimating the pose of a person in an image. Depending on the level of detail the pose is defined by a number of key-points that are placed on the person's body and refers to specific parts of the body such as head, shoulders, knee, hands etc. The BlazePose algorithm uses 33 key-points to estimate the pose of a person in an image as illustrated in Fig. 3. The key-points are used to estimate the position of the person's body parts and are used as input to human activity recognition algorithms that are able to estimate the activities that the person is carrying out in the image or frame.

3.3 Proxy Metric of Quantitative Job Demands

Job demands are defined as the psychological load that the employee experiences on a normal work day. This construct is not one-dimensional but consists of a number of different types of demands such as quantitative demands (e.g. number of work hours and pace of work), emotional demands (e.g. dealing with difficult customers) and cognitive demands (e.g. problem solving and decision making) [15]. Using a computational approach to estimate job demands from CCTV footage does not lay claim to be able to estimate all of these aspects of job demands but focuses on a subset of what could be considered elements of quantitative demands [14].

Our aim is to estimate the tuple $V_{\text{job demands}}$ that represents the quantitative job demands experienced by the employees in the shop.

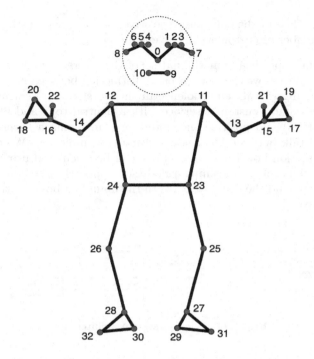

Fig. 3. Pose estimation example with 33 key-points

The tuple $V_{\text{job demands}}$ is defined as:

$$V_{\text{job demands}} = (T, C, S, D_{\text{total}}, D_{\text{avg}})$$

where:

- T total duration of work day (in minutes),
- S Set of all encounters $\{E_1, E_2, \ldots, E_n\}$,
- C Total number of customers, calculated as the sum of customers in each encounter: $C = \sum_{E_i \in S} n_i$.
- D_{total} total duration of the encounters (in minutes), calculated as $\sum_{E_i \in S}$ duration$_i$.
- D_{avg} average duration of the encounters (in minutes), computed as $\frac{1}{|S|} \sum_{E_i \in S}$ duration$_i$.

Each encounter E_i within the set S is defined as:

$$E_i = (\text{id}_i, \text{duration}_i, \text{class}_i, \text{count}_i)$$

where:

- id_i is the unique identifier of the encounter,
- dur_i is the duration of the encounter (in minutes),

- class$_i$ is the class of the encounter (positive, neutral, negative),
- n$_i$ is the number of customers in the encounter.

  Looking more specifically at the nature of the interactions between the customers and employees we can make a basic distinction between negative encounters (e.g. involving threats and violence in the worst case), neutral encounters (e.g. involving regular customer service with a neutral tone and blasé attitude from both parties) and positive encounters (e.g. involving a friendly tone and possibly small talk between the customer and the employee). We detail in the methodology section how these distinctions can be calculated using a combination of pose estimation and a simple rule-based approach based on the duration of the encounters and the distance between the bounding boxes of the customers and the employees.

Fig. 4. Overview of system architecture

4   Methodology

4.1   System Architecture

In Fig. 4, we present an overview of the system architecture that we use to estimate job demands from CCTV footage. As can be seen from the illustration, the system consists of a fundamental pipeline that detects and tracks persons in the video footage classifying them into customers and employees respectively. This classification is stored in a temporary database that is subsequently used to estimate job demands based on the number of customers, the number of encounters and their duration. Building on this classification, frames with at least two bounding boxes are selected for further analysis using the pose estimation algorithm as well as a simple rule-based approach (as explained below) to classify the interactions into positive, neutral or negative encounters. This enables us to estimate the final aspects of job demands arising from the nature of the interactions.

4.2   Object Detection and Tracking with YOLOv8 and DeepSORT

This section details the system employed for object detection and tracking in the video footage. We make use of a combination of two widely used deep learning algorithms: YOLOv8 [12] for object detection and DeepSORT [34] for object tracking. Unlike traditional methods that require separate stages for feature extraction and classification, YOLOv8 operates on a single-stage approach. This means it divides the input image into a grid and simultaneously predicts bounding boxes and class probabilities for objects contained within each grid cell. We restrict the object detection to be persons only, as we are only interested in being able to distinguish between customers and employees in the footage. The unique approach of YOLOv8 allows it to achieve real-time object detection speeds without compromising on detection accuracy. Although our system is not designed to be used in real-time, the efficiency of YOLOv8 is beneficial for processing large amounts of video footage. This would also be a requirement if the system should be set up to run on the hardware on-site used for recording the CCTV footage (i.e. some kind of webcam with limited computational resources).

The detection from YOLOv8 (in the form of bounding boxes, class predictions and confidence scores) is saved in a temporary database and subsequently used as input to the DeepSORT algorithm. DeepSORT utilizes these detections and extracts features from the objects to associate these across frames, assigning unique IDs and maintaining track information for each object throughout the video. We use the pre-trained model based on the MARS dataset [37] which is a large-scale dataset for person re-identification trained on a large number of pedestrian images. This provided us with a quick and efficient way to track persons across frames without the need to train the model on our own dataset. Because of the basic assumptions of the DeepSORT algorithm, however, this can lead to errors in tracking objects across frames. The Kalman filter used as the basis for DeepSORT assumes that the objects move in a linear fashion and that the velocity of the objects is approximately constant [33]. While this is a reasonable assumption for pedestrians walking around in public spaces, this is a more problematic assumption in the context of the retail sector. For this reason, DeepSORT IDs is a suboptimal approach. In some cases, the same object might be assigned to a different ID, especially in situations with occlusions, similar-looking objects, changes in the shape of the bounding box associated with an object or with movement of persons that are not linear. This is particularly the case in our footage in situations where the employee bow downs to pick up something or when the employee serves the customers by reaching out to the shelves. This will lead to errors when calculating properties or tracking specific objects based solely on their DeepSORT IDs.

4.3 Re-identification of Bounding Box IDs and Classification of Customers and Employees

Because the object detection algorithm is only able to detect persons regardless of their role as customers or employees, we need to implement a method to distinguish between the two. Even if we had trained our algorithm on a dataset from the retail sector, it would be unlikely that it would be able to distinguish between the two classes of persons based solely on their appearance. For this reason, we have implemented a simple rule-based approach that classifies the persons based on their initial position in the frame. As can be seen from the illustration in Fig. 5, we have defined two regions of interest (ROI) in the frame based on the line l that divides the frame into a *customer area* where the entrance to the shop is located and a *staff area* where the counter is located and the employee can exit to a back room. The classification of objects is based on the y-coordinate of the bottom-right corner of the bounding box y_2: bounding boxes with $y_2 < y_l$ (i.e. less than the y-coordinate of l) are classified as *employees* while bounding boxes with $y_2 > y_l$ are classified as *customers*. This simple rule helps reduce the computational load for re-identifying IDs for employees, as all IDs of bounding boxes in the staff area is reassigned to the employee. This is build on an assumption that there is only one employee in the staff area at a time. In more complex settings, this definition of the ROI should be extended to be able to account for multiple employees. In addition, a more sophisticated division of the frame using information from the shop's layout could be used to improve the classification of customers and employees.

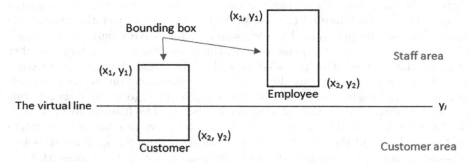

Fig. 5. Line l dividing the frame into two regions of interest (ROI) for classification of customers and employees

In an attempt to supplement the tracking IDs derived from DeepSORT, we have implemented a combination of three additional methods that analyse features within the bounding boxes identified by YOLO. These methods include Convolutional Neural Networks (CNNs) (and more specifically the EfficientNet-B0 model [29]) for feature extraction, Histogram of Oriented Gradients (HOG) for shape analysis, and K-Means clustering for color analysis. If the similarity score between two bounding boxes based on the features extracted by the three methods is greater than a predefined threshold, the program re-identifies the objects and assigns them the same ID, ensuring consistent tracking. By combining the three methods, we aim to achieve more robust and accurate results compared to using the individual methods in isolation. Our solution is inspired by Ye and colleagues [35] who reviewed state-of-the-art methods for re-identifying objects in video footage and points to the importance of combining multiple methods to achieve the best results. Our solution is designed to be able to weight the contribution of each of the three re-identification methods to the total similarity score.

The process for re-identifying IDs for objects is performed following these steps:

- Scan all bounding boxes to calculate CNN, HOG, and K-Means features for each ID assigned by DeepSORT.
- For each pair of IDs $(Object_1, Object_2)$, calculate the similarity between them based on their CNN, HOG, color (K-Means) features.
- Combine the similarities using a weighted average where the weights are chosen based on a predefined importance of the features in distinguishing between objects.
- Filter pair IDs that are greater than the threshold and sort them in descending order of similarities.
- Re-identify IDs by adding all bounding boxes of $Object_2$ to $Object_1$ and deleting $Object_2$.

This process is repeated for all pairs of IDs and is designed to be able to re-identify objects that e.g. have been occluded, whose bounding box have changed shape in the frame or have been wrongly assigned a new ID by DeepSORT. The weights for the CNN, HOG and color similarities are chosen based on the importance of the features in distinguishing between objects. In our setting, we priorize high-level features due to the relatively low level of detail in the footage which means attributing most weight (0.65) to the EfficientNet-B0 model as it is able to capture high-level features crucial for distinguishing between different objects based on their overall structure and appearance. The HOG features are given a moderate weight (0.20) as they capture shape and edge information that is useful but often less distinctive than high-level features from CNNs. Finally, the color features could help differentiate between customers and employees based on the color of their clothing and are given the remaining weight (0.15).

The re-identified IDs are used to estimate the number of customers entering the shop as well as the duration of their encounters. The duration of the encounters is calculated by taking the number of bounding boxes assigned to the customer and dividing it by the frame rate of the video footage. This approach assumes that the encounters begin when the customer enters the shop and ends when the customer leaves the shop. Using the pose-estimation approach we base the calculation of the duration of the encounters on the proximity of the bounding boxes of the customers and the employees. When the distance between the bounding boxes is less than a predefined threshold (distance $< 1.5\,\mathrm{m}$), the encounter is considered to have started.

4.4   Human Activity Recognition

As can be seen from the illustration in Fig. 4, the results from the object detection and tracking are subsequently used to select frames with at least two bounding boxes for further analysis, i.e. to identify *interactions* between customers and employees. We utilize *MediaPipe Pose solution* to estimate the landmark poses of the customers and employees in the selected frames. The algorithm is based on a pre-trained model that predict 33 keypoints of a person's skeleton, allowing us to track the movements and interactions of the individuals in the frame. While

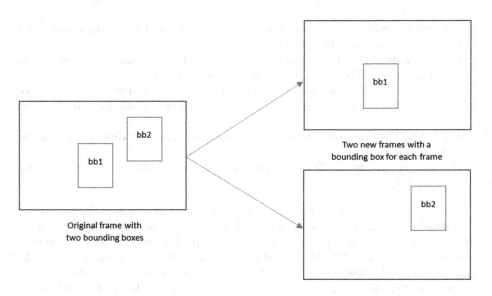

Fig. 6. Splitting the frame into multiple frames with isolated bounding boxes for pose estimation

MediaPipe Pose excels at pose estimation, it is designed to process a single person per frame only. To overcome this limitation when dealing with multiple people in a video, a potential approach involves strategically manipulating the frames as illustrated in Fig. 6. The procedure is thus as follows:

a. For each frame in the original video containing multiple people a new empty frame with the same dimensions and data type is created.
b. Loop through each bounding box detected by YOLOv8 in the original frame.
c. Copy the corresponding bounding box information (coordinates, width, height) from the original frame to the empty frame.
d. Apply the MediaPipe Pose algorithm to this newly created frame containing only the isolated bounding box to accurately estimate that person's key-point coordinates.
e. Repeat steps a-d for each detected bounding box in the original frame.

On the basis of the landmark poses obtained as well as information about the placement of the bounding boxes in the frame relative to each other, we then apply another rule-based approach to classify the interactions between customers and employees. The aim is to be able to distinguish between positive, neutral and negative interactions based on the combined information. As described above the distinction between the three types of interactions is based on three different criteria: *duration* of the encounter, *distance* between the bounding boxes of the two persons and their placement with respect to staff and customer area and finally, the *pose of the persons* in the frame.

Neutral Interactions. We assume that neutral interactions are the most common type of interaction in the retail sector and that overtly negative interactions are the least common. A neutral interaction is defined as a scenario where an employee situated in the staff area carries out tasks related to the servicing of customers such as retrieving bread from the shelves, packing goods and registering the payment at the counter. We assume that a neutral interaction of the encounter E_i is characterized by a duration of the encounter that is close to the average duration of all encounters or shorter than the average duration of all encounters (i.e. $dur_i \lesssim D_{\mathrm{avg}}$), and that the distance between the two persons equals the distance between a customer near the counter and the employee at the opposite side of the counter.

Positive Interactions. We assume that positive interactions are characterized by a friendly tone and possibly small talk between the customer and the employee. This implies that the duration of the encounter is longer than the average duration of all encounters (i.e. $dur_i > D_{\mathrm{avg}}$) and either

- that the employee is standing still at the counter without performing any tasks related to the servicing of customers or,
- that the employee is coming out from the staff area to the customer area.

We use the position of the bounding boxes to determine the placement of the persons in the frame in order to distinguish between the two scenarios.

Negative Interactions. Although negative interactions could be characterized by a number of different behaviours, we focus on one specific type of negative interaction in this study: threatening or violent behaviour. We assume that threatening behaviour is characterized by a customer trying to intimidate the employee by raising their hands above their head or hitting the employee. This means that the duration of the encounter is not relevant for the classification of the interaction. We use the landmark poses obtained from the Mediapipe algorithm.

As shown in Fig. 7, we can calculate the distance between the hands (19, 20) of one object and the head (0, 3) of another object within the same frame. An interaction is classified as negative if the calculated distance is less than the threshold, which typically ranges from 0 to 5 cm. This threshold is based on the assumption that threatening behaviour is characterized by a close proximity between the hands of the customer and the head of the employee.

It would be possible (and advantageous) to include more types of poses that are threatening e.g. a customer pointing a finger at the employee or poses signalling that the customer is angry or frustrated. This would require a more detailed analysis of the poses obtained from the Mediapipe algorithm and the implementation of a more complex rule-based approach to classify the interactions. As our study is a proof of concept we have chosen to only focus on this specific type of threatening behaviour despite the fact that it is highly unlikely for this to be prevalent in the video footage we analyse.

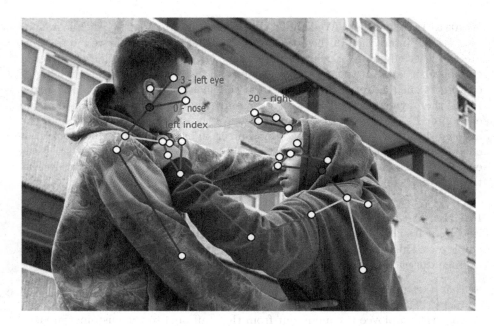

Fig. 7. Example of threatening pose with keypoint notations $(0, 3, 19, 20)$. Photo: Colourbox.com

4.5   Estimation of Psychosocial Work Environment Exposures

Based on the classification of customers and employees, we are able to estimate $V_{\text{job demands}}$ as described in the previous section. The total number of customers C is calculated as the sum of customers in each encounter and the total duration of the encounters D_{total} is calculated as the sum of the duration of each encounter. The average duration of the encounters D_{avg} is calculated as the average duration of all encounters. The duration of the encounters is calculated based on the frame rate of the footage and the number of frames in each encounter.

5   Experiments and Results

We use video footage captures from shops and malls. The footage is of low quality and the number of persons in the frame is quite limited, however, we believe that the material is representative of the type of footage that could be expected from CCTV cameras in the retail sector. As the aim of our paper is to provide a proof of concept that the method could be used to estimate aspects of the psychosocial work environment using CCTV footage, we find this fitting. We utilize a total of 1500 min of footage from a bakery and have analysed a subset of this footage consisting of 5 videos totalling 73 min. In the following, we describe the results of the experiments carried out as part of our study including information about the setup used.

5.1   Setup

The tests carried out as part of this study were all run on a laptop with an Intel Core i7-10750H CPU and 16 GB of RAM. The laptop was running Windows 11. We have made use of different existing libraries and have written our own code to implement the methodology described in the previous sections using Python 3.11. The code is available upon request from the first author including a small dataset of the footage used for the study to exemplify the methodology.

5.2   CCTV Footage Analysis

The CCTV footage was captured as MJPG which means that the frame rate is not constant across the footage. The frame rate most likely varies between 10–15 frames per second. For calculating the duration of the encounters, we have assumed a frame rate of 15 frames per second. The resolution of the footage is 640×480 pixels. The camera is placed in the ceiling of the workplace with a view of the counter and the entrance to the shop however without any information about the distance between the camera and the persons in the frame or the angle of the camera. These information could have helped improve the accuracy of the different algorithms used in the study for instance when estimating the distance between the bounding boxes of the persons in the frame. Depending on the way in which a customer enters the shop they might not be detected by the object detection algorithm as they are partly occluded.

5.3   Coding of Video Footage

In order to evaluate the performance of our methodology, we have coded the five videos by watching them and manually coding how many customers come into the shop and for how long they stay. In addition, we have coded the encounter as either positive, neutral or negative based primarily on the criteria described in the methodology section: positive encounters are characterised by the employee not performing any tasks related to the servicing of customers but seems to be talking to them and the duration of the encounter is therefore longer than the average neutral encounter. Neutral encounters are coded as such when the customer comes into the shop, buys an item and then exits the shop again immediately thereafter. We have not coded any negative encounters as the footage does not contain any threatening behaviour.

We decided not to annotate the bounding boxes of the persons in the frame as this is a time consuming task that would primarily be related to the accuracy of the object detection and tracking algorithm which is not the primary contribution of this study. The coding of aggregate measures related to the videos enables us to compare the results of the methodology with the manually coded data and calculate the accuracy of our proposed method with respect to three elements from $V_{\text{job demands}}$, namely the total number of customers C and the total D_{total} as well as average duration of the encounters D_{avg}. The accuracy of the predictions is calculated as the percentage of correctly identified customers and encounters as well as the average difference between the predicted and the manually coded values for the total and average duration of the encounters. These metrics are evaluated for each of the five videos and the average accuracy is calculated across the five videos. The results of these calculations are presented in table 1.

Table 1. Accuracy of object detection and tracking algorithm

Video Nr.	No. of customers	Accuracy (No. customers)	Recall (No. customers)	Average duration (min:sec)	Error (Duration)	Ratio of Positive interactions
1	6	86%	100%	1:23	30%	12%
2	14	43%	43%	1:54	33%	28%
3	1	100%	100%	1:09	7%	0%
4	4	80%	100%	1:05	17%	0%
5	4	31%	100%	3:46	58%	83%
Average		68%	89%		29%	

The results of the experiments carried out as part of this study show that the methodology is able to roughly estimate C, the number of customers in the footage with an accuracy of 68% and a recall of 89%. The approach, however, underestimates $D_{average}$, the average duration of the encounters by on average 29%.

5.4   Object Detection and Tracking

As can be seen from Fig. 8, the object detection and tracking algorithm is able to detect and track persons in the frame and applying our rule-based approach classify the persons as customers and employees respectively. The algorithm struggles primarily with re-identifying the employee across frames. This is likely due to the limitations of the DeepSORT algorithm as described in the methodology section, i.e. the assumption that the objects move in a linear fashion and that the velocity of the objects is approximately constant. The difficulties in re-identifying the employee across frames has consequences for the analyses of interactions as the employee is not detected in the frames in a high number of cases.

As can be seen in Table 1 the accuracy and precision of the object detection and tracking algorithm is best in videos with a low number of customers characterised by a neutral interaction pattern where the customer enters the shop, order an item, pays for it and then exists the shop immediately thereafter. In these cases (i.e. videos 3 and 4), the algorithm is able to detect and track the customers with a high degree of recall and accuracy. The worst performance is seen in video 5 where only 4 customers visit the shop (in the span of 15 min) and where one positive encounter takes a very long time. The algorithm detects this particular customer multiple times leading to an overestimation of the total

Fig. 8. Example of object detection and tracking with bounding boxes in the CCTV footage

number of customers as well as severely underestimating the duration of the encounters.

In video 2, the algorithm struggles because of the high number of customers and the fact that the customers are partly occluded when they enter the shop. In addition, identity switches occur when the customer that has been served exits the shop and in the process passes the other customers leading to the bounding boxes overlapping. An example of this can be seen in Fig. 8 where the customer at the entrance has not been detected by the algorithm. This leads to a severe underestimation of the total number of customers and is reflected in the low recall for this particular video. Overall this points to two weaknesses of our methodology: in cases where a high number of customers is present in the shop at the same time, the algorithm struggles to detect and track the customers accurately, and in cases where an encounter takes a long time and the customer does not exit the shop immediately this leads to a detection of the customer multiple times. In the next section of the paper, we discuss the implications of these limitations and how to address them in future studies.

Although the system is not designed nor optimized for real-time processing of video footage, the computational resources used is still an important part of the evaluation of the system. As can be seen from Table 2, the system is able to process on average 3 frames per second depending on the complexity of the footage. This means that e.g. video 2 with a length of 30 min takes around 3 h and 45 min to process. This is not problematic per se given the aim of the study which is to provide an estimate of the psychosocial work environment based on CCTV footage for use in research studies. In that respect, runtime is not a critical factor for evaluating the usefulness of the system.

Table 2. Runtime analysis of the system

Video Nr.	Length of video	No. offrames	Computationaltime (secs)	fps
1	08:52	7993	2736	2.92
2	30:00	27002	13108	2.06
3	10:00	9002	1973	4.56
4	09:59	8999	2589	3.48
5	15:00	13502	6912	1.95
Average				2.99

5.5 Interactions Between Customers and Employees

The results of the pose estimation algorithm and the rule-based approach to classify the interactions between customers and employees are unfortunately not very promising at the current stage. While the algorithm is quite capable of estimating the poses of the customers, the algorithm loses track of the employee in the frame at the current stage in a very high number of cases. The result shown in Fig. 9 is therefore not representative of the actual results of the pose estimation algorithm where the employee falls in and out of the frame in a high number of cases. This is likely due partly to the low quality of the footage and the fact that the employee is partly occluded in the frame. In addition, the pose estimation algorithm is not able to estimate the poses of the persons in the frame when they are too close to each other. This has the consequence that the estimated duration of the encounters based on the pose estimation severely underestimates the actual duration of the encounters in the footage. On average the estimated duration of the encounters is 8 s while the actual duration of the encounters is 1 min and 51 s. This is a major limitation of the methodology and more results of the pose estimation algorithm are therefore not included in the results of the study. Below we discuss whether this is due to a fundamental flaw in our proposed methodology or whether it is due to limitations of the pose estimation algorithm and the quality of the footage used at present.

Fig. 9. Example of pose estimation in the CCTV footage

6   Conclusion and Future Work

This paper has contributed with a proof of concept for a methodology that can be used for estimating certain aspects of the psychosocial work environment (more specifically quantitative job demands) using realistic CCTV footage. Drawing on several existing computer vision algorithms, we propose a pipeline that detects and tracks persons in the footage, classifies them as customers and employees respectively and based on these computations estimates core aspects of $V_{\text{job demands}}$. The results of the experiments carried out as part of this study show that the methodology is able to estimate the number of customers in the footage.

The results are best in videos with a few costumers and a neutral interaction pattern. The algorithm struggles in cases with a high number of customers or in situations where the duration of the encounters are longer than average. In particular, the algorithm fails in cases with positive interactions or when there are multiple customers waiting in line to be served. Then, at the current state, the pose estimation algorithm is unable to distinguishing between positive, neutral and negative, likely due to difficulties in estimating the pose of the employee in the frame.

Therefore, even when the proposed solution is promising, it cannot be used with 'out-of-the-box', so it still needs adjustments for the work place where it will be used, where hand-crafted rules are used to classify the interactions between customers and employees, limiting its scalability.

As future work, we suggest the following directions:

– Combining footage from multiple cameras in a shop could improve detection accuracy, particularly in crowded settings where occlusions are frequent, including more advanced tracking algorithms [21]
– Using a labeled dataset from the specific workplace to train models could improve interaction recognition. This includes annotating poses indicative of various interaction types, thereby enhancing the method's ability to distinguish between positive, neutral, and negative interactions, or employing deep learning models tailored to these specific interactions could yield better results [36].
– Comparing the algorithm's output with self-reported data from employees can validate its effectiveness. Collecting employees' perceptions of their job demands and interactions could provide a benchmark for refining the algorithm's accuracy.

References

1. Agarwal, P., Kahlon, S.S., Bisht, N., Dash, P., Ahuja, S., Goyal, A.: Abandoned object detection and tracking using CCTV camera. In: Mishra, D.K., Nayak, M.K., Joshi, A. (eds.) Information and Communication Technology for Sustainable Development. Lecture Notes in Networks and Systems, vol. 10, pp. 483–492. Springer, Singapore (2018). https://doi.org/10.1007/978-981-10-3920-1_49
2. Arbejdstilsynet: National Overvågning af Arbejdsmiljøet blandt Lønmodtagere (2021). https://at.dk/arbejdsmiljoe-i-tal/national-overvaagning-af-arbejdsmiljoe et-blandt-loenmodtagere/
3. Arshad, M.H., Bilal, M., Gani, A.: Human activity recognition: review, taxonomy and open challenges. Sensors 22(17), 6463 (2022). https://doi.org/10.3390/s22176463, https://www.mdpi.com/1424-8220/22/17/6463
4. Bazarevsky, V., Grishchenko, I., Raveendran, K., Zhu, T., Zhang, F., Grundmann, M.: BlazePose: on-device Real-time Body Pose tracking (2020). https://doi.org/10.48550/arXiv.2006.10204, arXiv:2006.10204 [cs]
5. Bewley, A., Ge, Z., Ott, L., Ramos, F., Upcroft, B.: Simple online and realtime tracking. In: 2016 IEEE International Conference on Image Processing (ICIP), pp. 3464–3468 (2016). https://doi.org/10.1109/ICIP.2016.7533003, arXiv:1602.00763 [cs]
6. Bosma, H., Stansfeld, S.A., Marmot, M.G.: Job control, personal characteristics, and heart disease. J. Occup. Health Psychol. 3(4), 402–409 (1998). https://doi.org/10.1037/1076-8998.3.4.402
7. Cao, Z., Hidalgo, G., Simon, T., Wei, S.E., Sheikh, Y.: OpenPose: realtime multi-person 2D pose estimation using part affinity fields. IEEE Trans. Pattern Analy. Mach. Intell. 43(1), 172–186 (2021). https://doi.org/10.1109/TPAMI.2019.2929257, https://ieeexplore.ieee.org/document/8765346

8. Dalal, N., Triggs, B.: Histograms of oriented gradients for human detection. In: 2005 IEEE Computer Society Conference on Computer Vision and Pattern Recognition (CVPR 2005), vol. 1, pp. 886–893 (2005). https://doi.org/10.1109/CVPR.2005. 177, https://ieeexplore.ieee.org/document/1467360. iSSN 1063-6919
9. Google: MediaPipe Solutions guide | Edge (2024). https://ai.google.dev/edge/ mediapipe/solutions/guide
10. Greiner, B.A., Krause, N., Ragland, D., Fisher, J.M.: Occupational stressors and hypertension: a multi-method study using observer-based job analysis and self-reports in urban transit operators. Soc. Sci. Med. **59**(5), 1081–1094 (2004). https:// doi.org/10.1016/j.socscimed.2003.12.006, https://www.sciencedirect.com/science/ article/pii/S0277953603006944
11. Griffin, J.M., Greiner, B.A., Stansfeld, S.A., Marmot, M.: The effect of self-reported and observed job conditions on depression and anxiety symptoms: a comparison of theoretical models. J. Occup. Health Psychol. **12**(4), 334–349 (2007). https:// doi.org/10.1037/1076-8998.12.4.334
12. Jocher, G., Chaurasia, A., Qiu, J.: Ultralytics YOLO (2023). https://github.com/ ultralytics/ultralytics
13. Karasek Jr, R.A.: Job demands, job decision latitude, and mental strain: implications for job redesign. Administrative science quarterly, pp. 285–308 (1979). https://www.jstor.org/stable/2392498
14. Kristensen, T.S., Bjorner, J.B., Christensen, K.B., Borg, V.: The distinction between work pace and working hours in the measurement of quantitative demands at work. Work Stress **18**(4), 305–322 (2004). https://doi.org/10.1080/ 02678370412331314005
15. Kristensen, T.S., Hannerz, H., Høgh, A., Borg, V.: The Copenhagen psychosocial questionnaire-a tool for the assessment and improvement of the psychosocial work environment. Scand. J. Work Environ. Health **31**(6), 438–449 (2005). https://www. jstor.org/stable/40967527
16. Luo, W., Xing, J., Milan, A., Zhang, X., Liu, W., Kim, T.K.: Multiple object tracking: a literature review. Artif. Intell. **293**, 103448 (2021). https://doi.org/ 10.1016/j.artint.2020.103448, https://www.sciencedirect.com/science/article/pii/ S0004370220301958
17. Niedhammer, I., Milner, A., LaMontagne, A.D., Chastang, J.F.: Study of the validity of a job-exposure matrix for the job strain model factors: an update and a study of changes over time. Int. Arch. Occup. Environ. Health **91**(5), 523–536 (2018). https://doi.org/10.1007/s00420-018-1299-2
18. Nieuwenhuijsen, K., Bruinvels, D., Frings-Dresen, M.: Psychosocial work environment and stress-related disorders, a systematic review. Occup. Med. **60**(4), 277–286 (2010). https://doi.org/10.1093/occmed/kqq081
19. Nobili, M., Gonnella, M.T., Mazza, B., Lombardi, M., Setola, R.: Review of measures to prevent and manage aggression against transport workers. Saf. Sci. **166**, 106202 (2023). https://doi.org/10.1016/j.ssci.2023.106202, https://www. sciencedirect.com/science/article/pii/S0925753523001443
20. Norris, C., McCahill, M., Wood, D.: The growth of CCTV: a global perspective on the international diffusion of video surveillance in publicly accessible space. Surveill. Soc. **2**(2/3) (2004). https://doi.org/10.24908/ss.v2i2/3.3369, https://ojs. library.queensu.ca/index.php/surveillance-and-society/article/view/3369
21. Omeragić, T., Velagić, J.: Tracking of moving objects based on extended kalman filter. In: 2020 International Symposium ELMAR, pp. 137–140 (2020). https://doi.org/10.1109/ELMAR49956.2020.9219021, https://ieeexplore.ieee.org/ abstract/document/9219021. iSSN 1334-2630

22. Paudel, P., Choi, K.-H.: A deep-learning based worker's pose estimation. In: Ohyama, W., Jung, S.K. (eds.) IW-FCV 2020. CCIS, vol. 1212, pp. 122–135. Springer, Singapore (2020). https://doi.org/10.1007/978-981-15-4818-5_10

23. Redmon, J., Divvala, S., Girshick, R., Farhadi, A.: You only look once: unified, real-time object detection. In: 2016 IEEE Conference on Computer Vision and Pattern Recognition (CVPR), pp. 779–788 (2016). https://doi.org/10.1109/CVPR.2016. 91, https://ieeexplore.ieee.org/document/7780460. iSSN 1063-6919

24. Ruiz-Santaquiteria, J., Velasco-Mata, A., Vallez, N., Bueno, G., Álvarez García, J.A., Deniz, O.: Handgun detection using combined human pose and weapon appearance. IEEE Access **9**, 123815–123826 (2021). https://doi.org/10.1109/ ACCESS.2021.3110335, https://ieeexplore.ieee.org/abstract/document/9529187

25. Salazar González, J.L., Zaccaro, C., Álvarez García, J.A., Soria Morillo, L.M., Sancho Caparrini, F.: Real-time gun detection in CCTV: An open problem. Neural Netw. **132**, 297–308 (2020). https://doi.org/10.1016/j.neunet.2020.09.013, https://www.sciencedirect.com/science/article/pii/S0893608020303361

26. Sivakumar, P., Jayabalaguru, V., Ramsugumar. R., Kalaisriram, S.: Real time crime detection using deep learning algorithm. In: 2021 International Conference on System, Computation, Automation and Networking (ICSCAN), pp. 1–5 (2021). https://doi.org/10.1109/ICSCAN53069.2021.9526393, https://ieeexplore.ieee.org/ abstract/document/9526393

27. Stansfeld, S., Candy, B.: Psychosocial work environment and mental health-a meta-analytic review. Scand. J. Work Environ. Health **32**(6), 443–462 (2006). https:// doi.org/10.5271/sjweh.1050

28. Takala, J., et al.: Global estimates of the burden of injury and illness at work in 2012. J. Occup. Environ. Hygiene **11**(5), 326–337 (2014). https://doi.org/10.1080/ 15459624.2013.863131

29. Tan, M., Le, Q.V.: EfficientNet: rethinking model scaling for convolutional neural networks (2020). https://doi.org/10.48550/arXiv.1905.11946, arXiv:1905.11946 [cs, stat]

30. Theorell, T., Hasselhorn, H.M.: On cross-sectional questionnaire studies of relationships between psychosocial conditions at work and health-are they reliable? Int. Arch. Occup. Environ. Health **78**(7), 517–522 (2005). https://doi.org/10.1007/ s00420-005-0618-6

31. Viola, P., Jones, M.: Rapid object detection using a boosted cascade of simple features. In: Proceedings of the 2001 IEEE Computer Society Conference on Computer Vision and Pattern Recognition. CVPR 2001, vol. 1, p. I (2001). https://doi.org/ 10.1109/CVPR.2001.990517, https://ieeexplore.ieee.org/document/990517. iSSN 1063-6919

32. Waldenström, K., et al.: Externally assessed psychosocial work characteristics and diagnoses of anxiety and depression. Occup. Environ. Med. **65**(2), 90–96 (2008). https://doi.org/10.1136/oem.2006.031252, https://oem.bmj.com/content/ 65/2/90

33. Welch, G., Bishop, G.: An Introduction to the Kalman Filter (1995). https://perso. crans.org/club-krobot/doc/kalman.pdf

34. Wojke, N., Bewley, A., Paulus, D.: Simple online and realtime tracking with a deep association metric. In: 2017 IEEE International Conference on Image Processing (ICIP), pp. 3645–3649 (2017). https://doi.org/10.1109/ICIP.2017.8296962, https://ieeexplore.ieee.org/document/8296962, iSSN: 2381-8549

35. Ye, M., Shen, J., Lin, G., Xiang, T., Shao, L., Hoi, S.C.H.: Deep learning for person re-identification: a survey and outlook (2021). https://doi.org/10.48550/ arXiv.2001.04193, arXiv:2001.04193 [cs]

36. Zheng, C., et al.: Deep learning-based human pose estimation: a survey. ACM Comput. Surv. **56**(1), 11:1–11:37 (2023). https://doi.org/10.1145/3603618, https://dl.acm.org/doi/10.1145/3603618
37. Zheng, L., et al.: MARS: a video benchmark for large-scale person re-identification. In: European Conference on Computer Vision. Springer (2016)
38. Zou, Z., Chen, K., Shi, Z., Guo, Y., Ye, J.: Object detection in 20 years: a survey. Proc. IEEE **111**(3), 257–276 (2023). https://doi.org/10.1109/JPROC.2023.3238524, https://ieeexplore.ieee.org/abstract/document/10028728

Wearable Devices and Health Monitoring

Objective Measurement of Stress Resilience: Is RSA a Possible Indicator?

Erik Endlicher[1]([envelope]) [iD], Gerald Bieber[1] [iD], Edda Jaleel[2], Angelina Schmidt[3] [iD], and Michael Fellmann[3] [iD]

[1] Fraunhofer IGD, Joachim-Jungius-Straße 11, 18059 Rostock, Germany
{erik.endlicher,gerald.bieber}@igd-r.fraunhofer.de
[2] Olavius GmbH, Auf dem Wolf 5, 4052 Basel, Switzerland
jaleel@olavius.com
[3] Department of Computer Science, University of Rostock, Albert-Einstein-Straße 22, 18059 Rostock, Germany
{angelina.schmidt,michael.fellmann}@uni-rostock.de

Abstract. Mental and physical health are interlinked. While there are many objective measurement methods and diagnostic tools for physical disorders, the factors influencing mental health are wide-ranging and very subjective. As a result, there is a need for an objective method for assessing stress and stress resilience. The main parameter used today is heart rate variability, which unfortunately varies according to age, gender and physical health. In this paper, we analyze the effects of respiratory sinus arrhythmia (RSA) on stress and promote RSA as a possible new and advanced parameter for stress resilience. In an evaluation we recorded the heart rate of 20 subjects via a PPG finger sensor and a rPPG method utilising only a webcam. Based on the recorded heart rate data we demonstrate RSA variation and define an RSA parameter that can be assessed remotely without physical contact using computer vision and a standard webcam.

Keywords: respiration · RSA · respiratory sinus arrhythmia · non contact · vital data recognition · stress

1 Introduction

Stress resilience, defined as the ability to adapt and recover from stressors, plays a crucial role in maintaining mental and physical well-being. It has even been shown to slow the effects of aging [10]. As the demands of modern life continue to increase, there is a growing interest in developing objective methods to assess stress resilience [18]. Since hypertension and increased heart rate are associated with stress, heart beat parameters are used to assess the effects of stress, but these have so far been very unspecific. One promising avenue of investigation is the study of respiratory sinus arrhythmia (RSA), a phenomenon characterized by the natural variation in heart rate that occurs during the breathing cycle.

O. Konak et al. (Eds.): iWOAR 2024, LNCS 15357, pp. 151–168, 2025.
https://doi.org/10.1007/978-3-031-80856-2_10

RSA reflects the dynamic interplay between the respiratory system and the autonomic nervous system, specifically the parasympathetic branch. During inhalation, heart rate tends to increase, while during exhalation, it tends to decrease. This rhythmic fluctuation in heart rate is believed to be an adaptive response, facilitating oxygen exchange and optimizing physiological functioning [25]. Importantly, alterations in RSA patterns have been associated with various stress-related conditions, including anxiety disorders, depression, and cardiovascular diseases [29].

Given the potential link between RSA and stress resilience, there is growing interest in exploring RSA as an objective measure of an individual's ability to cope with and recover from stress. By quantifying and analyzing RSA patterns, it may be possible to identify individuals with higher levels of stress resilience, as they might exhibit more efficient regulation of heart rate in response to stressors.

This paper aims to critically examine existing methods for the measurement of stress and stress resilience. After which a new way of measuring stress via a novel RSA parameter is introduced. To this end we conduct our own study to create a database of heart rate measurements, as well as a questionnaire about the stress levels of the participants. The database is then used to extract a novel parameter for the quantification of RSA. Lastly we aim to then link this newfound parameter to the occurrence of stress in our study.

Ultimately, understanding the potential of RSA as an objective measure of stress resilience could have significant implications for both research and clinical practice. By identifying individuals with lower stress resilience early on, appropriate interventions and strategies can be implemented to enhance their ability to cope with stress and promote overall well-being.

2   Related Work

Stress can be defined as a physiological and psychological response to external or internal pressures, often referred to as stressors, that challenge an individual's ability to cope [19]. It is a natural and adaptive response that helps us navigate demanding situations. Stress can manifest in various forms, including physical, emotional, or cognitive, and can have both short-term and long-term effects on overall well-being. It can also be divided into two general categories, distress and eustress.

Distress refers to a negative or unpleasant form of stress that exceeds an individual's ability to cope effectively. It is often associated with feelings of anxiety, sadness, and an overall sense of being overwhelmed [32]. Distress can have detrimental effects on physical and mental health if prolonged or left unmanaged. Examples of distressing events or circumstances may include traumatic experiences, chronic illness, or significant life changes.

Eustress is a positive form of stress that is typically associated with beneficial or exciting experiences. It is characterized by feelings of motivation, excitement, and a sense of fulfillment [3]. Eustress can arise from situations such as starting a new job, getting married, or participating in challenging activities that provide a sense of accomplishment. Unlike distress, eustress is believed to have a positive impact on performance, personal growth, and overall well-being.

It is important to note that the distinction between distress and eustress lies mainly in the individual's perception and interpretation of the stressor, which in turn is highly dependent on the resource state of the individual. If the individual has the ability and resources to manage the stressor, it will be perceived more positively as a challenge. If not, it will be perceived as a hindrance. Hence, what may be distressing for one person can be perceived as eustressful by another, depending on their subjective appraisal and ability to cope with the given situation [5].

2.1 Subjective Stress Determination

The assessment and evaluation of stress often requires a combination of different methods in order to be able to evaluate stress comprehensively. Each method has its strengths and limitations, and the choice of assessment method depends on the research or clinical objectives, context, and available resources.

Some stress monitoring methods are performed by the users itself or other observers. These assessment methods are highly subjective and might include a high variability and fuzziness.

Self-report Measures. Self-report measures involve individuals providing subjective information about their perceived stress levels, symptoms, and psychological well-being. This can be done through questionnaires, surveys, or rating scales specifically designed to assess stress [9]. Examples of self-report measures include the Perceived Stress Scale (PSS) and the Holmes and Rahe Stress Scale [22]. These measures provide insights into individuals' subjective experiences of stress but may be influenced by factors such as self-report bias and individual differences in introspection.

Behavioral Observation. Behavioral observation involves direct observation and assessment of behavioral indicators of stress. This can include changes in facial expressions, body language, vocal tone, or observable signs of agitation or distress. Behavioral observation can provide valuable insights into stress responses, especially in social or interactive contexts [31]. However, it may be subjective and influenced by the observer's interpretation and biases.

Psychometric Assessments. Psychometric assessments are standardized tests or inventories that measure specific aspects related to stress, such as coping strategies, resilience, or specific stress-related symptoms. These assessments provide quantitative data and can help identify individual differences in stress-related constructs. Examples include the Coping Strategies Inventory (CSI) and the Connor-Davidson Resilience Scale (CD-RISC) [7].

2.2 Objective Stress Determination

Objective assessment methods are independent by the observer but may also be error-prone because of indirect measurement and the individual feeling of the persons. Their advantage is reproducibility and objectivity.

Physiological Measures. Physiological measures assess stress by monitoring changes in the body's physiological responses to stressors. Common physiological measures include heart rate [12], blood pressure [28], body or skin temperature [11], and skin conductance [21]. These measures can indicate the activation of the autonomic nervous system and the body's stress response. Physiological measures are objective and can provide insights into the body's acute or chronic stress responses. However, they may not capture the full complexity of stress experiences and can be influenced by various factors such as environmental conditions and individual variability.

Biomarkers. Biomarkers are objective physiological or biochemical indicators of stress that can be measured in biological samples such as blood, saliva, or urine. These biomarkers can include cortisol, adrenaline, and inflammatory markers [4]. Biomarker analysis can provide insights into the body's stress response at a molecular level. However, biomarker assessments may require specialized laboratory analysis and may not be feasible for routine stress assessment in certain settings.

2.3 Respiratory Sinus Arrhythmia

Respiratory sinus arrhythmia (RSA) is a normal variation in heart rate that occurs in sync with the respiratory cycle. During inhalation, the heart rate increases, and during exhalation, it decreases. This rhythmic fluctuation is believed to be caused by the parasympathetic nervous system (PNS), which is mostly controlled by the vagus nerve [17]. The presence of a pronounced RSA in a subjects heart rate is considered as an indicator of good cardiovascular health, as well as psychological well-being [33,34].

3 Application of RSA

Measuring RSA is an established procedure to check for the function of the autonomic nervous system, autonomic balance and specifically the activity of the parasympathetic system as well. It is also generally relevant in infant research [1], risk assessment for patients with cardiac issues [13] and diabetes patients [6].

3.1   Applications in Cardiovascular Medicine

RSA can be used as an indicator of cardiovascular health. RSA reflects the heart's ability to adapt to changes in physiological demands and is often measured during cardiac health assessments to evaluate the autonomic nervous system's control over heart rate. When the RSA is present, it typically indicates good cardiovascular health [27].

3.2   Applications in Psychophysiological Medicine

RSA is used in psychophysiological medicine to assess emotional regulation and stress response. It is often used to evaluate how the nervous system responds to stress and relaxation, and can be an indicator of psychological resilience and emotional well-being. In more detail, a study of RSA-based biofeedback training (RSA-BF) on managers by Munafò et al. [20] indicated that higher RSA values are associated with increased vagal control. Also, RSA-BF decreased sympathetic arousal and lowered emotional interference and hence reduced negative psychophysiological outcomes of stress. In a similar study on healthy adults with increased stress levels by Sherlin et al. [26], RSA-BF had a carryover effect that reduced HR reactions to a repeated stressor, thus lowering stress reactivity. Given these insights, the RSA indeed seems to be indicative for stress reactivity and thus how good individuals cope with stressful events which is closely connected to the concept of stress resilience, further highlighting the need for an easily applicable RSA parameter.

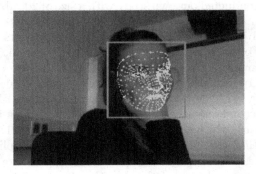

Fig. 1. Non contact heart rate detection during controlled respiration.

3.3   Problems in the Application

RSA is already widely applied, both in science and in clinical contexts. However, its use still brings issues with it, which have not been completely solved at this point in time.

RSA is a special characteristic of the variability of heartbeats. Unfortunately, heart rate variability (HRV) is not a single parameter, but is described by many, including in the time and frequency domain [23]. With expert knowledge one might be able to estimate the quality of RSA from multiple HRV parameters, however it would be much simpler if RSA could be described by a single parameter, that is also understandable with only surface level knowledge of the topic.

There is even some parameters, which aim to describe RSA directly, as shown by e.g. Lewis et al. [15]. However, these largely suffer from the same problems as other HRV parameters, as in that they are either not intuitive, don't communicate the magnitude of RSA well or require additional information about the breathing frequency. While information about respiration would be helpful for determining RSA, the focus in this paper is on heart rate data only which makes our approach more widely applicable even in scenarios where only a heart rate sensor is available.

The question therefore arises as to whether stress or stress resilience can be described by a new RSA parameter that is easy to record, use and understand, but still precise. To this end we created an evaluation to calculate a diverse range of HRV parameters and develop a suitable RSA parameter from those.

4   Evaluation of RSA

This section's goal is to evaluate a range of diverse HRV parameters and their potential link to RSA. The motivation behind this evaluation is that these parameters and the gained understanding of their relation to RSA can then be used later for the development of a new and more sophisticated RSA parameter.

In order to properly evaluate RSA as a possible measure for stress and stress resilience we have conducted our own study with a size of 20 subjects for that very purpose. The mean age of the subjects was 35 with a standard deviation of 12.4 years. 18 of the subjects were male and 2 female. All subjects were healthy, did not have a history of heart related diseases and gave written, informed consent prior to the experiment.

During the study each participant's heart rate was recorded for six minutes with two measuring methods. The first one being a standard PPG-sensor (Pulox PO-300) and the second one a system for remotely measuring the heart rate via a webcam (CareCam), which can be seen in operation in Fig. 1. The PPG-Sensor is a finger sensor that measures the pulse wave with a sampling rate of 60 Hz. The CareCam [14] is a technology that retrieves the pulse rate of the subject by analysing the chromatic change of the skin that is caused by every heart beat because of the varying blood flow at the forehead of the subject. The webcam (standard VGA resolution) records the videosignal with 30 fps.

The six minute experiment time was divided into three phases with a length of two minutes each in order satisfy common recommendations for cardiovascular science [24]. During the first phase, the resting phase, the participants were asked to sit in an upright position and to breathe freely. During the second phase, the reactivity phase, the participants were asked to match their breathing to on-screen instructions, in the form of a breathing cycle, which matched a breathing frequency of about 6 bpm (breaths per minute) in order to maximize the occurrence of RSA. During the last phase, the recovery phase, the participants were asked to breathe freely again. These three phases and the effect they have on the RSA-related heart rate are illustrated below in Fig. 2.

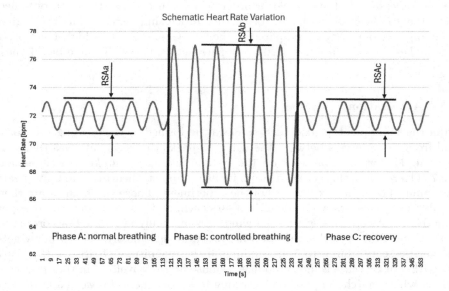

Fig. 2. Phases of the evaluation, resting phase A, reactivity phase B, recovery phase C.

After the experiment was completed, every subject answered a brief questionnaire in order to get additional contextual information about the measurement and the stress of the subject before, after and during the experiment. The most relevant contents of the questionnaire were as follows:

1. Did you feel stressed at the beginning of the experiment?
    − scale of 1 (not stressed) to 5 (very stressed)
2. Do you feel less stressed after the experiment?
    − scale of 1 (not stressed) to 5 (very stressed)
3. Did the breathing exercise have a relaxing effect on you?
    − scale of 1 (very stressful) to 5 (very relaxing)
4. Did you have air problems during the breathing exercise?
    − scale of 1 (no problems) to 5 (respiratory distress)

After all experiments of the study are done, there are now two largely similar, but still distinct, heart rate datasets. One is from the PPG-sensor recordings and one from the CareCam recordings. The general quality of the recorded data is mostly similar between the two, as can be seen when comparing Figs. 3 and 4. The two figures demonstrate that the fluctuations in the heart rate caused by

RSA can be captured by both methods. A more in-depth comparison of the two methods and the results they each produce would surely be interesting and worthwhile. However, it would take too much of the limited space available for the paper and also distract further from the main goal of developing a parameter for the assessment of stress. So in order to remain concise, the data obtained from the PPG-sensor is chosen for further processing, since it has the higher sampling rate of 60 Hz, as compared to the CareCam's 30 Hz. A higher sampling rate makes the calculation of heart rate parameters, especially time-based ones, more precise.

4.1 Annotation

After the experiment, peak detection [8] was performed on the raw ppg-waveform and from the intervals between the detected peaks the heart rate was then calculated. This was performed with the Python package *Neurokit 2* with version 0.2.7. The result of this is then a graph for each subject's heart rate in bpm (beats per minute) over the six minutes of the experiment. Those six minutes are then divided into windows with a length of 40 s each, so there are nine windows per experiment. After windowing, each window is manually annotated, according to how strong RSA is visible in that window. More specifically, each window gets assigned a score from 0 to 5, depending on the magnitude of RSA in the heart rate. RSA in this case is interpreted as a sinus-shaped waveform in the heart rate graph, which matches a possible breathing frequency, i.e. is between a frequency of 0.08 and 0.5 Hz. The criteria for the annotation scoring are as follows:

- 0: Heart rate is constant, with no variations.
- 1: Slight variations in the heart rate of up to 5 bpm, but not necessarily in a shape matching RSA.
- 2: Variations in the heart rate from 5 up to 10 bpm, matching the shape of RSA.
- 3: Variations in the heart rate from 10 up to 15 bpm, matching the shape of RSA.
- 4: Variations in the heart rate from 15 up to 20 bpm, matching the shape of RSA.
- 5: Variations in the heart rate of over 20 bpm, matching the shape of RSA.

4.2 Metrics

A diverse range of parameters is calculated for each of the 40 s windows of recorded heart rate data. For calculating the parameters *Neurokit 2* is used again and a total of 34 different parameters are calculated for each window [16]. The parameters can roughly be partitioned into three distinct categories. 18 of these 34 parameters fall into the first category of *time-based parameters*[1], those being e.g. the mean of the NN-intervals or the pNN50-value. 8 of the 34

---

[1] https://neuropsychology.github.io/NeuroKit/functions/hrv.html#hrv-time.

parameters are from the second category of *frequency-based parameters*[2], those being e.g. the spectral power in the low-frequency band or the LF/HF-ratio. The remaining 8 parameters belong to the third category, which consists of *RSA-based parameters*[3], i.e. parameters which are already designed to quantify RSA, but might not be suitable for the reasons discussed at the end of Sect. 3.

All 34 parameters are extracted from the heart rate data and then normalized along with the annotation. The *StandardScaler* function from *Scikit-Learn* with version 1.4 was used for normalization. After this, the Pearson correlation coefficient of each of the parameters with the annotation is calculated for each subject. This is done as a way of evaluation and to get an understanding of how well each parameter is able to represent RSA. In practice this means that for every subject and parameter the correlation coefficient with the respective annotation vector is calculated. For example, given a subject x with annotation vector $anno = [1, 1, 1, 5, 5, 5, 1, 1, 1]$, each value represents the annotated RSA value for the respective 40 s window and one parameter vector could be $meanNN = [1000, 1000, 1000, 800, 800, 800, 1000, 1000, 1000]$, where again each value represents the calculated parameter for the respective 40 s window and the vector as a whole represents one six minute experiment of a subject. The correlation coefficient between the annotation- and parameter-vector would then be $r = -1$. This way of calculating the correlation coefficient is then done for the other 33 parameter-vectors for that subject and then the same is done for every other subject. The result of this is a matrix with the correlation coefficient of every parameter-vector of every subject with their respective annotation-vector.

4.3   Results

In order for a parameter to be regarded as indicative of RSA within a subject it has to achieve a "moderately strong" correlation with the annotation, i.e. a correlation coefficient of greater than 0.6 or smaller than -0.6 [2]. In order for a parameter to be further regarded indicative of RSA in general, and not only within a subject, it needs to be indicative of RSA within at least half of the subjects, i.e. for 10 or more. With this general criterion in mind, a total of 14 parameters turn out to be indicative of RSA. A brief overview of them can be found in Table 1.

The table displays the mean value of the correlation and also the median p-value for each parameter. Each of them are calculated for the respective parameter and over all subjects. Because of this there are also the correlation values included in the calculation of the mean, which did not meet the threshold of 0.6 or -0.6. This fact in conjunction with the circumstance that there is also a high inter-subject variability leads to some of the correlation mean values in the table to be lower than 0.6, despite still meeting the general criterion defined earlier.

For displaying the p-values of the parameters, their respective median was chosen instead of their mean, as some heavy outliers were significantly skewing

---

[2] https://neuropsychology.github.io/NeuroKit/functions/hrv.html#hrv-frequency.

[3] https://neuropsychology.github.io/NeuroKit/functions/hrv.html#hrv-rsa.

the mean value for many of the parameters. Yet still, some of the median p-values do not meet the generally accepted threshold for statistical significance of being lower than 0.05. For this however, one has to take into consideration that each p-value is calculated based on a rather small sample size, which vastly increases the influence of random error on the p-value and means that the threshold of 0.05 shouldn't be taken too seriously [30].

Four of those 14 parameters even manage to be indicative of RSA in at least 75% of subjects, i.e. for 15 or more subjects. Those four parameters are *RespPSD, GatesSD, IQRNN* and *LF/HF*. In this context it is also worth mentioning, that for two subjects no single parameter had a moderately strong correlation with the annotation and indeed those subjects' heart rate shows no visible signs of RSA, so it can be expected that there is a significantly lesser degree of correlation between those subjects' parameters with what is essentially "noise", at least in regards to RSA.

Table 1. Overview of HRV parameters that have a link to RSA and the mean of their absolute correlation over all subjects

Parameter	Correlation Mean	P Median
RespPSD: Absolute Power Spectral Density around the common respiratory frequency	0.71	0.02
P2T: Median of the Peak-to-Trough values	0.64	0.08
PB: Porges-Bohrer value	0.54	0.09
GatesSD: Standard Deviation of the Gates values	0.74	<0.01
SDNN: Standard Deviation of NN-Intervals	0.56	0.11
CVNN: Standard Deviation of the NN-Intervals divided by the mean of the NN-Intervals	0.59	0.09
MadNN: Median Absolute Deviation of NN-Intervals	0.60	0.04
MCVNN: Median Absolute Deviation of the NN-Intervals divided by the median of the NN-Intervals	0.64	0.02
IQRNN: Interquartile Range of the NN-Intervals	0.76	<0.01
Prc20NN: 20th percentile of the NN-Intervals	0.65	0.03
HTI: Total Number of NN-Intervals divided by the height of the NN-Intervals histogram	0.58	0.07
LF: Power Spectral Density of the Low Frequency Band (0.04 to 0.15 Hz)	0.67	0.04
LFn: Normalized PSD of the Low Frequency Band	0.60	0.04
LF/HF: Ratio of Low Frequency Band to High Frequency Band PSD	0.63	0.06

To summarize this section, a heart rate dataset was created with the aim of evaluating RSA on its basis, which was then divided into windows and annotated. The dataset was then analyzed by extracting a diverse range of HRV parameters. These parameters were then further evaluated in regards to their potential link with RSA.

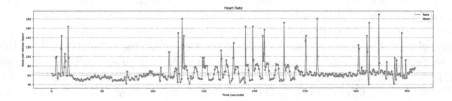

Fig. 3. Finger sensing of RSA.

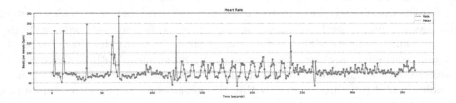

Fig. 4. Non contact RSA measurement.

5   New Qualitative Estimate for RSA

In the previous section, multiple parameters were found to be strongly indicative of RSA. However, none of these give an intuitive understanding of RSA. This means that, given a value, it is difficult to have an immediate understanding of how the heart rate looks like in regards to RSA. However, such a parameter has already been introduced in the context of this paper in the form of the annotation, which gives a very concise estimate of RSA from an intuitive standpoint from "nonexistent (0)" over "moderate(3)" to "strongly present (5)".

It would then be useful to have an application or model, which takes some piece of heart rate data, calculates the diverse parameters from the previous section and then gives an intuitive value based on the parameters, that is directly representative of the RSA occurring in the heart rate data similar to the scale used during the annotation. In addition it would also be interesting to get insight into the decision making process of the model, i.e. to see how the model reaches its result. The implementation of this model and its relevance then for stress detection is described in the following section.

5.1 Implementation

The objective in the calculation of an estimate for RSA is twofold. Firstly, to create a model, that takes the parameters derived from the heart rate and gives an estimate of RSA that is as accurate as possible. Secondly, to get an idea of how the model got to its estimate.

For each subject there are nine 40-s windows and the study includes twenty subjects in total, which leads to a number of 180 instances in the dataset. Since that is not a lot of data, a deep-learning approach seems ill-suited. From the more classical machine-learning methods the Decision-Tree-Algorithm seems the most promising, due to the relatively high number of parameters in the dataset and the circumstance that decision trees are easy to visualize and understand, if they don't get too complex. This means, that in order to understand how the model determines the value for the RSA parameter, one can simply look at the visualization of a decision-tree model with an acceptable performance. Once that model has been created it can then be optimized beyond it's purpose of visualization to achieve the best performance possible. For the implementation and evaluation of all models the Python package *Scikit-Learn* is used.

For the first model, the objective is to get a decision tree model, which is small and has acceptable performance, it doesn't need to be outstandingly accurate, but humanly understandable instead. In order to keep the decision tree small, certain parameters are restricted, namely the maximum depth of the tree and the minimum amount of samples needed to form a leaf. To find the optimal combination of these parameters within the restrictions, hyperparameter-tuning via Grid-Search is used with the resulting maximum depth having a value of 6 and the minimum number of samples needed to form a leaf being 10. It is also worth noting, that the decision tree has been created as a regressor, not a classifier, since the value it is trying to predict can be interpreted as being an element of a real-valued interval-scale. This model has then been evaluated by utilising a test-set, with a test-split size of 0.2. Calculating the Root-Mean-Square-Error (RMSE) on it gives a result of $RMSE = 1.14$. This result isn't too great, but also not bad, considering that the range of possible values is from 0 to 5.

When observing the tree, which is displayed in Fig. 5, one interesting piece of information arising is that the error largely comes from samples with a RSA-value in the middle range, i.e. somewhere around 2 to 3. But with RSA-values that are closer to either extreme, i.e. values around 1 or 5, the decision tress has significantly less trouble. To optimize the model AdaBoost should be a good approach, since the AdaBoost algorithm puts emphasis on samples that produce a larger error. So this algorithm should work well in order to teach the model how to handle samples with RSA-values in the middle range as well.

Again, Grid-Search is used to find the best hyperparameters for the optimized model, which in this case results in a value of 2 for the learning rate and a value of 25 for the number of estimators. The base estimator is a Decision-Tree-Regressor, similar to the simple model. The optimized model is then also evaluated on the same test-set, that was used previously in order to have a better understanding of how this model performs relative to the previous one. The evaluation leads to a result of $RMSE = 0.83$, which means a significant improvement compared to the simple model. The remaining error can, at least in part, be attributed to measuring errors during the experiment, e.g. sudden peaks of over 160 bpm in the heart rate data, as well as human error during the annotation. It could be possible to achieve an even better performance with a deep-learning approach, however, due to the low amount of data this doesn't seem sensible to try for now.

In summary, theses two models demonstrate two different things. The more sophisticated model made with the AdaBoost algorithm shows that it is generally possible to get a qualitative estimate of RSA only from heart-rate data, which is suitably accurate. Meanwhile, the simpler model gives a rough understanding of how one can infer RSA from heart-rate data. The next step now is to try to link that qualitative value of RSA to stress.

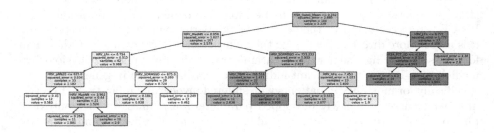

Fig. 5. Visualisation of the simple Decision Tree without optimization.

5.2 Relevance for Stress-Detection

In order to now show the relevance of this new RSA parameter in regards to stress it would make sense to compare the RSA values from the study, described in Sect. 4, to the stress values in the questionnaire from the study. This turns out to be difficult however, since the dataset from the study is unbalanced, as almost none of the participants reported that they feel stressed either before or after the experiment. In total only two participants reported they were at least moderately stressed (3 or greater on the scale) before the experiment and three participants reported so after the experiment. The mean of the stress level across all participants lies at 1.55 both before and after the experiment. Meanwhile the mean value of RSA during the reactivity phase of the experiment lies at 3.97. So in general one could say that stress levels in the study are generally low while RSA levels are generally high, which is indeed in accordance with the current state of the art. These observations also demonstrate that the design of the study succeeded in its goal of eliciting a strong RSA response from the subjects. However, at the same time it is unfortunately not possible to test whether the inverted assumption, that high stress leads to a low RSA value, also holds true, which would have been closer to the actual objective of the paper.

So in summary, while the developed RSA parameter so far works in accordance with the current state of the art, it is not possible to infer a relevant link between this RSA-parameter and stress yet, due to a lack of suitable data, that is representative for stress. It is thus left open to future work to conduct another study in which more stress is induced in participants using established methods, e.g., the Trier Social Stress Test, the Stroop Color Word Test or the Serial Seven Test, where participants have to count backwards.

6   Discussion

In this paper we introduced a new parameter for the quantification of RSA, which can potentially be used as a factor to detect stress and assess the stress resilience of a person. This new parameter is better suited for stress detection than other HRV parameters, as those tend to be more age-dependent. In addition, since RSA is strongly related to the activity of the parasympathetic nervous system, it is also a more direct indicator for the neurological effects of stress. Other than for stress measuring, the new RSA parameter can also be applied in physiological medicine, as RSA is a significant indicator for cardiac health in general and also specifically for mortality in patients who suffered myocardial infarction. However, in order to asses the newly developed parameter's usefulness in the context of physiological medicine, a separate evaluation on a more suitable clinical dataset would have to be conducted.

Looking a bit closer on the study, more specifically on the Peak-to-Trough (P2T) parameter, which describes the difference between the maximum heart rate during inhalation and the minimum heart rate during exhalation. The evaluation of the mean P2T value for each phase and over all subjects shows values of $P2Ta = 6.84 \pm \sigma = 5.35, P2Tb = 12.3 \pm \sigma = 7.49$, and $P2Tc = 7.92 \pm \sigma = 6.32$, each value is given in beats per minute. This shows that the subjects were more relaxed at the end of the evaluation in comparison to the start. It is worth mentioning however that during the study there were no ground truth measurements of respiration and thus the respiration signal for the calculation of the P2T values was derived from the heart rate. This means that those values are not fully reliable, but nevertheless provide a good estimation about the overall range of RSA. Indeed, these findings are further underlined when looking at the mean annotation values over the three phases: $ANNOa = 6.05 \pm \sigma = 4.75, ANNOb = 19.8 \pm \sigma = 6.75$, and $ANNOc = 8.75 \pm \sigma = 6.3$, again each values is in beats per minute. These observations also demonstrate that the design of the study succeeded in its goal of eliciting a strong RSA response in the subjects.

During the study we also showed that RSA measurement can also be achieved by a contactless assessment using the CareCam technology. This enables a continuous monitoring, e.g. during office work, and supports the idea of an unobtrusive stress assistance in the application field of occupational health. A deeper look into the data obtained via the CareCam would be worthwhile, since only some of the data was compared to the ground truth in the context of this paper. Through a deeper evaluation it could be possible to evaluate, if methods like the CareCam could potentially also be used to obtain ground truth data and if so, under which circumstances.

Other potential avenues for the application of the RSA parameter, as a parameter of stress and stress resilience, lie in estimating the efficiency of traditional stress training courses. While many coaching methods are costly and might be ineffective, RSA provides a promising new approach for educating individuals or treating patients, potentially including younger populations as well. It would be particularly interesting to explore how soldiers, who undergo significant behavioral changes during their service, are affected by intense training programs, such as boot camps or even a deployment both before and after their completion.

7   Conclusion and Outlook

In this paper a new method to objectively and unobtrusively measure a persons stress and stress resilience was developed. For this purpose a study was conducted with a focus on obtaining heart rate data, that had both pronounced RSA, as well as comparative baseline values. Additionally, the subjects' stress was also recorded via a questionnaire. Heart rate data was obtained in two ways. The first one being a PPG-sensor, attached to the finger of the subject and the second one a contactless method, working only with a RGB-video of the subject, called CareCam. It was demonstrated that both methods can achieve comparable quality in their results.

After data acquisition and annotation, a diverse range of HRV related parameters were extracted from the dataset. These parameters were then evaluated as to how strong their connection to RSA is. This was done by calculating each of their correlation coefficient with the RSA annotation, with the result being, that many of them have a moderate degree of connection and a few even have a strong connection. It was also found however, that none of the evaluated parameters give an intuitive understanding of the magnitude of RSA present in a given instance of heart rate data.

Thus a new parameter was introduced that is directly and intuitively communicating the degree of RSA present and is calculated on the basis of the evaluated HRV parameters. For this purpose a classical machine-learning approach has been applied, consisting of the Decision Tree and AdaBoost algorithms. The resulting model has then been evaluated on a test set with good results.

After calculating the newly developed RSA parameter it was then attempted to demonstrate its link with the stress related data from the questionnaire. This was unfortunately not possible in this way, since almost none of the subjects were even moderately stressed before or after the study. Meaning that the RSA parameter could not be linked to stress, due to a lack of data representative for stress in the study. This however does not contradict the concept of the RSA parameter, since the results in general are still in accordance with the state of research in this area, i.e. stress values were generally low and RSA values were generally high.

For continuing research it would definitely be advisable to conduct another study with a stressor built into its design in order to elicit a measurable stress response in the subjects, so it can be compared to the data acquired in this papers study. It would also be interesting to have a more in depth comparison between the two heart rate measuring methods, as especially the unobtrusiveness of the CareCam offers an advantage over more classical methods like PPG or ECG.

Acknowledgements. We would like to thank our test subjects for their participation in the many tests and for taking the necessary time out of their day. This work was funded by the Federal Ministry for Economic Affairs and Climate Action, Germany.

Disclosure of Interests. The authors have no competing interests to declare that are relevant to the content of this article.

References

1. Aikele, P.: Untersuchungen zur Entwicklung der kardiorespiratorischen Interaktion anhand gemeinsamer Rhythmen von Atmung und Herzaktion: Longitudinalstudie der ersten sechs Lebensmonate gesunder Säuglinge. Ph.D. thesis, Humboldt-Universität zu Berlin, Medizinische Fakultät - Universitätsklinikum Charité (1998). https://doi.org/10.18452/14413
2. Akoglu, H.: User's guide to correlation coefficients. Turk. J. Emerg. Med. **18**(3), 91–93 (2018). https://doi.org/10.1016/j.tjem.2018.08.001
3. Bienertova-Vasku, J., Lenart, P., Scheringer, M.: Eustress and distress: neither good nor bad, but rather the same? BioEssays **42**(7), 1900238 (2020). https://doi.org/10.1002/bies.201900238
4. Boucher, P., Plusquellec, P.: Acute stress assessment from excess cortisol secretion: fundamentals and perspectives. Front. Endocrinol. **10**, 461220 (2019). https://doi.org/10.3389/fendo.2019.00749
5. Bovier, P.A., Chamot, E., Perneger, T.V.: Perceived stress, internal resources, and social support as determinants of mental health among young adults. Qual. Life Res. **13**, 161–170 (2004). https://doi.org/10.1023/B:QURE.0000015288.43768.e4
6. Brown, C.M., Marthol, H., Zikeli, U., Ziegler, D., Hilz, M.J.: A simple deep breathing test reveals altered cerebral autoregulation in type 2 diabetic patients. Diabetologia **51**(3), 756–761 (2008). https://doi.org/10.1007/s00125-008-0958-3
7. Connor, K.M., Davidson, J.R.: Development of a new resilience scale: the connor-davidson resilience scale (CD-RISC). Depress. Anxiety **18**(2), 76–82 (2003). https://doi.org/10.1002/da.10113
8. Elgendi, M., Jonkman, M., De Boer, F.: Frequency bands effects on QRS detection. In: BIOSIGNALS 2010 - Proceedings of the Third International Conference on Bioinspired Systems and Signal Processing, pp. 428–431. INSTICC Press (2010)
9. Endler, N.S., Parker, J.D.: Stress and anxiety: conceptual and assessment issues. Stress Med. **6**(3), 243–248 (1990). https://doi.org/10.1002/smi.2460060310
10. Faye, C., Mcgowan, J.C., Denny, C.A., David, D.J.: Neurobiological mechanisms of stress resilience and implications for the aged population. Curr. Neuropharmacol. **16**(3), 234–270 (2018). https://doi.org/10.2174/1570159X15666170818095105

11. Herborn, K.A., et al.: Skin temperature reveals the intensity of acute stress. Physiol. Behav. **152**, 225–230 (2015). https://doi.org/10.1016/j.physbeh.2015.09.032
12. Katmah, R., Al-Shargie, F., Tariq, U., Babiloni, F., Al-Mughairbi, F., Al-Nashash, H.: A review on mental stress assessment methods using EEG signals. Sensors **21**(15), 5043 (2021). https://doi.org/10.3390/s21155043
13. Katz, A., Liberty, I., Porath, A., Ovsyshcher, I., Prystowsky, E.N.: A simple bedside test of 1-minute heart rate variability during deep breathing as a prognostic index after myocardial infarction. Am. Heart J. **138**(1), 32–38 (1999). https://doi.org/10.1016/S0002-8703(99)70242-5
14. Kraft, D., Van Laerhoven, K., Bieber, G.: CareCam: concept of a new tool for corporate health management. In: The 14th PErvasive Technologies Related to Assistive Environments Conference, pp. 585–593 (2021)
15. Lewis, G.F., Furman, S.A., McCool, M.F., Porges, S.W.: Statistical strategies to quantify respiratory sinus arrhythmia: are commonly used metrics equivalent? Biol. Psychol. **89**(2), 349–364 (2012). https://doi.org/10.1016/j.biopsycho.2011.11.009
16. Makowski, D., et al.: NeuroKit2: a Python toolbox for neurophysiological signal processing. Behav. Res. Methods **53**(4), 1689–1696 (2021). https://doi.org/10.3758/s13428-020-01516-y
17. Mccraty, R., Shaffer, F.: Heart rate variability: new perspectives on physiological mechanisms, assessment of self-regulatory capacity, and health risk. Glob. Adv. Health Med. **4**(1), 46–61 (2015). https://doi.org/10.7453/gahmj.2014.073
18. McEwan, B.S., Akil, H.: Revisiting the stress concept: implications for affective disorders. J. Neurosci. **40**, 12–21 (2020). https://doi.org/10.1523/jneurosci.0733-19.2019
19. Morton, M.L., Helminen, E.C., Felver, J.C.: A systematic review of mindfulness interventions on psychophysiological responses to acute stress. Mindfulness **11**(9), 2039–2054 (2020). https://doi.org/10.1007/s12671-020-01386-7
20. Munafò, M., Patron, E., Palomba, D.: Improving managers' psychophysical well-being: effectiveness of respiratory sinus arrhythmia biofeedback. Appl. Psychophysiol. Biofeedback **41**(2), 129–139 (2015). https://doi.org/10.1007/s10484-015-9320-y
21. Nardelli, M., Greco, A., Sebastiani, L., Scilingo, E.P.: ComEDA: a new tool for stress assessment based on electrodermal activity. Comput. Biol. Med. **150**, 106144 (2022). https://doi.org/10.1016/j.compbiomed.2022.106144
22. Noone, P.A.: The Holmes-Rahe stress inventory. Occup. Med. **67**(7), 581–582 (2017). https://doi.org/10.1093/occmed/kqx099
23. Rajendra Acharya, U., Paul Joseph, K., Kannathal, N., Lim, C.M., Suri, J.S.: Heart rate variability: a review. Med. Biol. Eng. Comput. **44**, 1031–1051 (2006). https://doi.org/10.1007/s11517-006-0119-0
24. Shaffer, F., Ginsberg, J.: An overview of heart rate variability metrics and norms. Front. Public Health **5**, 258 (2017). https://doi.org/10.3389/fpubh.2017.00258
25. Shaffer, F., McCraty, R., Zerr, C.: A healthy heart is not a metronome: an integrative review of the heart's anatomy and heart rate variability. Front. Psychol. **5**, 1040 (2014). https://doi.org/10.3389/fpsyg.2014.01040
26. Sherlin, L., Gevirtz, R., Wyckoff, S., Muench, F.: Effects of respiratory sinus arrhythmia biofeedback versus passive biofeedback control. Int. J. Stress. Manag. **16**(3), 233–248 (2009). https://doi.org/10.1037/a0016047
27. Soos, M.P., McComb, D.: Sinus arrhythmia. In: StatPearls [PMID: 30725696]. StatPearls Publishing (2022)

28. Suter, P., Maire, R., Holtz, D., Vetter, W.: Relationship between self-perceived stress and blood pressure. J. Hum. Hypertens. **11**(3), 171–176 (1997). https://doi.org/10.1038/sj.jhh.1000409

29. Thayer, J., Lane, R.: A model of neurovisceral integration in emotion regulation and dysregulation. J. Affect. Disord. **61**(3), 201–216 (2000). https://doi.org/10.1016/S0165-0327(00)00338-4

30. Thiese, M.S., Ronna, B., Ott, U.: P value interpretations and considerations. J. Thorac. Dis. **8**(9) (2016). https://doi.org/10.21037/jtd.2016.08.16

31. Thomassin, K., Raftery-Helmer, J., Hersh, J.: A review of behavioral observation coding approaches for the trier social stress test for children. Front. Psychol. **9**, 2610 (2018). https://doi.org/10.3389/fpsyg.2018.02610

32. Wheaton, B., Montazer, S., et al.: Stressors, stress, and distress. In: A Handbook for the Study of Mental Health: Social Contexts, Theories, and Systems, vol. 2, pp. 171–199 (2010). https://doi.org/10.1017/CBO9780511984945.013

33. Yasuma, F., Hayano, J.: Respiratory sinus arrhythmia: why does the heartbeat synchronize with respiratory rhythm? Chest **125**(2), 683–690 (2004). https://doi.org/10.1378/chest.125.2.683

34. Ćosić, K., Šarlija, M., Ivkovic, V., Zhang, Q., Strangman, G., Popović, S.: Stress resilience assessment based on physiological features in selection of air traffic controllers. IEEE Access **7**, 41989–42005 (2019). https://doi.org/10.1109/ACCESS.2019.2907479

Robust Wearable-Based Real Life Cognitive Fatigue Monitoring by Personalized PPG Normalization

Adonis Opris, Mohamed Benouis, Elisabeth André, and Yekta Said Can[✉]

Chair for Human-Centered Artificial Intelligence, University of Augsburg,
86159 Augsburg, Germany
{adonis.opris,mohamed.benouis,elisabeth.andre,
yekta.can}@uni-a.de

Abstract. Cognitive fatigue may have significant results if not intervened in factories, automobiles, and office environments. Development of a system for monitoring cognitive fatigue in real-life settings using unobtrusive wearable devices can help to minimize health problems, and work and car accidents. Photoplethysmography (PPG) sensors offer an unobtrusive way to track changes in heart rate and heart rate variability (HRV), which are indicative of cognitive fatigue levels. In this study, we propose a personalized PPG normalization technique to reduce inter-subject variability and enhance the performance of machine learning algorithms in classifying cognitive fatigue. The best-performing model, a Random Forest Classifier, achieved an accuracy of 80.5% in binary classification and demonstrated robust performance in regression tasks as well. The study highlights the potential of PPG-based wearables for non-obtrusive, long-term monitoring of cognitive fatigue, which could aid in preventing health issues associated with chronic fatigue.

Keywords: physiological signals · affective computing · cognitive fatigue · machine learning · neural networks · wearable computing

1 Introduction

When ongoing stress at work isn't handled well, one of the possible outcomes is a cognitive fatigue state. Although it's not a medical disorder, it can happen in any stressful work or home setting and is acknowledged by the World Health Organization (WHO) as a syndrome Ul Alam (2021). In the short term, cognitive fatigue can lead to problems like trouble sleeping, anxiety, irritability, and hormonal issues. Over time, it can cause more serious health problems, including multiple sclerosis, Parkinson's disease, and traumatic brain injury Karim et al. (2024).

Cognitive fatigue can be evaluated by examining the autonomic nervous system (ANS) Yue et al. (2021). One way is to monitor changes in physiological signals. The ANS includes the sympathetic nervous system (SNS) and the

O. Konak et al. (Eds.): iWOAR 2024, LNCS 15357, pp. 169–180, 2025.
https://doi.org/10.1007/978-3-031-80856-2_11

parasympathetic nervous system (PSNS). Research shows that physiological signals are good indicators of cognitive fatigue levels over time Lin et al. (2018) and Huang et al. (2018). Detecting cognitive fatigue using physiological signals offers several advantages, including non-obtrusive device options, user-friendly systems, objectivity, accuracy, and reliability Cos et al. (2023).

Currently, various physiological signals are tested to recognize cognitive fatigue levels. These signals include electrocardiography (ECG), electroencephalography (EEG), photoplethysmography (PPG), electrooculogram (EOG), electromyogram (EMG), electrodermal activity (EDA), skin temperature and respiratory system signals. EEG is one of the most commonly employed modalities for cognitive fatigue because it directly measures the signal from neurons. In one study, researchers collected EEG data obtained from the Muse band during N-back tasks. They obtained 88% accuracy with EEGNet architecture for binary cognitive fatigue detection Karim et al. (2023). ECG signals are also used for cognitive fatigue monitoring and robust performances are obtained. Bhardwaj et al. used ECG with a Stacked Autoencoders algorithm to predict driver fatigue with 90% accuracy based on HRV features Bhardwaj et al. (2018).

Although robust performances were obtained with ECG and EEG modalities, using them in real life can be inconvenient. It might be plausible to use these devices in short term laboratory experiments but they are not comfortable and obtrusive to use in real life environments such as offices, driving environments, daily life for long term. Users provided chest bands, electrodes and head bands lower comfort, long term use, social acceptance, wearablity and social acceptance scores Umair et al. (2021). At this point, PPG-based devices offer a more practical alternative. They have relatively lower data quality when compared to abovementioned technologies but they provide comfort, social acceptance and aesthetics for long term use. Some studies used mobile phone PPG sensors Yue et al. (2021) and wearable PPG sensors Chen et al. (2023) for monitoring cognitive fatigue during laboratory experiments.

Another issue with most of the studies in the literature is the usage of tests in laboratory environments. N-back tests, arithmetical tasks, simulations and VR-based tasks are used in laboratory environments. However, these are short-term and artificially applied stimuli. Studies showed that artificially induced affects are different from the ones that occur naturally in the wild Picard (2016). For these reasons, recognizing cognitive fatigue in more realistic environments and tasks for longer terms will contribute more to developing real-life monitoring systems.

In this study, we used a real-life PPG dataset consisting of one-day data Ul Alam (2021) from 5 participants and developed a personalized system for recognizing cognitive fatigue levels. We cleaned the PPG signals, extracted distinctive features, employed suitable machine learning algorithms. After that, we employed subjectwise PPG normalization to reduce the effect of interpersonal variability and improved the cognitive fatigue recognition performance. We further provided feature-based analysis and the importance of personalized evaluation in the discussion section (Fig. 1).

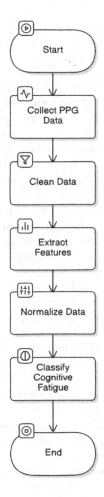

Fig. 1. A block diagram of cognitive fatigue monitoring system.

2   Related Work

As mentioned, the cognitive fatigue monitoring studies using heart activity started in laboratory environments. Lee et al. (2019) introduced a method for detecting driver fatigue using 2-minute signal segments from wearable ECG/PPG sensors, achieving a 70% accuracy in binary classification through 10-fold cross-validation. Kundinger et al. (2020) developed a non-intrusive fatigue detection system using a wrist-worn ECG sensor, which utilized a 5-minute sliding window with 2-second increments to generate heart rate variability features, achieving a top accuracy of 92.31% for binary classification, comparable to a medical-grade ECG device. Bhardwaj et al. employed the Stacked Autoencoders algorithm to predict driver fatigue based on HRV, attaining a 90% accuracy and noting that HR and LF decreased while HF increased during the transition from alertness to fatigue Bhardwaj et al. (2018). Despite the effectiveness of these methods, their reliance on long-term ECG signals hinders real-time performance. To address this, Lei et al. applied a support vector machine (SVM) to short-term ECG signals, each 5 s long, for fatigue recognition Lei et al. (2018).

After demonstrating the robust performance of ECG-based mental fatigue systems, researchers also tested PPG sensors for the same task. The main reason is the unsuitability of ECG sensors for real life environments especially for long term use. In one study, researchers investigate the real-time detection and prediction of mental fatigue using heart rate (HR) and heart rate variability (HRV) as classification features, extracted from short-term photoplethysmography (PPG) signals via smartphones, offering a more convenient alternative to ECG recordings. The researchers processed PPG data by removing baseline wander and smoothing waveforms using polynomial fitting and Savitzky-Golay filtering, then applied an adaptive peak-seeking algorithm to extract R-peaks and calculate HR. Welch spectrum estimation was used to obtain HRV frequency domain characteristics, including high-frequency (HF) and low-frequency (LF) components and the LF/HF ratio. The analysis revealed that HR and HRV features change throughout the day with mental activity, with HR increasing in the afternoon and decreasing in the evening as mental fatigue sets in. The classification of mental fatigue achieved an accuracy of 92.26% and a specificity of 96.12%, indicating that HR and HRV can effectively detect mental fatigue levels in practice, potentially aiding in the prevention of health issues associated with fatigue.

In another study, Alam developed a cognitive fatigue assessment tool, emphasizing the need for contextual evaluation rather than generalized approaches. The authors propose a novel Activity-Aware Recurrent Neural Network (AcRoNN) framework that leverages physiological data from wearable sensors to assess cognitive fatigue. The framework is designed to recognize activities and align them with physiological responses, accounting for artifacts introduced by physical activity. The study evaluates AcRoNN on three datasets, demonstrating significant improvements in cognitive fatigue assessment over baseline models, with a maximum of 19% improvement reported.

Although, there are some recent studies using PPG sensors for real life cognitive fatigue monitoring, the performance of these systems need improvement. In this study, we used the Gamer's Fatigue dataset Ul Alam (2021) collected in real-life environments for 24 h. First, we tested machine learning algorithms for classifying binary cognitive fatigue. We then applied personalized PPG normalization to decrease intersubject differences and showed improvement in terms of performance. We also tested some regression algorithms for levels from 1 to 7. Our results showed the need for alleviating interpersonal variability to obtain more robust performances.

3   Methodology

The analysis process involved the following steps: cleaning the raw PPG signals, dividing them into frames, extracting features that capture the characteristics of the PPG data, labeling the frames based on the self-assessment of sleepiness, and finally, predicting fatigue using machine learning algorithms.

3.1   Preprocessing

The PPG signals were cleaned using the Toolbox for Neurophysiological Signal Processing Neurokit2 Makowski et al. (2021). A Butterworth filter was applied with a low-cut frequency of 0.5 Hz Pilt et al. (2013), a high-cut frequency of 8 Hz Mejía-Mejía et al. (2022), and order 3. Figure 2 illustrates the results of cleaning the PPG signal. It can be observed that the noise has been reduced and the baseline corrected.

3.2   Feature Extraction

The extraction of features was conducted via a segment-wise analysis, utilising the Heartpy Toolbox Van Gent et al. (2019). The signal was divided into 300-second segments, with 50% overlap between segments. From each segment, time-domain features were extracted, as well as frequency-domain features. The time domain measures include: beats per minute (bpm), inter-beat interval (IBI), standard deviation of NN intervals (SDNN), standard deviation of successive differences (SDSD), root mean square of successive differences (RMSSD), proportion of NN20 (PNN20), proportion of NN50 (PNN50), breathing rate (breathingrate), and some others. The frequency domain features include: very low frequency (VLF), low frequency (LF), high frequency (HF), the ratio of low frequency to high frequency (LF/HF), total power (P_total), percentage of very low frequency (VLF_perc), percentage of low frequency (LF_perc), and percentage of high frequency (HF_perc).

3.3   Feature Level Analysis and Personalized PPG Normalization

Figure 3 shows the distribution of four different features in both fatigue and non-fatigue states. The green box plot represents the fatigue state and includes the frames in which the subject reported the maximum fatigue score. The maximum score varies from subject to subject, there are participants whose maximum fatigue score was 4/7 and others who also used the score 7/7. The yellow ones represents the non-fatiguing state, where participants reported the lowest fatigue score.

When we analyzed the features, the results aligned with the literature Bhardwaj et al. (2018). HF component is higher during fatigue state (see Fig. 3). These features showed that variance of RR distribution and heart rate variability is higher during fatigue which corresponds to more relaxed conditions as expected.

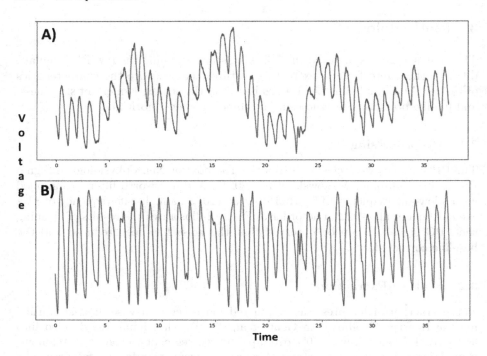

Fig. 2. A) PPG signal before cleaning, B) same signal after cleaning. Cleaned and uncleaned PPG signal

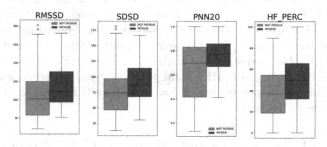

Fig. 3. PPG features distribution over the two states, fatigued and non-fatigued

Once the features had been extracted, the PPG feature values were scaled using the following standardization formula for each subject, where μ is the mean and σ is the standard deviation of the given distribution.

$$z = \frac{x - \mu}{\sigma} \tag{1}$$

In order to train machine learning algorithms, we used the Stanford Sleepiness Scale (SSS) as labels. This was completed by participants after each hour. For regression, we used the scale with its seven values. For classification, we used two classes, with a threshold set at the value of 4 (somewhat foggy, let down) on the SSS scale. This was based on our belief that this is a point where action should be taken to avoid mistakes caused by sleepiness.

3.4   Machine Learning Models

In order to predict sleepiness, we trained a number of machine learning models with different configurations. For classification, we used a k-Nearest Neighbours (kNN) model with different numbers of neighbours, a Naive Bayes model, an Support vector machine (SVM) model with different kernel functions and C values, a Random Forest (RF) classifier with different depths, and also an MLP model. For regression, we used kNN, Linear Regression (LR), a Random Forest Regressor, and SVM. Table 1 shows the details of the hyperparameters used in the machine learning algorithms.

Table 1. Hyperparameters for Selected Machine Learning Algorithms

Model	Hyperparameter	Values
kNN	N Neighbors	3, 5, 7, 9, 11, 13, 15
SVM	Kernel	linear, poly, rbf, sigmoid
	C	1, 6, 11, 16, 21, 26, 31, 36
RF	N Estimators	10, 30, 50, 70, 90
	Max Depth	1, 4, 7, 10, 13, 16, 19, 22, 25, 28

4   Experimental Results

After the pre-processing and feature extraction phase, we removed the rows with missing values and proceeded with training the ML algorithms.

4.1   Classification

The final data set comprised 82.21% instances of fatigue and 17.79% instances of non-fatigue. To ensure the models were not biased towards the majority class, we balanced the data set through random undersampling of the majority class. We trained several machine learning models using the balanced data set and validated them using a five-fold cross-validation process. The best results were achieved with a k-nearest neighbour model, which achieved 61.2% accuracy, and a random forest classifier, which achieved 73.8% accuracy. Figure 5 presents the results obtained with balanced but non-standardised data.

We standardised the data as described in the previous section and trained and validated the models using the same approach with a stratified 5-fold cross-validation. The results of the best-performing machine learning algorithms without balancing the standardised data are shown in Fig. 4.

176   A. Opris et al.

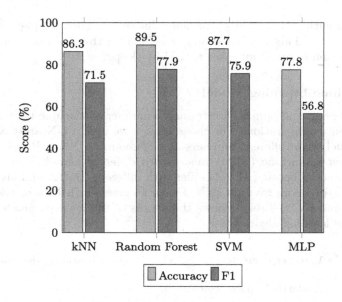

Fig. 4. Accuracy and F1 of the best-performing models on unbalanced dataset

After getting results for the original imbalanced dataset, we balanced the dataset by random undersampling and showed the results in Fig. 5. As it can be seen, the performance metrics decreased drastically due to losing the advantage of leaning towards majority class.

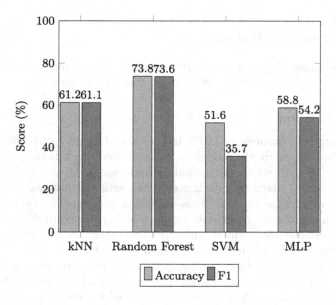

Fig. 5. Accuracy and F1 score on non-standardized balanced data set

The results of the best-performing models after balancing and personalized normalization are shown in Fig. 6. The kNN achieved 72.6% accuracy with 9 neighbours, the Random Forest Classifier had 80.5% accuracy using 50 trees and a maximum depth of 13, and the SVM used a radial basis function kernel.

The Random Forest Classifier demonstrated the best overall performance in the classification task, which utilized binary classes. Table 2 shows the F1 score, precision, recall for this model, offering additional insights into its performance. Table 3 shows the F1 scores for the Random Forest classifier using different numbers of trees and different depths.

Table 2. Best performing Random Forest Classifier detailed scores

Accuracy	F1 Score	Precision	Recall
80.5	80.5	80.7	80.5

4.2 Regression

In order to perform the regression analysis, we utilised the standardised features as input. The target values ranged from one to seven, in accordance with the Stanford Sleepiness Scale. The performance of the models was evaluated using mean squared error (MSE), mean absolute error (MAE), and R2 score, which

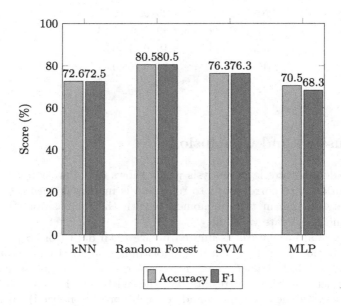

Fig. 6. Accuracy and F1 of the best-performing models

Table 3. Random Forest F1 scores in percent with different parameter configurations

Max Depth	Number of Trees				
	10	30	50	70	90
1	60.9%	61.3%	63.2%	64.5%	63.4%
4	72.6%	75.7%	76.8%	75.4%	76.5%
7	76.1%	77.7%	77.3%	80.2%	77.2%
10	77.4%	78.4%	78%	79.6%	78.3%
13	77.2%	77.3%	80.5%	78.6%	78.7%
16	76.6%	76.9%	77.4%	77.4%	77.6%
19	75.5%	79.7%	77.1%	78.2%	77.9%
22	76.5%	78.7%	76.7%	77.9%	77.7%
25	75.7%	77.3%	79.1%	78.4%	79.5%
28	77.2%	77.1%	78.3%	78.9%	78.7%

are presented in Table 4. Similarly to the classification task, in the regression task, the best model was the Random Forest Regressor, this time with 90 trees and a maximum depth of 10.

Table 4. Regression models scores

Model	MSE	MAE	R2 score
kNN	1.23	0.84	0.29
Linear Regression	1.49	0.97	0.14
SVM	1.16	0.81	0.33
RF	0.85	0.70	0.51

5   Discussion and Conclusion

We first made a feature level analysis which shows that Parasymphathetic Nervous System activity corresponds to relaxness is increased during fatigue. Our feature analysis confirm this phenomenon with the increase of HF, standard deviation and heart rate variability.

Since our real life dataset is limited in size (24 h data from 5 participants), we chose traditional machine learning algorithms instead of more complex ones such as CNN, LSTM, Transformers. From the results, it can be seen that Random Forest achieves the best results. We showed both F1 scores and accuracy for both cases. For the imbalanced and general (not personalized) case, accuracy scores are much higher than F1 scores because of ML algorithms' tendency to classify the label as majority class. Therefore, we need to compare the performances before and after personalization from F1 scores. We obtained around 2.6% increase in the binary classification performance for the best result. A different amount of performance increases are demonstrated except for kNN algorithm. We further provided regression results by using the perceived cognitive fatigue scale from 1 to 7. Random Forest Regressor achieves the best results.

We chose a PPG dataset collected with unobtrusive wearables during real world tasks continuously for one day. The reason for that is to obtain more realistic results that can be applied to real world applications. Laboratory induced short term cognitve fatigue will be different than cognitive fatigue caused by a real life task. Furthermore, PPG sensors can be used without disrupting users for longer times. We also improved the performance by applying personalized normalization to decrease the effect of interpersonal variability.

We believe that our system can be applied for especially decreasing cognitive fatigue related work and car accidents by unobtrusive continuous monitoring and giving a chance to intervene before fatigue reaches high levels.

This work was carried out within the framework of the AI Production Network Augsburg. This work was partly funded by the German Research Foundation under the project Health-relevant effects of different urban forest structures (LEAF). This work presents and discusses results in the context of the research project ForDigitHealth. The project is part of the Bavarian Research Association on Healthy Use of Digital Technologies and Media (ForDigitHealth), which is funded by the Bavarian Ministry of Science and Arts.

References

Bhardwaj, R., Natrajan, P., Balasubramanian, V.: Study to determine the effectiveness of deep learning classifiers for ECG based driver fatigue classification. In: 2018 IEEE 13th International Conference on Industrial and Information Systems (ICIIS), 98–102 (2018). https://doi.org/10.1109/ICIINFS.2018.8721391

Chen, Y.-X., et al.: Fatigue estimation using peak features from PPG signals. Mathematics 11, 16 (2023). https://doi.org/10.3390/math11163580

Cos, C.-A., Lambert, A., Soni, A., Jeridi, H., Thieulin, C., Jaouadi, A.: Enhancing mental fatigue detection through physiological signals and machine learning using contextual insights and efficient modelling. J. Sens. Actuator Netw. 12, 6 (2023). https://doi.org/10.3390/jsan12060077

Huang, S., Li, J., Zhang, P., Zhang, W.: Detection of mental fatigue state with wearable ECG devices. Int. J. Med. Inform. 119, 39–46 (2018). https://doi.org/10.1016/j.ijmedinf.2018.08.010

Karim, E., et al.: An EEG-based cognitive fatigue detection system. In: Proceedings of the 16th International Conference on PErvasive Technologies Related to Assistive Environments (Corfu, Greece) (PETRA 2023), pp. 131–136. Association for Computing Machinery, New York (2023). https://doi.org/10.1145/3594806.3594848

Karim, E., et al.: Examining the landscape of cognitive fatigue detection: a comprehensive survey. Technologies 12, 3 (2024). https://doi.org/10.3390/technologies12030038

Kundinger, T., Sofra, N., Riener, A.: Assessment of the potential of wrist-worn wearable sensors for driver drowsiness detection. Sensors **20**, 4 (2020). https://doi.org/10. 3390/s20041029

Lee, J.-S., Bae, Y.-S., Lee, W., Lee, H., Yu, J., Choi, J.-P.: Emotion and fatigue monitoring using wearable devices. In: Hwang, S.O., Tan, S.Y., Bien, F. (eds.) ICGHIT 2018. LNEE, vol. 502, pp. 91–96. Springer, Singapore (2019). https://doi.org/10. 1007/978-981-13-0311-1_17

Lei, J., et al.: Study on driving fatigue evaluation system based on short time period ECG signal. In: 2018 21st International Conference on Intelligent Transportation Systems (ITSC), pp. 2466–2470 (2018). https://doi.org/10.1109/ITSC.2018.8569409

Lin, C.-T., Nascimben, M., King, J.-T., Wang, Y.-K.: Task-related EEG and HRV entropy factors under different real-world fatigue scenarios. Neurocomputing **311**, 24–31 (2018). https://doi.org/10.1016/j.neucom.2018.05.043

Makowski, D., et al.: NeuroKit2: a Python toolbox for neurophysiological signal processing. Behav. Res. Methods **53**(4), 1689–1696 (2021). https://doi.org/10.3758/ s13428-020-01516-y

Mejía-Mejía, E., Allen, J., Budidha, K., El-Hajj, C., Kyriacou, P.A., Charlton, P.H.: 4 - Photoplethysmography signal processing and synthesis. In: Allen, J., Kyriacou, P. (eds.) Photoplethysmography, pp. 69–146. Academic Press (2022). https://doi.org/ 10.1016/B978-0-12-823374-0.00015-3

Picard, R.W.: Automating the recognition of stress and emotion: from lab to real-world impact. IEEE Multimed. **23**(3), 3–7 (2016). https://doi.org/10.1109/MMUL.2016. 38

Pilt, K., Ferenets, R., Meigas, K., Lindberg, L.-G., Temitski, K., Viigimaa, M.: New photoplethysmographic signal analysis algorithm for arterial stiffness estimation. Sci. World J. **2013**(1), 169035 (2013)

Ul Alam, M.A.: Activity-aware deep cognitive fatigue assessment using wearables. In: 2021 43rd Annual International Conference of the IEEE Engineering in Medicine Biology Society (EMBC), pp. 7433–7436 (2021). https://doi.org/10.1109/ EMBC46164.2021.9630729

Umair, M., Chalabianloo, N., Sas, C., Ersoy, C.: HRV and stress: a mixed-methods approach for comparison of wearable heart rate sensors for biofeedback. IEEE Access **9**, 14005–14024 (2021). https://doi.org/10.1109/ACCESS.2021.3052131

Van Gent, P., Farah, H., Van Nes, N., Van Arem, B.: Analysing noisy driver physiology real-time using off-the-shelf sensors: heart rate analysis software from the taking the fast lane project. J. Open Res. Softw. **7**(1), 1–9 (2019)

Yue, Y., Liu, D., Fu, S., Zhou, X.: Heart rate and heart rate variability as classification features for mental fatigue using short-term PPG signals via smartphones instead of ECG recordings. In: 2021 13th International Conference on Communication Software and Networks (ICCSN), pp. 370–376 (2021). https://doi.org/10.1109/ICCSN52437. 2021.9463614

The Supervised Learning Dilemma: Lessons Learned from a Study in-the-Wild

Kristina Kirsten[1]([✉]), Robin Burchard[2], Olesya Bauer[1], Marcel Miché[3],
Philipp Scholl[4], Karina Wahl[3], Roselind Lieb[3], Kristof Van Laerhoven[2],
and Bert Arnrich[1]

[1] Digital Health - Connected Healthcare, Hasso Plattner Institute,
University of Potsdam, Potsdam, Germany
`kristina.kirsten@hpi.de`
[2] Ubiquitous Computing, University of Siegen, Siegen, Germany
[3] Department of Psychology, University of Basel, Basel, Switzerland
[4] ABB Corporate Research, Baden, Switzerland

Abstract. The increasing popularity of conducting studies in real-life settings, known as "studies in-the-wild", is a valuable addition to the traditional controlled clinical trials. These studies enable the observation of long-term effects and account for the complex influences of everyday life. Body-worn sensors facilitate the continuous and unobtrusive collection of motion data in its user's natural, everyday life environment. However, studies in-the-wild require careful planning regarding equipment usability, accessibility, and the creation of efficient study protocols to maximize the quality and output of the collected data. This paper presents insights from our recent study on compulsive handwashing, highlighting the challenges and strategies in study design, implementation, and label acquisition in order to perform supervised machine learning. We present approaches as well as the benefits and limitations of annotating data retrospectively so that participants are impacted minimally during the study. Finally, we list our learning and insights for upcoming studies of that kind.

Keywords: human-activity-recognition · sensor data · wearables · real-life study

1 Introduction

Conducting studies outside the controlled setting, also referred to as "in-the-wild", has gained enormous popularity in recent years. The concept of observational studies in natural environments without intervention began to emerge along with the questions of what studies outside the laboratory should look like [6]. This specific kind of study offers many benefits. On the one hand, findings from clinical trials can be reassessed in everyday life and observed over a longer period to study long-term effects. On the other hand, for many research

O. Konak et al. (Eds.): iWOAR 2024, LNCS 15357, pp. 181–195, 2025.
https://doi.org/10.1007/978-3-031-80856-2_12

questions, the influences of ordinary life play a major role in the results. These influencing factors can only be observed in a real and realistic environment where the participant is not controlled or monitored. Studies that additionally use sensors can also be carried out outside the lab through the rapid development of portable sensors, known as wearables to collect physiological signals and motion data. Wearables, such as smartwatches, make collecting data constantly but unobtrusively in everyday life possible.

Although studies in-the-wild have great advantages, they also require special precautions in their design and implementation. These are characterized by the choice of equipment concerning usability and accessibility for the participant and a study protocol that is simple to implement but provides the desired output.

Wearables can be used to record physiological parameters as well as motion data continuously. The latter can be used to recognize movement patterns and assign activities. The research field of human activity recognition in-the-wild is popular but poses many challenges. Distinguishing activities in everyday life without further (e.g. contextual) information is highly complex. Thus, when it comes to developing a (machine learning) model that recognizes certain activities, researchers still rely on supervised machine learning methods. For those approaches, the beginning and end of an activity needs to be known. These so-called labels can be received from the study participants during data collection. Nevertheless, it is a significant effort for the participant to provide information not only about the time of an activity but also about the duration, i.e. start and end. However, since we want to influence the subject's everyday behavior as little as possible, we often accept collecting only the information about the time of the activities. This means that for the supervised machine learning model, it is necessary to find a way to determine the start and end time of the activity after the data has been recorded.

In this paper, we show what we have learned from our recent study on (compulsive) handwashing in terms of study design, implementation, and label acquisition. We explore various strategies for addressing noisy labels, coming from real-life situations, in supervised machine learning. We delve into the insights and impacts of manual inspections and annotations and discuss the Inter-Annotator Agreement (IAA). Lastly, we share our lessons learned and insights to guide future research in this area.

2   Background

Since the present work is essentially concerned with the aspects of studies outside the laboratory and the associated challenge of data annotation, we will explain the fundamental aspects below.

2.1   Studies in-the-Wild

Over a decade ago, researchers identified the need for "in-the-wild" studies with wearable devices, arguing that research in participants' natural environments is crucial for understanding the real-life impact of technology and minimizing behavior changes from observation awareness [6,9].

Schlögl et al. emphasized the importance of involving more users in these studies to validate data from wearable technologies. Their research highlighted that real-life interactions with wearables are affected by technical knowledge and device discomfort, recommending a user-centered approach [15].

Overall, scientific literature indicates that including participants as early as possible in the study design is essential for understanding their needs, ensuring compliance, and achieving high-quality data in unsupervised, real-life studies.

2.2   Time-Series Data Annotation and IAA

Even though research in the area of machine learning is increasingly moving in the direction of deep learning, there are still use cases that are better suited to classic machine learning due to their novelty and limited amount of data. When talking about classic machine learning, a distinction is made between supervised, semi-supervised, and unsupervised learning. While the former requires a considerable amount of annotated data, the advantages in terms of accuracy, interpretability, performance evaluation, and reliability make it the preferred choice for many applications, especially those where precision and reliability are of major importance [2,5].

Despite the benefits, obtaining high-quality annotated data in a real-world study with wearables can be challenging when it comes to capturing participants' natural behavior without additional burden. To keep the effort and influence to a minimum, it is common practice to have third parties enrich the data with additional information (annotations, labels) afterwards. In the following, the terms annotation and labeling are used synonymously.

Annotating data retrospectively by external persons, e.g. by visual inspection, involves a certain risk, especially concerning the introduction of a personal bias. Several annotators are often used for the same data to keep this to a minimum. Approaches such as the calculation of IAA are used to evaluate the success and degree of agreement of the manually annotated data. Prominent metrics for calculating the IAA are, i.e., the Percent Agreement, Krippendorff's Alpha, and Cohen's Kappa (κ) [7]. The latter will be used in this paper and is defined as follows:

$$\kappa = \frac{P_o - P_e}{1 - P_e}$$

where P_o is the observed agreement and P_e is the expected agreement by chance.

3   Related Work

In their systematic literature review, the authors of [1] explicitly highlight that one of the primary obstacles in real-world activity recognition is the necessity for labeled data. However, the review did not identify a simple, high-quality label creation solution. As a possible solution, the paper by Garcia-Ceja and Brena is referenced, where the authors recommend labeling only a small part of the dataset with available annotated data and using it to train personalized models, as these outperformed general models [8].

The paper by Larradet et al. explores various aspects, including the challenges associated with self-reporting for emotion recognition in daily life. They draw attention to the subjective nature of labeling, which is influenced by individual perceptions. Moreover, they point out the likelihood of delays or inaccuracies in annotations due to the dynamic and unpredictable nature of everyday activities. To address these challenges, they propose implementing standardized annotation protocols to improve consistency and objectivity [13].

In a recent study presented in [11], conducted in real-world settings, the authors highlight significant challenges arising from delays encountered at various stages of the project. These delays range from acquiring ethics approval to facing technical difficulties upon the initiation of the main study. They suggest conducting pilot studies with distinct goals, e.g., to validate assumptions made in the study design or to test the devices in action. This again shows the need to involve future study participants in the planning phase, which is known as a user-centered approach.

4   Previous Works

In a series of previous studies [3,18,19] in preparation for the study presented in this paper, lab-recorded inertial measurement unit (IMU) data from the wrist, collected under controlled conditions, was used to simulate specific handwashing behaviors as it occurs in people suffering from obsessive-compulsive disorder (OCD). The researchers used detailed scripts of compulsive handwashing, based on descriptions from individuals with OCD, to enact specific sequences of handwashing gestures. The goal was to demonstrate that simulated compulsive handwashing could be distinguished from routine handwashing in healthy participants. This approach could later be utilized to support and enhance conventional therapies, such as psychotherapy or specifically exposure and response prevention (ERP) therapy, by automatically detecting and logging compulsive actions, and providing feedback to the patient to help them discontinue these behaviors.

In a subsequent study, the dataset was expanded to include other repetitive activities similar to handwashing [16]. This enhancement aimed to improve the robustness of the trained models against confounding activities, such as "rinsing a cup" or "peeling a carrot" which involved repetitive wrist motions resembling handwashing. The researchers successfully showed that simulated compulsive handwashing could be distinguished from these confounding activities, including routine handwashing.

These pilot studies in the laboratory served both technically and in terms of study design as the basis for the study-in-the-wild presented in the following.

5   Dataset Generation

The collected data is part of a study called OCDetect about compulsive hand-washing conducted in Switzerland. The study was approved by the Ethics Committee of North/West Switzerland (application number 2021-01317). We recruited 30 participants with excessive urge to wash their hands. All participants were examined by trained psychologists and had to complete interviews to guarantee their suitability for the study. To be part of the study, participants had to be aged between 18 and 75, non-suicidal, and meet the criteria for compulsive handwashing. In the end, 22 participants completed the study, and eight dropped out for personal or technical reasons.

The participants were asked to wear a smartwatch for at least six hours a day over a 28-day recording period and follow their normal daily routines. The Android-based smartwatches were adapted with a pre-trained machine learning model to recognize handwashing in daily life automatically. Therefore, we recorded the data from the three-axis accelerometer and gyroscope at a frequency of 50 Hz. The model was trained on simulated lab data so that its performance in real life was less than expected. Whenever the watch detected a possible handwashing activity, the user got a notification that could be affirmed or declined. Additionally, the participants could mark handwashing manually by tapping on the watch and also indicate the type of washing, i.e. compulsive or routine handwashing. By this, we received information, later called labels, about the point when a handwashing activity occurred.

We ended up with a cleaned dataset of 2600 h of daily-life activities and a total of 2930 handwashing sessions, of which 1526 were categorized as compulsive by users, while 1404 were identified as routine handwashing sessions.

6   Re-labeling Approaches

For the OCDetect study, we decided to collect only one label in the form of a timestamp for each handwashing event. We aimed to prevent patients with compulsive washing behavior from additional stress and we did not want to change their natural movement patterns unnecessarily. Thereby, we could collect data in a realistic scenario. Consequently, this also means that we have no information afterward about the start and possibly the end of the activity. However, this information is necessary for supervised machine learning approaches. For this reason, we enriched the data with this information retrospectively after completing the data acquisition. Since this step is not trivial without the information about the length of the activity as well as the start and exact end, we considered two different approaches. In the following, these two approaches are referred to as automatic re-labeling and manual re-labeling.

6.1   Automatic Re-labeling

First, we wanted to get a sense of how long participants spend washing their hands on average. Although we found evidence in the literature on the average duration of hand washing in the German population (more than half of the participants wash their hands for between 10s and 19s on average [14]), we could not assume that this behavior is the same in patients with compulsive handwashing. Therefore, we used the video footage we created during the first visit to the lab, where participants were asked to wash their hands while being filmed. Using the video material, we were able to derive a personal handwashing duration for each participant for whom we had a recording. Unfortunately, this was not the case for every participant, so for those where we had no lab video, we used the average duration of handwashing that we had calculated from all available videos. On average, handwashing in the lab took 38s, with 18s being the shortest and 60s the longest. This observation does not align with the typical handwashing duration seen in the general population, but it supports the naive assumption that individuals with a handwashing compulsion tend to wash their hands for a longer period. Finally, we labeled the activity up to 5s before the actual user label, as we assumed that the hand washing was already over by the time the user pressed the button on the watch to indicate a washing activity had happened.

6.2   Manual Re-labeling

As an additional approach, we opted for an elaborate manual approach to evaluate the extent to which the human factor can improve the labels and thus the result. Since manual annotation is very time-consuming, we decided to annotate only a subset of six participants manually, but with higher quality and less potential bias, rather than relying on quantity. This subgroup already has a sufficient number of participants and annotations to get a feel for the impact on the classification results (which will be published elsewhere).

To minimize personal bias, we opted to use two different annotators for each participant to manually label the handwashing events. With six participants and four annotators, we established unique participant-annotators pairs, we formed the following set of possible labeling assignments:

$$\mathcal{A} = \{(P_i, (A_j, A_k)) | i = 1, 2, ...6, j, k \in \{1, 2, 3, 4\}, j \neq k\} \tag{1}$$

We then selected assignments from $\mathcal{A}$ so that the following constraints were met:

$$\forall P_i \in P : P_i \text{ appears in } \mathcal{A} \text{ exactly twice} \tag{2}$$

$$\forall \text{Pairs } (A_j, A_k), j < k : (A_j, A_k) \text{ appears in } \mathcal{A} \text{ exactly once} \tag{3}$$

As an annotation tool, we decided on an open-source, easy-to-use, and collaborative online platform called Label Studio [17]. Since not every handwashing activity is clearly visible, the annotator could choose between four different label types: *Begin AND End uncertain* (if both the activity start and end are difficult to identify), *Begin uncertain* (if only the end can be clearly determined), *End uncertain* (if only the beginning is identifiable), or *Certain* (if the activity is fully recognizable). Additionally, the annotator may opted not to set a manual

Table 1. This table shows the amount of originally set user labels (*before, abbr. as bef.*) and those set by the individual annotator (abbr. as Annot.) for their assigned subject (A - F) afterward (*after*). Each absolute number of before and after labels, as well as the corresponding percentage share, is also provided.

Annot.	Subject A			Subject B			Subject C			Subject D			Subject E			Subject F		
	bef.	*after*	%	*bef.*	*after*	%	*bef.*	*after*	%	*bef.*	*after*	%	*bef.*	*after*	%	*bef.*	*after*	%
1	362	235	65	225	208	92				398	308	77						
2				225	212	94	130	115	89							195	169	87
3							130	127	98	398	347	87	366	343	94			
4	362	195	54										366	323	88	195	124	64

label at all, such as when there is no movement. This differentiation between label types allows for subsequent analyses of the relabeling process.

In Fig. 1, we illustrate visualizations of accelerometer data capturing two distinct handwashing activities performed by Subject E. While in Fig. 1a, the rapid handwashing movement is clearly identifiable, in Fig. 1b, this characteristic is not noticeable. Furthermore, in Fig. 1a, the original user label (depicted by a dotted black vertical line) coincides with ongoing motion, making it challenging to determine whether the activity had already concluded before the movement, merely indicating button pressing, or if the movement still constitutes part of the handwashing activity. However, segments with clearly no movements make it easier to isolate specific patterns, such as handwashing. In contrast, Fig. 1b presents a significant challenge because neither the beginning nor the end of the activity can be distinctly identified visually. This highlights some of the difficulties encountered during manual data annotation.

7   Re-labeling Results

To get a first impression of the quality of the manual re-labeling approach, we first create some overall statistics and visualize different aspects of the output.

In Table 1, the number of existing labels for the six different subjects (A-F) as well as the manually set labels (independent from their kind) for the respective annotator are listed. The differences in the number of newly set labels are due to the fact that an annotator could also decide not to set a label at all if he or she believed that there was most likely no activity there. Overall it can be seen that already the amount of user labels differs between the subjects which can be a sign of the severity of the disorder or a general lack of compliance. Subject A clearly shows that a high number of user labels does not mean that handwashing is more routinized and therefore more visually recognizable. Both annotators did not set new labels for almost half of the original user labels. In general, it can be said that the annotators (except for Subject F) were in reasonable agreement as to where handwashing had actually occurred and therefore needed to be labeled.

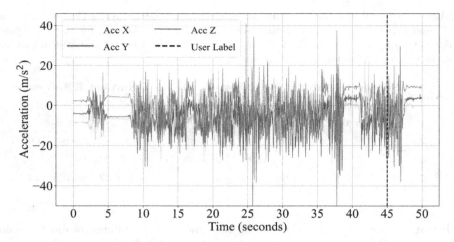

(a) Example of a handwashing activity where rapid movements are clearly visible. The start of the activity is visually identifiable (around second 8), but the endpoint labeled by the user appears to occur in the midst of a movement.

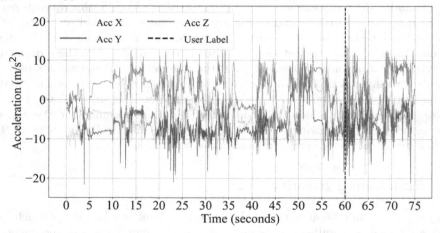

(b) Example of a handwashing activity where the beginning and end are not easily identifiable due to a less distinctive pattern.

Fig. 1. Visualizations of accelerometer data (in three axes: Acc x, Acc y, and Acc z) depicting two handwashing activities for Subject E. The subject's original labels are represented by dotted vertical lines.

Figure 2 and Fig. 3 give insights into the shares of the different kinds of labels. Figure 2 illustrates the frequency and distribution of label types utilized by the four annotators across all subjects to which they were assigned. This figure provides insights into various annotator behaviors, revealing significant variations in label types despite two annotators consistently relabeling the same subject.

Such discrepancies may stem from a lack of common understanding regarding the identification of handwashing activity patterns or uncertainty regarding which actions constitute handwashing (e.g., drying hands or opening the faucet).

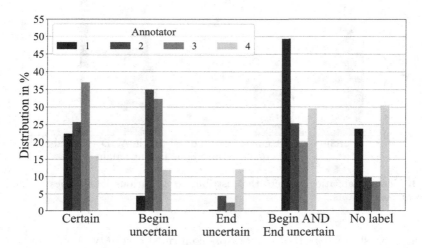

Fig. 2. The figure showcases the spread of different label types assigned by each annotator across all newly set labels.

Figure 3 shows the same label types but in relation to the different participants. This plot aids in identifying subjects where handwashing was visually easier to discern (labeled as *Certain*), as well as instances where the pattern was less clear (labeled as *Begin AND End uncertain*). It also highlights the participants for which incorrect previous user labels may have occurred, potentially indicating no movement and thus no newly set label.

The mean handwashing durations for compulsive as well as routine handwashing in seconds for each subject after re-labeling the data are illustrated in Fig. 4. Therefore, the two annotations for each activity have been combined. It becomes apparent that the duration of handwashing is extremely different not only across participants but also within a participant (recognizable by the high standard deviation). This may be due to natural human behavior, but may also be influenced by the annotators and the ambiguous visual pattern. Since no clear statement can be made about different durations between the two different types of hand washing (compulsive and routine), no conclusions can be drawn here either. Without differentiation between compulsive and routine handwashing, the overall mean duration is 52.30 s with a standard deviation of 39.00 s. With differentiation, the mean durations are 56.09 s for compulsive and 53.84 s for routine behaviors, with standard deviations of 53.89 s and 30.96 s, respectively.

When considering activities where annotators were certain during re-labeling, the frequency of hand washes decreases. Figure 5 visualizes compulsive and rou-

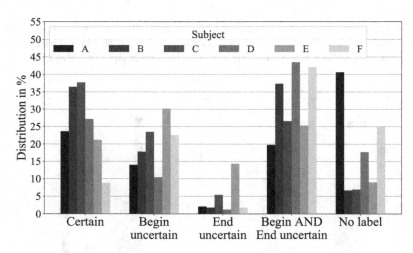

Fig. 3. The visualization depicts the distribution of various label types assigned to different participants.

tine hand washes where both annotators confirmed certainty about the activity pattern. This results in an overall mean duration of 32.02 s with a standard deviation of 13.85 s when not differentiating between handwashing types. When distinguishing between compulsive and routine handwashing, the latter has a mean duration of 36.11 s $\pm$ 17.41 s (with $n = 25$ instances). For $n = 102$ compulsive handwashing activities, the mean duration is 30.48 s $\pm$ 5.92 s. The unexpectedly shorter duration for compulsive handwashing should be interpreted cautiously, as it exhibits a significantly smaller standard deviation compared to routine handwashing activities, despite occurring four times more frequently.

8   IAA Evaluation

As introduced in Sect. 2.2, we used Cohen's Kappa to evaluate the level of agreement between different annotator pairs. The results, visualized in Fig. 6 as a heatmap, reveal considerable variation in agreement levels among the pairs. While annotator pairs (1, 4) and (3, 4) show a higher level of consensus, the other pairs demonstrate lower agreement. It is important to note that these discrepancies are likely to be explained by the different ways of washing hands even within the same participant. Furthermore, it cannot be said with complete certainty that all activities marked by the user were actually handwashing, as even an accidental press of the smartwatch button, for example, would be incorrectly counted as such without the possibility of validating this afterwards.

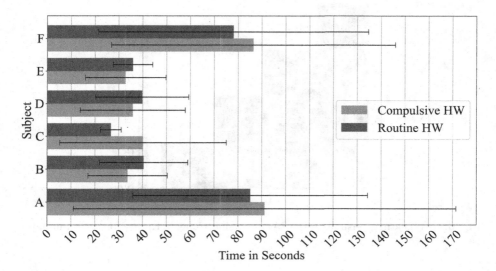

Fig. 4. The horizontal bar chart displays the mean handwashing durations in seconds categorized as compulsive and routine handwashing (abbrev. HW) activities, merged from annotations by each subject. Additionally, each bar also indicates the respective standard deviation.

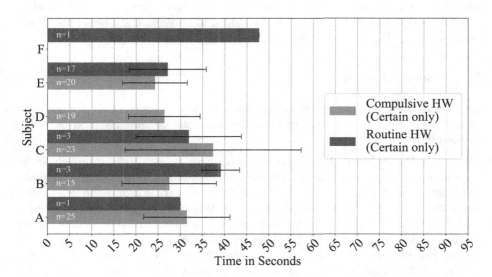

Fig. 5. The horizontal bar chart shows again the mean handwashing durations in seconds categorized as compulsive and routine handwashing activities, merged from annotations by each subject but only when both annotators labeled the activity as being *Certain*. The number of resulting activities is displayed as n if there was at least one.

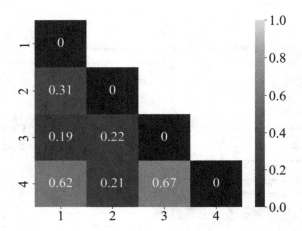

Fig. 6. The heatmap visualizes the IAA by using Cohen's Kappa for each annotator pair.

Cohen's Kappa, commonly used for measuring IAA, has several drawbacks. It is sensitive to an unbalanced distribution of categories, which is particularly relevant in our context. Moreover, it may not accurately reflect agreement when annotators have different tendencies. The simplified treatment of random matches and the sensitivity to annotations near category boundaries further complicate the interpretation. Since in our use case different types of hand washing often follow each other, these factors could lead to lower scores. These limitations underscore the importance of interpreting Kappa scores cautiously.

9   Lessons Learned

As a result of our OCDetect study, we can draw several lessons that are not only valuable for our future work but can also serve the community as a basis for studies in-the-wild.

Plan for Participant Involvement. Following user-centric approach while designing the study is essential. This can involve multiple approaches, ranging from using questionnaires to gather input from the target group about assumptions leading to the study design to incorporating concrete pilot studies as integral parts of the overall research. This might help to understand challenges and increase study results through greater participant commitment and compliance. In our specific case, it would have been helpful to give the participants some (technical) background knowledge on data recording with wearables and maybe even the basic machine learning concept. The lack of understanding of the connection between the time-series data recorded by the smartwatch and the annotation of a handwashing activity by the user led to poorer data quality. Later data exploration showed that some users apparently did not wear the watch, but nevertheless pressed the button to annotate, e.g. after washing their hands. This behavior is valuable from the user's point of view, as the information for washing hands was provided. From the point of view of automated machine learning, however, this leads to misinformation for the model, as there is no movement data but still a label. In future studies, we will ask users not to set a label if the smartwatch is not being worn. Even if the watch is worn, we will give an approximate time period of 10 min in which an annotation can be made afterwards and, in case of forgetting, simply not to set a label, since a label set much too late can hardly be assigned to the original activity.

Data Recording App Improvements. We have also noticed several times that labels occur in very short succession, where it is unlikely that several activities have taken place. We assume that the user has entered an incorrect label, for example, or that a label has been added several times due to a lack of feedback that a label has already been set. The user interface can be improved technically by introducing the option to take back a label and an overview of annotations that have already been made.

Interdisciplinary Team. In addition, as already demonstrated in our study, it is important to involve not only the user but also experts, such as trained psychologists in our case, in the study process. In this way, trust is created, responsibility is shared and the results can be correctly classified, categorized, and interpreted.

Annotation Guidelines. When it comes to manually annotating the data afterwards, it became apparent that defining annotation guidelines is essential. By doing so, a common understanding of the data and desired outcome is created, the data quality improves considerably, and personal bias is reduced to a minimum.

Multimodal Data Collection. Manual data annotation is time-consuming and requires additional knowledge, such as contextual information. Collecting further data modalities during the study can be beneficial [10]. For activities like handwashing, context, such as location within the room, is crucial. The direct link between specific activities and their spatial allocation (e.g., washing hands at the sink) can help determine the start and end of these activities.

Personalized Pre-model. As previously described in Sect. 5, the smartwatches used for data recording were equipped with a deep learning model pre-trained on lab data. This model aims to automatically recognize as many handwashing activities as possible, requiring confirmation from the user only. However, the study revealed significant variability in individual handwashing techniques, even within the same participant. This variability can lead to numerous incorrect detections, causing label fatigue [12]. To minimize this issue, the pre-trained model can be personalized for each user during the initial days of data recording through a combination of online and active learning with individual data [4]. This personalization reduces false-positives and enhances user compliance.

10   Conclusion

In conclusion, we have presented key findings and challenges in the study design, execution, and data annotation of our in-the-wild study OCDetect. Our findings highlight the importance of a user-centered approach to study design, engaging participants and experts to ensure robust data collection and participant compliance.

Wearable technology proved essential for continuous and unobtrusive data collection in naturalistic settings. However, it also posed a challenge to the accuracy and reliability of the data generated by participants. In our study, both automated and manual relabeling of handwashing activities were performed, showing considerable variability in labeling quality. This highlighted the need for standardized labeling protocols to reduce personal bias and improve data consistency. Although the process of manual relabeling was resource intensive, it provided valuable insights into the reliability of human annotations and IAA. Using Cohen's Kappa metric, we assessed the agreement between annotators.

In a detailed lessons learned section, we highlight the challenges faced during the study and provide potential solutions for future studies of this type, ranging from plans for participant involvement, over additional ideas for data collection and label acquisitions to advanced machine learning approaches.

Acknowledgments. We thank Lorenz Kautzsch and Lea Liekenbrock for their assistance in annotating the data. We would also like to express our gratitude to Silvan Wirth for his technical assistance during data collection and to Alexander Henkel for providing the data recording app.

Disclosure of Interests. The authors have no competing interests to declare that are relevant to the content of this article.

References

1. Allahbakhshi, H., Hinrichs, T., Huang, H., Weibel, R.: The key factors in physical activity type detection using real-life data: a systematic review. Front. Physiol. (2019)
2. Amodei, D., Olah, C., Steinhardt, J., Christiano, P., Schulman, J., Mané, D.: Concrete problems in AI safety. arXiv preprint arXiv:1606.06565 (2016)
3. Burchard, R., Scholl, P.M., Lieb, R., Van Laerhoven, K., Wahl, K.: WashSpot: real-time spotting and detection of enacted compulsive hand washing with wearable devices. In: Proceedings of the 2022 ACM International Joint Conference on Pervasive and Ubiquitous Computing. pp. 483–487. ACM, Cambridge United Kingdom (2022). https://doi.org/10.1145/3544793.3563428
4. Cacciarelli, D., Kulahci, M.: Active learning for data streams: a survey. Mach. Learn. (2024)
5. Caruana, R., Niculescu-Mizil, A.: An empirical comparison of supervised learning algorithms. In: Proceedings of the 23rd International Conference on Machine Learning (2006)

6. Chamberlain, A., Crabtree, A., Rodden, T., Jones, M., Rogers, Y.: Research in the wild: understanding 'in the wild' approaches to design and development. In: Proceedings of the Designing Interactive Systems Conference. DIS 2012, Association for Computing Machinery, New York, NY, USA (2012). https://doi.org/10.1145/2317956.2318078

7. Cohen, J.: A coefficient of agreement for nominal scales. Educ. Psychol. Meas. (1960)

8. Garcia-Ceja, E., Brena, R.F.: Activity recognition using community data to complement small amounts of labeled instances. Sensors (Basel, Switzerland) (2016). https://api.semanticscholar.org/CorpusID:6907811

9. Johnson, R., Rogers, Y., Van Der Linden, J., Bianchi-Berthouze, N.: Being in the thick of in-the-wild studies: the challenges and insights of researcher participation. In: Proceedings of the SIGCHI Conference on Human Factors in Computing Systems, pp. 1135–1144 (2012)

10. Kirsten, K., Arnrich, B.: Elements of a system for automatic monitoring of specific mental health characteristics at home. In: Proceedings of the 25th International Multiconference Information Society 2022, IS 2022, Ljubljana, Slovenia (2022)

11. Komoszyńska, J., Kunc, D., Perz, B., Hebko, A., Kazienko, P., Saganowski, S.: Designing and executing a large-scale real-life affective study. In: 2024 IEEE International Conference on Pervasive Computing and Communications Workshops and other Affiliated Events (PerCom Workshops), pp. 505–510. IEEE (2024)

12. Kumar, P., Chauhan, S., Awasthi, L.K.: Human activity recognition (HAR) using deep learning: review, methodologies, progress and future research directions. Arch. Comput. Methods Eng. (2024)

13. Larradet, F., Niewiadomski, R., Barresi, G., Caldwell, D.G., Mattos, L.S.: Toward emotion recognition from physiological signals in the wild: approaching the methodological issues in real-life data collection. Front. Psychol. (2020)

14. Mardiko, A.A., von Lengerke, T.: When, how, and how long do adults in germany self-reportedly wash their hands? compliance indices based on handwashing frequency, technique, and duration from a cross-sectional representative survey. Int. J. Hygiene Environ. Health (2020). https://doi.org/10.1016/j.ijheh.2020.113590, https://www.sciencedirect.com/science/article/pii/S1438463920305368

15. Schlögl, S., Buricic, J., Pycha, M.: Wearables in the wild: advocating real-life user studies. In: Proceedings of the 17th International Conference on Human-computer Interaction with Mobile Devices and Services Adjunct (2015)

16. Scholl, P.M., Wahl, K.: Ablutomania-set - a dataset for OCD and everyday handwashing detection from wrist motion (2021). https://earth.informatik.uni-freiburg.de/ablutomania/

17. Tkachenko, M., Malyuk, M., Holmanyuk, A., Liubimov, N.: Label Studio: data labeling software (2020–2022). https://github.com/heartexlabs/label-studio

18. Wahl, K., Scholl, P.M., Miché, M., Wirth, S., Burchard, R., Lieb, R.: Real-time detection of obsessive-compulsive hand washing with wearables: research procedure, usefulness and discriminative performance. J. Obsessive-Compulsive Related Disorders, 100845 (2023). https://doi.org/10.1016/j.jocrd.2023.100845, https://linkinghub.elsevier.com/retrieve/pii/S2211364923000660

19. Wahl, K., et al.: On the automatic detection of enacted compulsive hand washing using commercially available wearable devices. Comput. Biol. Med. 105280 (2022). https://doi.org/10.1016/j.compbiomed.2022.105280, https://linkinghub.elsevier.com/retrieve/pii/S0010482522000725

Novel AI and Machine Learning Approaches

FlyAI - The Next Level of Artificial Intelligence is Unpredictable! Injecting Responses of a Living Fly into Decision Making

Denys J.C. Matthies[1,2](✉), Ruben Schlonsak[1,2], Hanzhi Zhuang[1,3], and Rui Song[1,3]

[1] Technical University of Applied Sciences Lübeck, Lübeck, Germany
[2] Fraunhofer IMTE, Lübeck, Germany
denys.matthies@th-luebeck.de
[3] East China University of Science and Technology, Shanghai, China

Abstract. In this paper, we introduce a new type of bionic AI that enhances decision-making unpredictability by incorporating responses from a living fly. Traditional AI systems, while reliable and predictable, lack nuanced and sometimes unseasoned decision-making seen in humans. Our approach uses a fly's varied reactions, to tune an AI agent in the game of Gobang. Through a study, we compare the performances of different strategies on altering AI agents and found a bionic AI agent to outperform human as well as conventional and white-noise enhanced AI agents. We contribute a new methodology for creating a bionic random function and strategies to enhance conventional AI agents ultimately improving unpredictability.

Keywords: Artificial Intelligence · Bionic Random Function · Random Number Generation · Decision Making · Unpredictability

1 Introduction

If one asks an AI, particularly the Large Language Model (LLM) GPT4, the following question: *"What are the next big steps in AI development?"* it determinedly prompts 10 most important future developments, which are: General AI, Explainable AI, Ethical and Fair AI, Human-AI Collaboration, AI in Healthcare, Edge AI and AIoT, Quantum AI, AI-Driven Autonomous Systems, Improved AI Hardware, and AI for Scientific Discovery. While these might be useful research directions, it is important to recognize that this perspective comes solely from an AI standpoint. The limitations of AI creativity are evident in this LLM response, as it overlooks a crucial aspect. We argue that a significant next step in AI development is to humanize AI, which also includes making it less predictable (Fig. 1).

Does this imply that humans inherently know better? While it is true that AI has surpassed humans in measurable key performance indicators, such as reaction time [34], knowledge recall [15], and various basic tasks [12], the question of human superiority remains nuanced. In an increasingly intellectual and diverse

O. Konak et al. (Eds.): iWOAR 2024, LNCS 15357, pp. 199–219, 2025.
https://doi.org/10.1007/978-3-031-80856-2_13

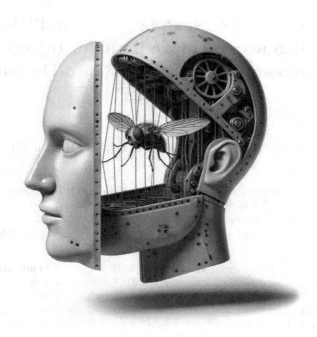

Fig. 1. A bionic element in form of a fly that adds the factor of unpredictability (partly generated by an AI - DALL·E 3).

society, we less and less compare ourselves to each other and rather highlight individual strengths. In this light, it remains the question why we still keep comparing humanity against AI [6]? Indeed, humans excel in emotional intelligence, creativity, and complex problem-solving, allowing for empathy, original thought, and adaptive thinking that AI has yet to truly replicate [24]. Humans possess context-based ethical and moral reasoning [31], rich social interaction skills, and the ability to build meaningful relationships [4].

While AI to date lacks these capabilities, it seems to stand as solid as a rock when it comes to providing us with support in our everyday life situations and anywhere [35]. There may not be a need to discuss whether the responses of an AI are true or not [17]. However, it is striking that AI responses are usually quite solid – based on the learned ground truth. While this is important when we use AI as a tool, it at the same times makes it easy for a human to identify whether we are chatting with an actual human or with AI, such as in the form of an LLM. To be more specific, providing the same input will provide exactly the same output. In machine learning, this is denoted as the concept of model robustness which plays an integral role in establishing trustworthiness in AI systems [1]. While system's robustness has certainly positive aspects, it makes an AI tremendously predictable, from a human's perspective as well as for a controlling or correcting AI [8].

In this paper, we developed some type of bionic AI that counteracts the aspect of high predictability by injecting an unpredictable response from a living organism, the insect of a fly, into the agent's decision making process. This idea has not been largely explored yet. Until now, researchers primarily focused on mimicking animals or insects in their movement capabilities [19] or attaching sensors and actuators to their body in order to partly or fully control the organism [30].

Contrary to existing literature, our research focuses on the natural responses of a living organism. In this project, we captured a fly, which resides unharmed in a transparent box. We trigger the fly's response by activating a fan momentarily. While the fly exhibits similar reactions on some days, its trajectory and flying speed vary on others. We harness several of the fly's evoked parameters to develop a bionic random number generator (bRNG). This bRNG is then integrated into the decision-making process of an AI agent, specifically for the game of "Gobang" [42]. We ran a study to understand how such a bionic response would impact the AI's performance and how this factor of unpredictablity would impact the overall outcome. In this paper, we contribute with:

- a new methodology to create bionic random number generator based on flying trajectories of a fly held in a box,
- an artifact and an empirical investigation of different strategies to enhance conventional agents, while ultimately improving unpredictability of AI.

2   Related Work

2.1   A Weaknesses of AI

It is no question that Artificial Intelligence (AI) is superior to humans in terms of measurable key performance indicators, such as reaction time [34], recall of knowledge [15] and all other basic tasks [12]. AI systems have achieved remarkable performance across numerous fields, such as rapid and accurate image categorization, photorealistic image synthesis, superior performance in competitive games, and precise natural language processing [3]. However, the weakness of the AI may lay in the perfection of following deterministic models. We claim that one significant weakness of AI is its lack of humanity. AI, composed of machines and algorithms, does not possess the same form of imperfect intelligence as humans. It remains a tool that can handle information efficiently but cannot feel or truly understand our emotions.

2.2   (Un)predictability in AI

Unpredictability in AI refers to the inability of humans to consistently and precisely predict the actions an intelligent system will take to achieve its goals, even when the ultimate goal of the algorithm is known [41]. Similar to predicting the outcome of a physical process without understanding the behavior of every atom, we can often foresee the ultimate goal of an AI system without comprehending every intermediate decision it makes. This contributes to the robustness of an AI system, ultimately establishing trustworthiness in AI [1]. Although complex AI systems may naturally exhibit some unpredictable behaviors, most of their actions display patterns and clues that can be recognized by humans. No machine has yet passed the Turing test, and current AI algorithms often show discernible patterns. For example, hackers have sometimes deciphered the principles of specific AI systems by determining the seed of their random generators. In 2010, an individual installed backdoor malware on a U.S. lottery machine to steal the generated random numbers and won millions of dollars in prizes [22]. A less predictable AI system is deemed to be safer. With diverse and unpredictable initiation conditions, capturing detailed characteristics of the system's behavior is difficult. Making systems safe with such chaos approach is a common strategy in cryptography [23]. In a typical encryption, the generation of secret and symmetric keys is based on chaos theory, which utilizes diffusion and confusion to ensure randomness of keys [39] aiming for unpredictability.

2.3   Decision Making in AI

Decision-making by artificial intelligence is widely used today, allowing people to enjoy interactions with game agents and obtain targeted information from smart machines. Although models and algorithms vary, they typically follow similar principles. An AI agent perceives input from its environment, processes it through a decision-making system, and then generates a result. Based on this result, the agent acts or provides an output, which can influence its environment. For example, the simplest algorithm may be decision trees (DT), which are predictive models that map characteristics to values, where non-leaf nodes store attributes for classification, branch nodes store outcomes for specific states, and leaf nodes store final values for decision-making [28]. They are typically readable and easy for human analysis, with methods such as CART, C4.5, CHAID, and QUEST used for development [32]. Building on DT, random forests (RF) generate multiple decision trees from training data and choose the best decisions from this ensemble. A more sophisticated approach are Artificial Neural Networks (ANN), which simulate human neural networks, with interconnected processing elements that calculate inputs to make decisions and provide outputs [21]. ANNs possess self-learning capabilities and can process data to find better solutions, making them more efficient than other complex decision-making models [16].

As decision support systems (DSSs) integrate with modern AI techniques, they are finding exciting applications in decision-making. These systems often mimic human decision-making behaviors, with Artificial Neural Networks (ANNs) and Recurrent Neural Networks (RNNs) being prominent examples. ANNs simulate human neural networks with interconnected nodes, while RNNs use recurrent connections for more complex tasks. For scenarios difficult to model mathematically, techniques like fuzzy logic are employed [27]. AI has diverse applications in decision-making, with early successes in gaming. In 2016, Deep-Mind's AlphaGo defeated professional Go champion Lee Sedol, and its successors, AlphaGo Master and AlphaGo Zero, continued to achieve significant victories, demonstrating advanced AI capabilities through supervised learning, Monte Carlo Tree Search, and deep reinforcement learning [5]. Beyond gaming, AI is revolutionizing fields like self-driving technology. Self-driving cars use either rule-based decision-making, such as Ford and Carnegie Mellon University's BOSS, which follows traffic regulations [37], or learning algorithms that simulate real driving environments using large datasets [26].

2.4   Using Randomize Functions with AI

Utilizing randomized functions is a traditional method to introduce unpredictability in AI systems. This approach is frequently employed in game-based AI, which often relies on either hard-coded rules or conventional machine learning techniques, such as decision trees, or statistical and probabilistic models.

While a random function can to a certain point provide an artificial uncertainty, it can also be used to stabilize results in Neuronal Networks (NN). NN, like any other ML-approach, aim to provide reliable and precise results, but they can suffer from overfitting due to multiple parameters. Overfitting results in an "over sensitive" model prone to incorrect classifications with ambiguous inputs. The "Dropout" technique addresses this by randomly omitting some units in a feedforward neural network with a probability p, enhancing generalization by preventing the model from focusing too narrowly on specific characteristics [9]. Another randomization method is "Random Initialization," used at the initial state of a neural network. In the McCulloch-Pitts "M-P neural model" [20], formalized by $y = f(Wx + b)$, we initialize weights W and biases b randomly preventing identical influence of inputs on the output, avoiding identical gradients [14]. This method is crucial for Q-learning, a reinforcement learning algorithm. Q-learning generates a Q-table to evaluate actions based on states and rewards. Initially, random exploration helps the agent learn optimal actions by trying different steps and observing the resulting rewards [33].

A typical random function outputs values in an equally distributed manner, similar to a white noise signal. Therefore the AI system still retains some kind of predictability. If replacing the random function with a bionic random function that has unpredictable outputs, such as the responses of a fly, the AI system becomes more unpredictable, which is the focus of this work.

3   Bionic Random Function

Using a Bionic Random Function we aim to introduce biological variability into AI, enhancing decision diversity and making AI behavior less predictable. By mimicking natural randomness, a bionic random function may enable AI systems to exhibit a wider range of responses and simulate human-like emotional influences, leading to more dynamic interactions. In research there has not made many attempts to develop a bionic random function. Wan et al. [38] introduced a bionic true random number generator (TRNG) in form of a plant tissue film,

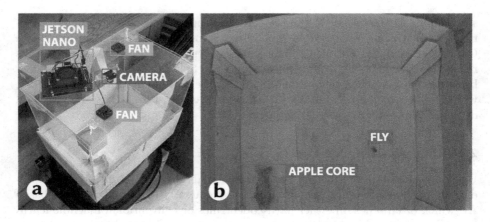

Fig. 2. a) The plexi glas box prototype with a Jetson Nano, two fans, and a camera connected to it. b) Camera image showing the fly and the remains of an apple.

a ginkgo leaf, which is shined through with a laser, resulting in a somewhat random absorption and reflection. Typically, other researchers rely on transistor- [2,7] or memristor- [10,18,40] based technology for random number generation. However, all these approaches do not include factors such as the mood and lust of an actual living organism. Utilizing a living fly for that might be novel and viable way to generate a random number (Fig. 2).

3.1   Implementation

Hardware Prototype. A custom container was designed for housing a fly and integrating a camera system, as depicted in Fig. 4. The container was constructed with specific criteria:

- Using a laser cutter, the plastic walls of the container were perforated with numerous holes to ensure adequate ventilation for the flies, allowing for sufficient oxygen consumption during experiments.
- Half of the container was made from translucent, colorless plastic to provide ample brightness for illuminating the interior, ensuring well-exposed photographs could be captured.
- The inner walls of the container were lined with clean-colored plastic, white, and brown cardboard to provide a neat background for photographs, facilitating easier detection of flies by the algorithm.
- The container was designed in two parts: a cardboard base and a plastic cover, allowing for easy access and modifications to the interior setup as needed during experiments.
- A Jetson Nano was chosen as our hardware platform. A fan that could harshly blow air into the box could triggered, while a camera was recording the fly's movements.

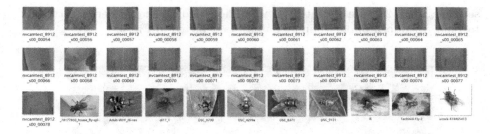

Fig. 3. A snipped of our training dataset to create a refined YOLOv5 model.

Software Prototype. There is many different ideas on how to extract the movements of the fly. We decided to follow a straight-forward approach of using a state-of-the-art framework for real-time object detection "You Only Look Once (YOLO)" that was introduced by Joseph Redmon et al. [29]. We utilized YOLOv5 as it builds on the strengths of previous YOLO versions, offering pre-trained models adaptable to various tasks with advantages like easy availability, low computational cost, and high performance. It has been particularly effective in optimizing object detection applications, surpassing other algorithms in tasks such as vehicle recognition [25]. Unlike its predecessors written in C, YOLOv5 is implemented in Python, enhancing ease of installation and integration on IoT devices. Leveraging the PyTorch framework's extensive community support, YOLOv5 benefits from ongoing contributions and future development potential [36]. YOLOv5s specifically excels in processing deep neural networks quickly and efficiently, making it ideal for projects with limited computational resources and requirements for real-time detection [13].

Model Training. The YOLOv5 series, encompassing models like YOLOv5n, YOLOv5s, YOLOv5m, and others, leverages the Microsoft Common Objects in Context (MS COCO) dataset for pretrained models. This dataset, widely used in computer vision, contains 80 object categories but lacks flies, which are crucial for this project. Due to the unique challenges of capturing fly images-blurry and poorly lit-the decision was made to train YOLOv5s specifically with collected fly data. Transfer learning was employed to adapt YOLOv5s, known for its excellence in detecting complex objects, ensuring rapid adaptation despite limited fly samples. This approach bridges the gap between existing pretrained models and the specific demands of fly detection in this study.

To train the YOLO network for fly detection, a dataset of 125 fly images was meticulously prepared. This included 113 images captured by ourselves, showcasing flies in various angles and positions within the experimental box (see Fig. 4). Additionally, 12 high-resolution fly images were sourced from the internet to enhance sample diversity. Each image was annotated using the Roboflow application to mark the fly locations, resulting in a dataset stored in JPEG format at 720px * 480px resolution. For training, 88 images were randomly selected, while 25 were allocated for validation, and 12 images were reserved for testing. A snipped of our training dataset is depicted in Fig. 3.

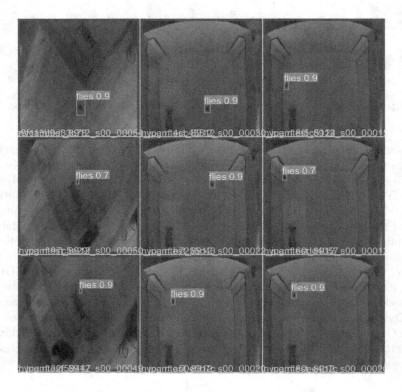

Fig. 4. Real-time fly detection: displaying a label with calculated accuracy.

The YOLOv5s network was trained on a dataset of fly images, achieving an average accuracy of 91.4%. Training was completed on 27/4/2022 using a Tesla T4 GPU on Google Colab, with Python 3.7, Pytorch 1.11.0, CUDA 10.1, and CUDNN 7.6, spanning 300 epochs in approximately 25 min.

The custom trained YOLOv5s model was successfully deployed on the Jetson Nano 2 GB. Deploying the model required resolving dependencies to ensure compatibility with the ARM-based Ubuntu 14.0.1 platform and the specific requirements of YOLOv5s, which was challenging due to version compatibility issues. Upon successful deployment, the system achieved an image inference speed of 0.06 s on average, allowing for real-time object detection at approximately 15 frames per second. This performance is notable considering the embedded system's limited hardware configuration.

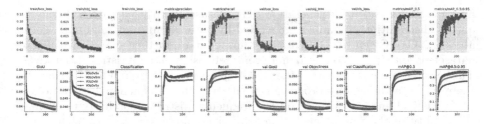

Fig. 5. Top: Charts of box loss, object loss, classification loss, precision, recall and mean average precision (mAP) over the training epochs for the training and validation set. Bottom: YOLOv5 series in charts of box loss, object loss, clas- sification loss, precision, recall and mean average precision (mAP) over the training epochs for the training and validation set.

Model Performance. In Fig. 5, the post-training, statistical analysis is presented, including performance metrics illustrating various aspects of model performance during both training and validation phases. The figure shows three types of losses: box loss, object loss, and classification loss. Box loss assesses the accuracy of object localization and bounding box prediction, while object loss indicates the likelihood of an object being present within the predicted region. Given that only one object type was trained, classification loss is not pertinent in this study.

Performance analysis reveals consistent improvement in recall, precision, and mean average precision (mAP) until approximately 200 epochs, where performance reaches saturation. Both box loss and object loss exhibit rapid declines in early epochs, plateauing near zero after 200 epochs. To further evaluate model performance, the loss function curves and mAP at IoU 0.5 are compared with standard YOLOv5s statistics.

The convergence of box and object losses in our custom model closely mirrors the original YOLOv5s, with our model achieving lower final losses, indicating effective convergence (see Fig. 5). The mAP at IoU 0.5 measures detection model quality, with our model achieving a peak of approximately 92% after stabilizing around 91% post-200 epochs. While our model converges slower than the standard YOLOv5s, it surpasses its performance with higher accuracy, demonstrating effective enhancements.

3.2 The Random Number Generator (RNG)

Once we detected the fly, we can have multiple approaches to design a bionic RNG. In this section, we will describe multiple design.

In our data collection process, a total of 1050 samples were gathered from flies. Various environmental factors potentially invoking a very specific fly behavior were carefully managed by altering photographing times, weather conditions, lighting setups within the box, and positions within the experimental lab. This approach aimed to minimize environmental biases that could affect fly movements and data generation. The dataset is utilized to assess the frequency distribution of numbers generated by our custom random number generators (RNGs). Given the constraints of limited data, further analysis with larger datasets is anticipated to reveal more comprehensive characteristics of the RNGs. The selected number range for the RNGs spans integers from 0 to 49, balancing the need for a sufficiently broad range with adequate frequency distribution.

Statistical analysis focused on the frequency distribution charts to evaluate the quality of the randomness of generated numbers. Cluster bar charts were chosen over line graphs for displaying frequency distributions due to the discrete and independent nature of frequency data points. We particularly looked at the following features describing our bionic RNG.

- **Mean**: Provides the average value of a dataset.
- **Median**: Identifies the midpoint value separating the higher and lower halves of a dataset.
- **Standard deviation**: Quantifies the degree of variation within a dataset.
- **Kurtosis**: Measures the peakedness or flatness of a distribution. A value less than three denotes platykurtic, while values greater than three indicate leptokurtic distributions.
- **Skewness**: Assesses the asymmetry of a distribution. A value within the range of $(-0.5, 0.5)$ indicates symmetry, while values outside this range suggest significant skewness.

Approaches. We generated four bionic RNG (**bRNG1**, **bRNG2**, **bRNG3**, **bRNG4**) based on different ideas and compared it to the an ideal random function (**RNG**) and to a random function provided by Phyton (**pRNG**) as seen in Table 2.

- We created **bRNG1** on the basis of fly's flying vector (direction and length). The sum of the two-dimensional vector is than scaled to the targeted integer range of 0 to 49.
- The **bRNG2** is also created on the basis of fly's flying vector (direction and length). The two-dimensional vector is first converted into raw bytes, and then, the raw bytes are fed into the SHA256 hash function. A 32 bytes sequence with random values between 0 and 255 is generated. Then, the first four bytes are taken to be interpreted as an integer and finally scaled to the integer range between 0 and 49.
- The **bRNG3** is created on the basis of fly's coordinate. The average value of the four numbers, which are x, y coordinate, 10 times width and height, is calculated and then scaled to the targeted integer range between 0 and 49.
- Finally, **bRNG4** is created on the basis of fly's coordinate as well, with a little difference. The whole line, including the object class number, two-dimension coordinate and the width and height of the bounding box, is first converted into raw bytes together and then, the raw bytes are fed into the SHA256 hash function. A 32 bytes sequence with random values between 0 and 255 is then

generated. After that, the first four bytes are taken to be interpreted as an integer and finally scaled to the integer range between 0 and 49.

Results. It is striking that Python's random function, which uses Mersenne Twister (MT) as the core generator, generates pseudo random numbers for a different distribution than what is expected from ideal white noise (**RNG**). MT is one of the most extensively tested RNG method with great performance, which generates 53-bit floats and has a long period of 2*19937-1. The **pRNG** somewhat compares to our **bRNG4**. We consider **bRNG1** and **bRNG3** to demonstrate the greatest deviations and therefore having a greater chance to create unpredictable results (Table 1).

Table 1. Comparing the bionic RNG to a white noise RNG. 1050 samples are used to calculate and compare the mathematical features.

	RNG	pRNG	bRNG1	bRNG2	bRNG3	bRNG4
Mean	24.5	21	21	21	21	21
Median	24.5	21.5	4	21	14.5	21
Std.	14.41	4.14	30.96	4.04	21.72	4.51
Kurtosis	−1.2	−0.48	6.31	−0.39	−0.84	0.54
Skewness	0	−0.35	2.15	−0.36	0.69	0.43

4 Enriching AI with Bionic Random Function

Current advancements in AI, such as integrating AI with self-driving cars and implementing methods like Dropout with random functions, focus on enhancing AI's logical decision-making capabilities, which benefits industrial production by providing more profitable methods. However, in human-interactive or service-industry contexts, achieving goals is not the sole priority; the human experience during the interaction also matters. As Johnson [11] notes, humans rarely make purely rational decisions, so an AI that always thinks rationally might make user feel uncomfortable. Therefore the goal is to make an AI less predictable and more human-like.

4.1 Implementation

Application. Human decisions are often unpredictable, influenced by various factors such as personal emotions and environmental interruptions. This unpredictability poses a challenge for today's AI systems, which tend to perform poorly in such contexts. For instance, when faced with two identical situations, such as in a game, a conventional AI will consistently choose the same "best move".

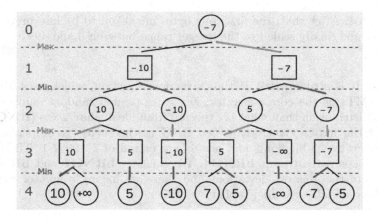

Fig. 6. Following the evaluation process in the Minimax algorithm, scores from various paths propagate upwards through the decision tree. The child node aligning with the score at the root node signifies the optimal path identified by the algorithm.

Our main objective is to enhance current AI algorithms to exhibit more unpredictability while still achieving specific goals. When modifying AI to incorporate randomness, it is essential to maintain the core objective: the AI must still aim to succeed, such as winning a game. Therefore, the fundamental algorithms should either remain unchanged or be only partially modified to incorporate random functions. In line with this principle, our work begins with traditional AI methods, focusing on the well-known Gobang game [42], where the goal is to achieve "five in a row." This game implemented in python will serve as a testbed for developing and evaluating our approach to making AI behavior more unpredictable while maintaining its effectiveness. We have chosen the application of a game environment, as it is a safe space, unlike an AI assistive self-driving car application.

Minimax Algorithm. The Gobang AI agent is fundamentally based on the Minimax and Alpha-Beta Pruning algorithms, commonly used in zero-sum games like chess. The Minimax Algorithm, particularly effective in zero-sum scenarios where one player's gain is another's loss, underpins the AI's strategy in Gobang. In such games, potential outcomes are represented in a decision tree, with each node assigned a score indicating the result's utility. For instance, in a simplified tree for Tic-Tac-Toe, the AI (MAX) aims to maximize its score (+1 for a win) while the opponent (MIN) seeks to minimize it (-1 for a loss). This structured approach ensures that the AI consistently strives for the best possible outcome.

The Gobang AI agent plays as MAX aiming to maximize benefits by exploring the entire decision tree depth-first and selecting paths with maximum scores. Conversely, the MIN agent minimizes benefits. Each node in the decision tree represents a game state, with scores propagated up from leaf nodes to determine optimal moves (see Fig. 6). In practice, the AI, represented as MAX in this scenario, evaluates potential moves several steps ahead to strategize its current best move based on game rules and board positions.

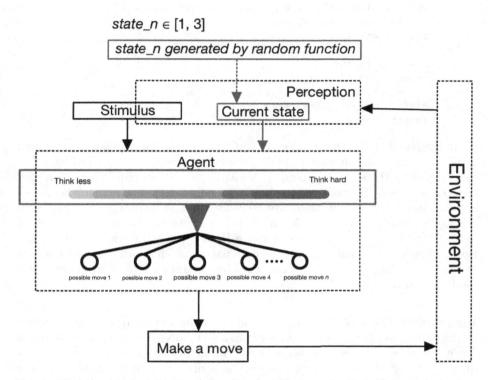

Fig. 7. Injection Method A: The adjustment of thinking depth in the agent involves assigning an integer value from a random function to represent the agent's current mental state. A lower integer value, closer to 1, indicates a more carefree state, prompting the agent to perform a shallow tree search with a depth of 1 (Think Less). Conversely, higher integer values indicate a more cautious state, prompting a deeper tree search (Think More). The search yields a result based on this depth configuration.

Injection Method A. The implementation of the first idea is straightforward. The simulated "emotional state" of the AI agent dictates the depth of its decision-making process, similar to a mapping relationship where each state corresponds to a specific search depth during iterations.

```
function minimax (node, depth, maximizingPlayer, state):
  if state == state n
    return state n mapped thinking depth n
  if depth n == 0 or node is a terminal node then
```

```
      return static evaluation of node
  if MaximizingPlayer
      maxEva = -infinity
      for each child of node do
          eva = minimax (child, depth n - 1, false, state n)
          maxEva = max (maxEva, eva)
          return maxEva
  else
      minEva = +infinity
      for each child of node do
          eva = minimax (child, depth n - 1, true, state n)
          minEva = min (minEva, eva)
          return minEva
```

In the pseudo code, the parameter "*state*" represents the simulated "emotional state" derived from our bionic random function, where "$state_n$" and "$depth_n$" form a pair in the state mapping table. Analogous to human behavior, a cautious or serious state prompts the agent to conduct deeper searches, whereas an imprudent state results in shallower considerations. The procedure outlined in the figure details this approach: the agent's current mental state, denoted by "$state_n$," translates into a numeric range [1 to 3] reflecting the extent of caution. Following the completion of the designated search depth, the agent selects the move yielding the highest score, thereby determining its next action. This method is also illustrated in Fig. 7.

Injection Method B. The implementation of the second idea involves a more intricate process. To enable our AI agent to select among various potential moves during its turn, we create an ordered list containing all possible moves. Subsequently, the agent's decision-making process is driven by an input stimulus that influences the selection from this list of moves. The pseudo-code for this approach is as follows:

```
function minimax (node, depth, maximizingPlayer, stimulate):
  if stimulate == stimulate n
      return stimulate n mapped tendency to choose choice n
  new scorelist []
  if depth n as 0 or node is a terminal node then
      return static evaluation of node
  if MaximizingPlayer
      maxEva = -infinity
      for each child of node do
          eva = minimax (child, depth_n - 1, false, stimulate_n)
          if maxEva < eva then
              scorelist.add (eva)
              maxEva = eva
      scorelist.ordered (MaxToMin)
      return scorelist [choice n]
  else
      minEva = +infinity
```

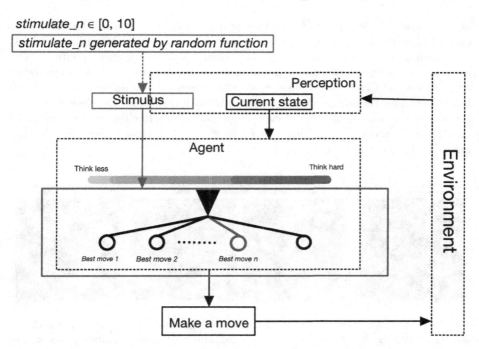

Fig. 8. Injection Method B: The procedure involves providing stimulation to the agent after conducting the tree search. Once an integer representing the level of stimulation is inputted into the agent, it selects from the available moves. Higher levels of stimulation increase the likelihood that the agent will opt for less optimal moves-those with lower scores.

```
for each child of node do
    eva = minimax (child, depth _n - 1, true, stimulate_n)
    if minEva > eva then
        scorelist.add (eva)
        minEva = eva
scorelist.ordered (MinToMax)
return scorelist[choice n1]
```

Similar to the *"state"* parameter in the previous method, the *"stimulate"* input is also generated by our bionic random function. In this case, an integer ranging from 0 to 10 is chosen to represent varying degrees of stimulation. A higher stimulation value increases the likelihood that the AI may opt for a sub-optimal move. This parameter may mimic an impulsive human decision-making-where curiosity or mood may influence risk-taking behavior. External interruptions during gameplay can also affect decision-making, similar to the influences represented by the random function in our agent's environment. Assuming the scores of each route equate to their winning probabilities, these are stored in *"scorelist"*. For efficiency, not all routes need preservation; obviously disadvantageous ones can be discarded. Based on the specific *"stimulate"* value, denoted as "*stimulate_n*", our agent determines which routes to consider. In the subsequent Fig. 8, the agent selects the "*bestmove_n*" based on the "*stimulate_n*" input.

A common yet noteworthy scenario arises when two or more routes in the decision-making process yield identical or very similar scores. For instance, in the aforementioned Fig. 8, "*Best move 1*" and "*Best move 2*" could correspond to different positions but share identical scores. In such instances, the choice between these routes has minimal impact on the current stage's likelihood of winning. To emulate human decision-making, our agent resorts to chance-randomly selecting one of these options to make its move.

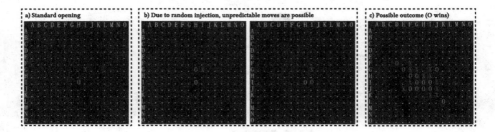

Fig. 9. Pink X: original AI agent, Green O: our modified AI agents. a) Showing a standard opening. b) Our agent is able to continue with unpredictable moves due to the RNG inject. c) Five connecting chars in a row win the game – our AI agent won. (Color figure online)

4.2   Evaluation

It would be interesting to know whether the human would find playing against a bionic AI more unpredictable and difficult than playing against a simple rule-based AI agent, which is already provided by the Gobang Python implementation [42] (see Fig. 9). This rather subjective opinion may or may not arise in the player. The issue is that a non-experienced player is likely to lose against against a simple rule-based and bionic AI, as we quickly figured out in our pilot tests. We assume that only professional players may identify the difference of the varying game styles introduced by the different AIs in this particular application.

Study Design. Hence, we decided to utilize the provided rule-based AI as a benchmark, and testing several other modified copies against it. We calculated the win-rate based on 10 trails run in 50 blocks, resulting in 500 games played against every agent (2000 played games in total). To understand the strength of the modified agents, we additionally we asked 11 players to play against the standard AI 10 times, resulting in 110 played games.

Agent A is a copy of the original AI with the difference of using the Injection Method A, where we use the Python's random function (**pRNG**). **Agent B**

relies on the Injection Method B, also using **pRNG**. **Agent C** combined both injection methods A+B using **pRNG**. **Agent Fly** combined both injection methods A+B using our bionic random dunction (**bRNG1**).

Results. Agent C, which exhibits random injections at several points results in a somewhat comparably low winning rate ($M = 0.34$) to our amateur human players ($M = 0.39$). Both are still able to win, however, inserting white noise at so many points into the **Agent C**, impacts the decision-making process negatively. **Agent A** ($M = 0.61$) and **Agent B** ($M = 0.59$) have just a single point of noise injection and surprisingly perform slightly better than the original AI. However, we also see a high standard deviation ($SD = 0.21$) with a peak win-rate between 0.84 and 0.15. However, we can still see that inserting random noise is not a disadvantage and is somewhat confusing the original AI. Looking at the **Agent Fly**, we can see the highest win-rate ($M = 0.68$) with a relatively low standard deviation ($SD = 0.12$). Here, the bionic RNG inserted specific noise patterns that could be interpreted as a strategy from a human point of view. Apparently, the original AI was unable to counter this unpredictable behavior and therefore demonstrated the greatest loss against our bionic AI agent.

Table 2. Average win-rates of different agents playing against the original AI. A high win-rate > 0.5 indicates the opponents, such as the Agent A, B... to have a greater chance to win against the original AI agent.

AI vs.	Human	Agent A	Agent B	Agent C	Agent Fly
Win-Rate	0.39	0.61	0.59	0.34	0.68

5   Discussion

Bionic Random Function Generator (bRNG): In essence, the term "bionic" typically denotes a fusion of biological principles with mechanical or electronic technology. Therefore, a "bionic random function", could theoretically be used to refer to a random function that is inspired by or mimics biological processes. While the term "bionic random function" isn't commonly used in scientific literature or technology, there is a concept that somewhat aligns with with it: a true random number generator (TRNG) [38]. This concept draws inspiration from natural phenomena such as the unique and random architectures found in leaves, where a laser pointing through the tissue and an optical sensor is used to generate random numbers. In contrast, our bionic random number generator (bRNG) incorporates responses from a living organism, reflecting the complexity of emotions and mood variations.

Practical and Ethical Challenges: While the concept of leveraging a living organism raises intriguing ethical considerations, we chose an insect and designed an environment to mitigate many potential issues. Our aim was to create a habitat that is sufficiently spacious and provides adequate food to ensure the fly's well-being. However, our current setup has practical limitations: the device is bulky, and the process of triggering the fly's response via a fan activation may not be rapid enough for real-time applications. While effective for prototyping purposes, a miniaturized and portable device would be advantageous for practical implementation in various applications.

System's Robustness: Obtaining a bionic random value isn't always guaranteed due to the fly's occasional periods of rest when it might not respond to the fans. Moreover, the fly could sometimes hide in areas not fully captured by the camera, or go unnoticed if the YOLOv5s model, despite its high accuracy (91.4%), missed identifying it.

A Quick and Dirty Approach: We employed a powerful machine learning approach to accomplish a straightforward task: identifying the fly and tracking its flight vectors and coordinates for number generation. Alternatively, a simpler method could involve using a histogram of the camera image, which would enhance robustness and reduce computational costs.

Mission Accomplished: We confirmed that our bRNG, incorporating the fly's responses, significantly enhanced the AI agent, making it more unpredictable and successful. In comparison, both a human player and a conventional AI agent, even when enhanced with a white-noise RNG, exhibited lower performance levels.

Application in Game AI and Beyond: We initially tested our approach in the Gobang game, implementing our bionic RNG with the Minimax Algorithm to enhance decision-making unpredictability. This demonstrates significant potential, particularly also for other games such as chess. Adding unpredictability in various other AI applications, including LLMs, humanized robots, etc. could be a game changer particularly when it comes to making AI creative. Additionally, using a bRNG to generate cryptographic keys presents a promising avenue to bolster cybersecurity.

The Danger: This unpredictability poses risks, particularly in critical applications such as healthcare and finance, where reliability is essential. To balance these benefits and risks, unpredictability should be introduced in specific areas and in a controlled manner only. Although it is a necessary step in humanizing AI, it can be dangerous, as we might train AI to make mistakes, which might need to be covered up by an LLM creating lies.

6   Conclusion

In this research, we presented a novel bionic AI system that leverages the natural, unpredictable responses of a living fly to enhance the decision-making unpredictability of an AI agent in the game of Gobang. Traditional AI systems, despite their reliability and precision, often fall short in replicating the nuanced and sometimes erratic decision-making processes characteristic of humans. By integrating a fly's diverse reactions into the AI's decision-making process, we introduced a level of unpredictability that mimics human-like spontaneity. Our comparative study showcased that the bionic AI agent not only outperformed human players but also surpassed conventional AI agents and those enhanced with white-noise randomization. This suggests that incorporating biologically inspired randomness can significantly improve AI performance in tasks that benefit from unpredictability.

References

1. Braiek, H.B., Khomh, F.: Machine learning robustness: a primer. arXiv preprint arXiv:2404.00897 (2024)
2. Brown, J., et al.: Random-telegraph-noise-enabled true random number generator for hardware security. Sci. Rep. **10**(1), 17210 (2020)
3. Brundage, M., et al.: The malicious use of artificial intelligence: forecasting, prevention, and mitigation. arXiv preprint arXiv:1802.07228 (2018)
4. Chater, N., Zeitoun, H., Melkonyan, T.: The paradox of social interaction: shared intentionality, we-reasoning, and virtual bargaining. Psychol. Rev. **129**(3), 415 (2022)
5. Fu, M.C.: Alphago and monte carlo tree search: the simulation optimization perspective. In: 2016 Winter Simulation Conference (WSC), pp. 659–670. IEEE (2016)
6. Fuchs, T.: Human and artificial intelligence: a critical comparison. In: Intelligence-Theories and Applications, pp. 249–259. Springer (2022)
7. Gaviria Rojas, W.A., et al.: Solution-processed carbon nanotube true random number generator. Nano Lett. **17**(8), 4976–4981 (2017)
8. Greenblatt, R., Shlegeris, B., Sachan, K., Roger, F.: Ai control: improving safety despite intentional subversion. arXiv preprint arXiv:2312.06942 (2023)
9. Hinton, G.E., Srivastava, N., Krizhevsky, A., Sutskever, I., Salakhutdinov, R.R.: Improving neural networks by preventing co-adaptation of feature detectors. arXiv preprint arXiv:1207.0580 (2012)
10. Jiang, H., et al.: A novel true random number generator based on a stochastic diffusive memristor. Nat. Commun. **8**(1), 882 (2017)
11. Johnson, J.: Designing with the Mind in Mind: Simple Guide to Understanding User Interface Design Guidelines. Morgan Kaufmann, Burlington (2020)
12. Jones, N.: Ai now beats humans at basic tasks-new benchmarks are needed, says major report. Nature **628**(8009), 700–701 (2024)
13. Kasper-Eulaers, M., Hahn, N., Berger, S., Sebulonsen, T., Myrland, Ø., Kummervold, P.E.: Detecting heavy goods vehicles in rest areas in winter conditions using yolov5. Algorithms **14**(4), 114 (2021)
14. Katanforoosh, K., Kunin, D.: Initializing neural networks. DeepLearning. ai (2019)
15. Korteling, J.H., van de Boer-Visschedijk, G.C., Blankendaal, R.A., Boonekamp, R.C., Eikelboom, A.R.: Human-versus artificial intelligence. Front. Artif. Intell. **4**, 622364 (2021)
16. Kukreja, H., Bharath, N., Siddesh, C., Kuldeep, S.: An introduction to artificial neural network. Int. J. Adv. Res. Innov. Ideas Educ. **1**(5), 27–30 (2016)
17. Lebovitz, S., Levina, N., Lifshitz-Assaf, H.: Is AI ground truth really true? the dangers of training and evaluating AI tools based on experts' know-what. MIS Q. **45**(3) (2021)

18. Li, X., Zanotti, T., Wang, T., Zhu, K., Puglisi, F.M., Lanza, M.: Random telegraph noise in metal-oxide memristors for true random number generators: a materials study. Adv. Func. Mater. **31**(27), 2102172 (2021)
19. Manoonpong, P., et al.: Insect-inspired robots: bridging biological and artificial systems. Sensors **21**(22), 7609 (2021)
20. McCulloch, W.S., Pitts, W.: A logical calculus of the ideas immanent in nervous activity. Bull. Math. Biophys. **5**, 115–133 (1943)
21. Mishra, M., Srivastava, M.: A view of artificial neural network. In: 2014 International Conference on Advances in Engineering & Technology Research (ICAETR-2014), pp. 1–3. IEEE (2014)
22. Nestel, M.L.: Inside the biggest lottery scam ever. The Daily Beast (2015). https://www.thedailybeast.com/articles/2015/07/07/inside-the-biggest-lottery-scam-ever
23. Noll, L.C., Mende, R.G., Sisodiya, S.: Method for seeding a pseudo-random number generator with a cryptographic hash of a digitization of a chaotic system (1998). uS Patent 5,732,138
24. Oritsegbemi, O.: Human intelligence versus AI: implications for emotional aspects of human communication. J. Adv. Res. Soc. Sci. **6**(2), 76–85 (2023)
25. Ouyang, L., Wang, H.: Vehicle target detection in complex scenes based on yolov3 algorithm. In: IOP Conference Series: Materials Science and Engineering, vol. 569, p. 052018. IOP Publishing (2019)
26. Pan, X., You, Y., Wang, Z., Lu, C.: Virtual to real reinforcement learning for autonomous driving. arXiv preprint arXiv:1704.03952 (2017)
27. Phillips-Wren, G., Ichalkaranje, N.: Intelligent Decision Making: An AI-Based Approach, vol. 97. Springer, Heidelberg (2008)
28. Quinlan, J.R.: Learning decision tree classifiers. ACM Comput. Surv. (CSUR) **28**(1), 71–72 (1996)
29. Redmon, J., Divvala, S., Girshick, R., Farhadi, A.: You only look once: unified, real-time object detection. In: Proceedings of the IEEE Conference on Computer Vision and Pattern Recognition, pp. 779–788 (2016)
30. Romano, D., Donati, E., Benelli, G., Stefanini, C.: A review on animal-robot interaction: from bio-hybrid organisms to mixed societies. Biol. Cybern. **113**, 201–225 (2019)
31. Segovia-Cuéllar, A.: Revisiting the social origins of human morality: a constructivist perspective on the nature of moral sense-making. Topoi **41**(2), 313–325 (2022)
32. Song, Y.Y., Ying, L.: Decision tree methods: applications for classification and prediction. Shanghai Arch. Psychiatry **27**(2), 130 (2015)
33. Sutton, R.S., Barto, A.G.: Reinforcement Learning: An Introduction. MIT Press, Cambridge (2018)
34. Swaroop, S., Buçinca, Z., Gajos, K.Z., Doshi-Velez, F.: Accuracy-time tradeoffs in AI-assisted decision making under time pressure. In: Proceedings of the 29th International Conference on Intelligent User Interfaces, pp. 138–154 (2024)
35. Talati, D.: Ai (artificial intelligence) in daily life. Authorea Preprints (2024)
36. Thuan, D.: Evolution of yolo algorithm and yolov5: the state-of-the-art object detention algorithm (2021)
37. Urmson, C., et al.: Autonomous driving in urban environments: boss and the urban challenge. J. Field Robot. **25**(8), 425–466 (2008)
38. Wan, Y., et al.: A flexible and stretchable bionic true random number generator. Nano Res. **15**(5), 4448–4456 (2022)
39. Wang, X., Zhao, J.: An improved key agreement protocol based on chaos. Commun. Nonlinear Sci. Numer. Simul. **15**(12), 4052–4057 (2010)

40. Wen, C., et al.: Advanced data encryption using 2D materials. Adv. Mater. **33**(27), 2100185 (2021)

41. Yampolskiy, R.V.: Unpredictability of AI. AI and Ethics, pp. 1–19 (2019). https://arxiv.org/pdf/1905.13053

42. Zhou, R.: Gobang game with artificial intelligence in 900 lines !! (2015). https://github.com/142857why/gobang-python

Raising the Bar(Ometer): Identifying a User's Stair and Lift Usage Through Wearable Sensor Data Analysis

Hrishikesh Balkrishna Karande⊙,
Ravikiran Arasur Thippeswamy Shivalingappa⊙, Abdelhafid Nassim Yaici⊙,
Iman Haghbin⊙, Niravkumar Bavadiya⊙, Robin Burchard(✉)⊙,.
and Kristof Van Laerhoven⊙

University of Siegen, 57076 Siegen, Germany
robin.burchard@uni-siegen.de
https://ubicomp.eti.uni-siegen.de/

Abstract. Many users are confronted multiple times daily with the choice of whether to take the stairs or the elevator. Whereas taking the stairs could be beneficial for cardiovascular health and wellness, taking the elevator might be more convenient but it also consumes energy. By precisely tracking and boosting users' stairs and elevator usage through their wearable, users might gain health insights and motivation, encouraging a healthy lifestyle and lowering the risk of sedentary-related health problems. This research describes a new exploratory dataset, to examine the patterns and behaviors related to using stairs and lifts. We collected data from 20 participants while climbing and descending stairs and taking a lift in a variety of scenarios. The aim is to provide insights and demonstrate the practicality of using wearable sensor data for such a scenario. Our collected dataset was used to train and test a Random Forest machine learning model, and the results show that our method is highly accurate at classifying stair and lift operations with an accuracy of 87.61% and a multi-class weighted F1-score of 87.56% over 8-second time windows. Furthermore, we investigate the effect of various types of sensors and data attributes on the model's performance. Our findings show that combining inertial and pressure sensors yields a viable solution for real-time activity detection.

Keywords: Real-time activity recognition · Wearable inertial sensing · Barometric pressure sensing · Stairs and lift taking detection

1 Introduction

The proliferation of wearable technology in recent years has significantly transformed how we monitor and understand human physical activities. Wearable devices, equipped with a variety of sensors, have emerged as pivotal tools in numerous fields including health monitoring, fitness tracking, and medical diagnostics [10,14]. Activity recognition, a key application of wearable technology,

O. Konak et al. (Eds.): iWOAR 2024, LNCS 15357, pp. 220–239, 2025.
https://doi.org/10.1007/978-3-031-80856-2_14

involves the identification and classification of various physical actions performed by an individual, such as walking, running, sitting, or in our case more complex activities like climbing stairs or using an elevator [4,16].

Differentiating between activities such as stair climbing and lift use is especially important since each activity places different physiological and bio-mechanical demands on the body [12]. Stair climbing is a physically challenging activity that can yield useful information on cardiovascular health, lower body strength, and overall mobility. It is also connected with a high caloric expenditure, making it an important exercise to track in fitness and weight control settings [3,6]. In contrast, using an elevator indicates stationary behavior, emphasizing times of immobility that are critical to understanding overall activity patterns and such behavior [18].

The use of pressure sensors in wearable electronics provides a precise and effective approach for capturing the finer details of these actions. Pressure sensors detect differences in pressure at different positions or in various situations, providing extensive information on an individual's gait and posture [8]. For example, the pattern of pressure changes while ascending stairs differs significantly from the pressure change while standing still in an elevator. Using these sensors, we can improve the accuracy of activity recognition, allowing us to distinguish between the energy demands of stair climbing and the passive nature of the elevator use.

The ability to accurately recognize and differentiate various activities offers profound implications across multiple domains. In personalized healthcare, it enables tailored interventions and monitoring, enhancing treatment plans and preventive care [24]. Additionally, In the context of elderly care, detecting the specific activity of stair climbing versus elevator use becomes critical in ensuring safety. Many older adults are at a higher risk of falls when ascending or descending stairs, and timely detection of stair use can help caregivers monitor and prevent potential accidents or offer immediate assistance when needed [7]. In this way, monitoring specific activities can contribute to safer and more secure living environments for vulnerable populations. In the fitness industry, these technologies allow for more customized exercise plans and real-time feedback on performance, aiding in achieving personal fitness goals [20]. Furthermore, In workplace ergonomics and occupational health, recognizing whether employees are using stairs or elevators can assist in designing more efficient movement patterns within the workplace. Employers can encourage healthier habits such as stair climbing, which can reduce sedentary behavior, improve cardiovascular health, and enhance overall well-being among workers [9]. Additionally, analyzing activity patterns can help assess whether employees are adhering to ergonomic safety protocols, potentially reducing the risk of workplace injuries associated with improper movements or excessive inactivity.

Our dataset[1] and this paper's preliminary experiments offer several contributions:

---

[1] Both the code and data (raw and resampled form) for the project are publicly accessible on GitHub: https://github.com/iiMox/project_work_stairs_lift_detection.git.

- Introduction of a stairs and lift taking dataset: We present a dataset specifically dedicated to distinguishing between lift usage and stair climbing with multiple sensors and a high variability between participants.
- Characterization of barometric pressure sensor data: We provide a proof of concept for the application of pressure sensor data in activity recognition.
- Examination of Window Size for Time-Series Data: We investigate the impact of various window sizes on the pre-processing of time-series data.
- Feature Importance Analysis: We analyze the importance of different features, highlighting the critical role of pressure measurements in accurately classifying activities.

2   Related Technologies

2.1   Sensors

The field of activity recognition using wearable technology has seen significant advancements due to the integration of various sensor technologies and data analysis techniques [25]. In our study, we utilized accelerometer and barometer sensors to capture the necessary data for activity recognition. The accelerometer measures the acceleration forces acting on the device, providing detailed information about movement and orientation. The barometer, on the other hand, measures atmospheric pressure, which can be useful in detecting changes in elevation, such as when a person uses stairs or an elevator [15].

2.2   State of the Art and Limitations

The development and validation of activity recognition systems have heavily relied on various publicly available datasets. These datasets contain sensor data collected from wearable devices, which were placed on participant's bodies and recorded during different physical activities. The datasets are crucial for training and evaluating machine learning models. This section reviews some of the most commonly used datasets in the field that include stair usage, highlighting their contributions.

Among the prominent datasets, the UCI HAR [2] dataset includes activities such as "walking upstairs" and "walking downstairs" performed by participants wearing smartphones on their waists. Similarly, the PAMAP2 [17] dataset captures a range of activities including "ascending stairs" and "descending stairs" using multiple sensors placed on participants' bodies. The MHealth dataset [5] also includes "climbing stairs" along with other physical exercises. Table 1 lists some of the public activity recognition datasets that contain "stairs" as one of their activities. The table also includes information about the recorded sensors and the overall size of the datasets mentioned.

None of the datasets we examined that included stair usage involved the activity of taking lifts. Furthermore, to our knowledge, there are no datasets that specifically involve the activity of using lifts. There are also devices like "Fitbit" that can detect if you are taking the stairs [19], using sensors such as altimeters to measure elevation changes. However, these devices do not focus on differentiating between the usage of lifts and stairs specifically, and user reports [1, 21] indicate that they cannot reliably detect the difference between lifts and stairs.

In addition to these datasets, other related works pursue the same goal of promoting healthy living through wearable technology. For instance, Neves et al. [11] explore the use of wireless sensor networks to monitor health metrics and encourage healthier behaviors. Similarly, Ohtaki et al. [13] developed a system that automatically classifies ambulatory movements and estimates energy consumption using accelerometers and a barometer. Although these studies do not focus on differentiating between lift and stair usage, they contribute to the broader objective of using wearable devices and sensor technologies to enhance health by monitoring physical activity and energy expenditure, aligning closely with our study's focus on leveraging sensor technology for health promotion.

Our study, therefore, aims to fill this gap by providing extensive sensor data from participants specifically using lifts and stairs.

Our focus is on capturing the use of lifts and stairs, and not just having incidental usage. Our study, therefore, aims to fill this gap by providing extensive sensor data from a larger cohort of participants specifically using lifts and stairs. This level of detail and focus on lift versus stair usage is not comprehensively covered by existing datasets, making our publicly available dataset the first with this focus.

3 Data Collection and Analysis

A total of 20 participants were involved in the data collection process. These participants varied in age (26.0 ± 10.75), gender (10 male and 10 female), and physical fitness levels to ensure a diverse dataset that reflects different human movement patterns. Prior to participation, each individual signed a consent form, acknowledging their voluntary involvement and understanding of the experiment's procedures and objectives. Additionally, we submitted a detailed proposal to The Council for Ethics in Research (Ethics Council) of the University of Siegen, which reviewed and approved the study, allowing us to proceed with the experiment. The data was gathered using the Bangle.js 2 smartwatch, which is equipped with both accelerometer and barometer sensors. The accelerometer measures the acceleration forces acting on the device in three-dimensional space, while the barometer provides data on atmospheric pressure, which can be used to infer altitude changes.

3.1 Data-Collection Procedure

The experiment was conducted in a university building that comprises a total of eight floors that can be switched between by either flights of stairs or a set of elevators. This environment was chosen due to its accessibility and the availability of both stairs and elevators. To ensure variability and reduce systematic bias, we employed randomization in our experiment in several ways:

Table 1. State-of-the-art datasets that are related to activity recognition and contain going up or down the stairs as an activity. The datasets differ in the contained activities, numbers of participants, and sensors used, as well as in their sizes. Our newly created dataset is the only available dataset that includes taking the lift as an activity and uses a barometric pressure sensor.

Dataset	Activities	Stairs	Lift	Users	Sensors used	Dataset size
UCI HAR (Human Activity Recognition Using Smartphones) [2]	Walking, Walking Upstairs, Walking Downstairs, Sitting, Standing, Laying	Yes	No	30	Accelerometer, Gyroscope	10,299 Observations (Each 2.56 s)
PAMAP2 (Physical Activity Monitoring) [17]	18 total - basic, household, and exercise activities	Yes	No	9	Accelerometer, Gyroscope, Magnetometer, Heart Rate Monitoring	About 10 h (IMU data: 100 Hz Heart rate data: 9 Hz)
WISDM [22, 23]	18 total - ambulation-related activities, hand-based activities of daily living, and various eating activities	Yes	No	51	Accelerometer, Gyroscope	2754 min
MHealth [5]	12 total - Basic, Locomotion, and exercise activities	Yes	No	10	Accelerometer, Gyroscope, Magnetometer, Electrocardiogram (heart monitoring)	Not specified
Ours	Walking Upstairs, Walking Downstairs, Lift up, Lift down, Null	Yes	Yes	20	Accelerometer, Barometer	525.02 min (50 Hz)

- The next floor for each participant to visit was determined by a random number generator, ensuring an unpredictable sequence of floor visits. The floor from which the experiment would be started was also determined by the random number generator. Since the university building that we used has floors numbered from 2 (first accessible floor) to 8 (last accessible floor), our random number generator had been set to produce the lowest possible random number 2 and the highest possible random number 8.
- The choice between using the elevator or stairs for each transition was decided by a coin toss, ensuring an impartial probability of selecting either mode of movement.
- The participants were advised to act normal and try different variations of activities that they would ideally do while performing the movement of taking the stairs or taking the Lifts. Some participants chose to carry a handbag or a set of books with them, while others used their phones while taking the lifts or stairs. The participants were encouraged to do the experiment at their own pace and with their own choice of effort level. These variations of the different hand movements that the participants did while participating in the experiment were recorded using the accelerometer.

Each participant was instructed to wear the Bangle.js 2 smartwatch throughout the experiment. They were guided to move between floors based on the outcomes of the random number generator and the coin toss. The smartwatch continuously recorded accelerometer and barometer data during these activities at a frequency of 50 Hz. For each participant, the experiment was conducted over a period of approximately 30 min. Participants were given adequate breaks between movements to ensure they were not fatigued, which could affect the naturalness of their movements. The data collection sessions were scheduled to avoid peak hours in the building, minimizing external disruptions and ensuring safety.

Each participant was accompanied by four researchers, each one of these four were responsible for one of these tasks:

1. Video recording the participant's complete physique for the entire duration of the experiment.
2. Annotating the changes in the events that are taking place, classifying them into the 5 classes, and also noting down the time when this change took place.
3. Generating a random number to decide which floor to go to next.
4. Tossing the coin to decide whether to take the stairs or the lift to this floor.

During the data annotation phase, using the video recordings and based on the context data from the annotation data files, class labels were manually added to the sensor data CSV (Comma-Separated Values) files as ground truth for the experiment.

3.2 Activity Classes

The dataset was categorized into five distinct classes:

- **Null**: Periods in which none of the target activities was performed, includes idleness (such as sitting, standing still, walking, or pacing).
- **Lift Up**: Movement of participants using the elevator to ascend floors.
- **Lift Down**: Movement of participants using the elevator to descend floors.
- **Stairs Up**: Movement of participants using the stairs to ascend floors.
- **Stairs Down**: Movement of participants using the stairs to descend floors.

We gathered a total of 525 min (8:45 h) of data from the participants. The distribution of this data among the five classes can be seen in Fig. 1. The exact duration of each class in minutes is given in Appendix D Table 5 (Figs. 2, 3, 4 and 5).

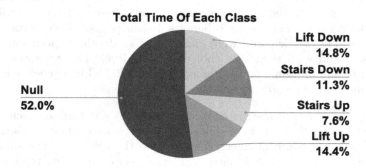

Fig. 1. The distribution of the activity classes contained in the recorded dataset. The Null class makes up 52 %, while the rest of the data consists of the four target classes (Lift Up, Lift Down, Stairs Up, Stairs Down).

3.3   Analysis

Sensor Data: The sensor data contains detailed information about the movement and pressure measurements taken at various time intervals. This data is evaluated to better comprehend movement patterns, acceleration variations, and possible activities or behaviors.

- Time: The timestamp indicating the time at which the data was recorded.
- Timestamp: A numerical representation of time, in milliseconds.
- X, Y, Z: Accelerometer data representing the acceleration along the X, Y, and Z axes, respectively.
- Magnitude: Magnitude of the acceleration vector.
- Pressure: Pressure data.
- Label: Ground truth label for the data. One of: Stairs Up, Stairs down, Lift up, Lift down &Null.

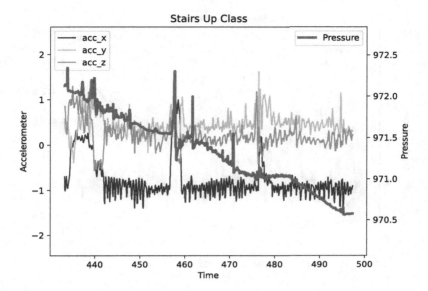

Fig. 2. Example accelerometer and barometer data for the 'Stairs Up' activity class. The accelerometer shows the typical patterns of walking. Meanwhile, the pressure steadily decreases, with short plateaus occurring on the stairway's landings. Additionally, the pressure sensor shows some spikes which are likely caused by the movement of the arm while walking.

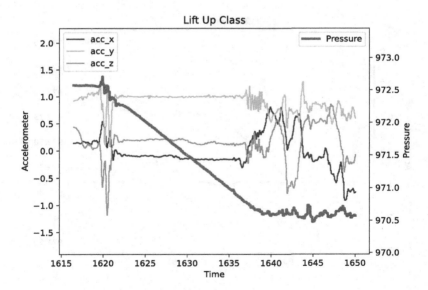

Fig. 3. Example accelerometer and barometer data for the 'Lift Up' activity class. While the lift is moving, the participant mostly stood still. We observe the pressure decreasing smoothly.

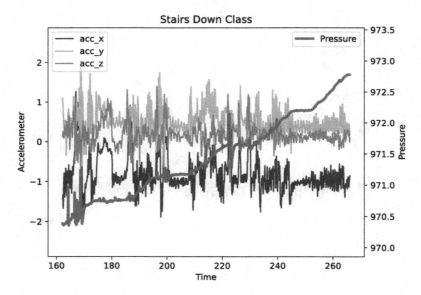

Fig. 4. Example accelerometer and barometer data for the 'Stairs Down' activity class. The accelerometer shows a lot of activity, with similar walking patterns as in 'Stairs Up'. In direct comparison, the magnitude and frequency of the movement sensors seem higher. The barometer detects the steadily rising pressure, also interrupted by short plateaus caused by the landings.

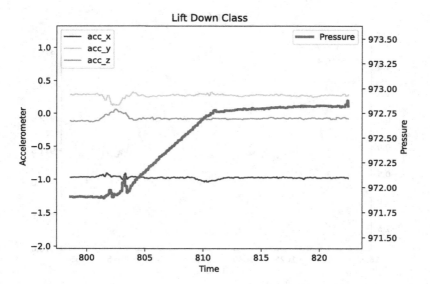

Fig. 5. Example accelerometer and barometer data for the 'Lift Down' activity class. The specific participant for this instance was standing very still during the descent. We can see the pressure increasing linearly and smoothly.

Annotation Data: The annotation data adds context to sensor data by designating specific time points as events or activities. This annotation can help segment or categorize sensor data based on various activities.

- Elapsedtime: The elapsed time since the start of the recording.
- Comment: Annotations or labels provided at specific time points, such as "Lift down", "Stairs up", etc.

During the initial study of the sensor data, it was discovered that the annotation for "Lift" occurrences was completely dependent on the user entering the lift. However, it became clear that this approach did not accurately represent the user's experience because the lift may remain stationary for an extended amount of time before moving. This difference resulted in an erroneous portrayal of lift utilization in the data.

To address this issue and ensure the lift data's accuracy, it was decided to manually annotate certain data points within the sensor data that corresponded to lift occurrences. This manual annotation entailed carefully studying the sensor data and determining the exact instant when the lift began moving.

4   Dataset Validation and Prediction Algorithm

When constructing a detection algorithm for evaluating sensor data, both the data separation method and the detection algorithm selection were carefully considered. To evaluate the collected dataset, a random forest classifier (from scikit-learn.ensemble libraries) has been chosen as the classification algorithm for this problem. Before feeding the raw data into the random forest classifier, we are pre-processing the data to extract features using sliding windows. We trained and evaluated the model on different window lengths of 4 and 8 s. For each of the windows, we are extracting 26 features from the data and the label is based on majority voting. During the window creation, windows are discarded if no label is assigned to at least 80% of the total number of observations within the window. We also discard windows that are too short or are missing data, e.g. at the end of a recording.

We use leave-one-participant-out cross-validation to get a subject-independent performance evaluation. In the prediction algorithm, the first step involves selecting a participant to serve as the test participant, while the remaining 19 participants are used for training the model. For these 19 participants, various features are computed as outlined in the data pre-processing stage. These features include statistical measures such as averages, minimums, maximums, variances, and standard deviations for accelerometer data (X, Y, Z), magnitude, and pressure, as well as additional metrics like range, slope, kurtosis, and skewness.

The class imbalance was addressed using the random oversampling technique, which duplicates randomly selected samples from the minority classes until all classes have the same number of samples. The *imblearn* library has been used to oversample the data with 'not majority' as the sampling strategy. This step is meant to prevent the model from being biased towards the majority class and to ensure it performs well across all classes. For this proof-of-concept study, we did not explore the use of undersampling or a combination of oversampling and undersampling. A more sophisticated sampling technique like SMOTE could improve our model's performance further, but was out of the scope of this work.

To optimize the random forest classifier's performance, a grid search was conducted to identify the best hyperparameters, specifically the depth of the trees (max_depth) and the number of trees in the forest (n_estimators). Grid search involves testing various combinations of these hyperparameters to find the combination that yields the highest performance, in our case based on 10-fold cross-validation results. We used 'GridSearchCV' from the scikit-learn library. With the optimal hyperparameters identified, the random forest model was trained using the 19 participants in each LOSO split's training data.

Finally, for each left-out participant, the trained Random Forest model was then used to make predictions and evaluate its performance. The model's performance was evaluated by calculating the accuracy of its predictions, which measures the proportion of correctly classified instances out of the total number of instances. Additionally, we report the F1-score in three modes of multiclass-averaging (Micro, Macro, Weighted).

To measure the impact of the addition of the pressure sensor to the data, we performed a small ablation study, repeating the same training and validation procedure, but without the pressure data. This enabled us to test the hypothesis, that pressure data contains viable information to detect stairs and lift usage, but also to distinguish between these two, as well as their directions (up or down).

5   Results and Discussion

We show the results of our machine learning experiments in Table 2. The results demonstrate significant performance improvements when the time-series data is pre-processed using an 8-second window for feature extraction compared to a 4-second window. The model's evaluation metrics, including accuracy and F1 scores, are notably higher with the 8-second window, reaching a macro F1 score of 0.86 (8 s) versus 0.76 (4 s). This substantial increase in accuracy highlights the importance of selecting an appropriate window size for pre-processing time-series data, as it can greatly enhance the classifier's ability to understand patterns and make accurate predictions.

When comparing the performance of a Random Forest model trained solely on acceleration data (IMU data) to one that incorporates both acceleration and pressure data, the results clearly show that the inclusion of pressure data significantly enhances the model's ability to accurately distinguish between stair use and lift. Without the barometric sensor, a macro F1-score of only 0.49 was reached. While acceleration data captures the dynamic movement patterns, pressure data can offer insights into altitude changes, such as those experienced when ascending or descending stairs. The altitude changes experienced when ascending or descending stairs are distinct from the relatively constant altitude changes during elevator use. For the evaluation metrics of each participant in both time-windows please refer to our GitHub repository.

Table 2. The model evaluation metrics averaged over all 20 participants for 8-second and 4-second time-window. The results are shown with and without the use of the recorded pressure data. The columns on the left show results when IMU and the pressure sensor were used, while the columns on the right show the results without the pressure data.

Sensors	IMU & Press.		IMU only	
Time-window	8 s	4 s	8 s	4 s
Accuracy	0.88	0.80	0.68	0.65
F1-Score (Micro-Avg)	0.88	0.80	0.68	0.65
F1-Score (Macro-Avg)	0.86	0.76	0.49	0.46
F1-Score (Weighted)	0.88	0.80	0.67	0.63

Evaluating F1 scores in micro, macro, and weighted modes offers a comprehensive understanding of the model's performance across different aspects of the data, especially when data is imbalanced. The macro F1 score is particularly informative in scenarios with class imbalance because it reveals the model's performance across each class individually. The weighted F1 score provides a balanced view that accounts for class imbalance while still reflecting the overall performance across all classes. The table of complete metrics for each participant in 8-second and 4-second time windows along with the best parameter values for max_depth and $n\_estimators$ hyperparameters while fitting random forest classifier can be found in Appendix B. 3 and C.4 respectively.

Figures 6 and Appendix A Fig. 7 present the confusion matrix of the model over an 8-second and a 4-second time window respectively. The confusion matrix offers a detailed breakdown of the model's performance by presenting the counts of true positives, true negatives, false positives, and false negatives for each class. In Fig. 6, we can observe that most prediction mistakes are related to the null class and that the classes related to taking stairs and taking the lift are rarely confounded.

In the feature importance analysis conducted across all 26 features for each of the 20 participants, it was observed that the feature "slope_pressure" consistently exhibited the highest importance score. This finding underscores the significance of pressure values in effectively distinguishing between the five distinct classes. The steepness or gradient of pressure changes, as represented by the slope feature, appears to be particularly informative in differentiating between activities involving changes in elevation, such as ascending or descending stairs and using lifts. The feature importance scores of all 26 features are presented in the Appendix E as Table 6.

Overall, the evaluation of the collected dataset with the explained methods shows that lift and stair usage can be distinguished and differentiated from the

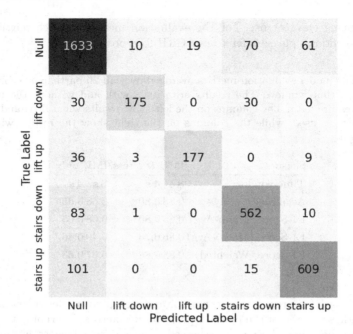

Fig. 6. Confusion Matrix for 8-second windows. Most predictions are correct (diagonal of the matrix). We observe that most mistakes revolve around the null class and that 'stairs' and 'lift' can be separated reliably by the model.

background class with a sufficiently high accuracy and F1 score, given the set of wearable sensors.

6   Conclusions

This paper presents the possibility of differentiating movement into five different classes with acceleration and pressure readings from a smartwatch. The feature importance score analysis depicts the importance of pressure measurement in this particular classification problem. Barometric measuring is a sensing modality seldom used in HAR. This work serves as a proof of concept, highlighting the potential of utilizing pressure data in activity recognition. The findings indicate that pressure-related features, particularly the slope of pressure changes, are highly informative for detecting and classifying different movement patterns related to altitude changes. This insight could pave the way for more advanced and accurate activity recognition systems, which have applications in various applications such as health monitoring, fitness tracking, and smart home environments.

Furthermore, the effectiveness of different window sizes for pre-processing time-series data in the context of activity recognition using a random forest classifier is also investigated. Our findings highlight once more the critical role of window size selection in enhancing model performance. This underscores the importance of capturing more comprehensive temporal information to better discriminate between activity classes.

We believe the main contributions of our dataset and this paper's experiments are relevant to the Activity Recognition community:

- A dataset dedicated specifically to taking lifts versus taking stairs detection was collected and annotated
- Our experiment serves as a proof of concept for the use of barometric air pressure data in Activity Recognition
- We have investigated especially the window size in such time-series data pre-processing
- We analyzed Feature Importance scores to investigate the impact of both sensors and features

7 Future Work and Enhancements

The dataset used in this study presents opportunities for further investigation, particularly in addressing imbalances among the five activity classes. Despite our efforts to collect data in an unbiased manner, the inherent variability in participants' activities has led to class imbalances. The lifts are faster than the stairs, which is one of the main reasons for the imbalance in data. In longer and real-world settings, the data is likely to be even more imbalanced. Future studies could explore strategies to mitigate this imbalance and to deal with it both during data collection and real-time inference.

Expanding the dataset size is another avenue for future research. Currently, data collection occurs within a single building, potentially limiting the generalizability of the model. By collecting data from diverse environments and settings, including outdoor and indoor scenarios, we can enhance the model's ability to generalize across different contexts. Additionally, increasing the dataset size by recruiting participants from various demographics and activity levels can enrich the diversity and representativeness of the dataset. With a larger dataset, implementing neural networks such as Long Short-Term Memory (LSTM) or transformer-based networks becomes feasible, allowing for the exploration of deep learning architectures capable of capturing even more complex temporal dependencies.

Furthermore, the definition of the Null class can be refined to incorporate a broader range of activities. While the null class primarily represents periods of inactivity, such as standing or sitting, future studies could consider including additional activities like cycling, jogging, or walking within this class. This expansion would provide a more comprehensive representation of daily activities, thereby improving the model's performance in real-world settings where activities may be more diverse and dynamic.

Acknowledgements. This project is funded by the Deutsche Forschungsgemeinschaft (DFG, German Research Foundation) - 425868829 and is part of Priority Program SPP2199 Scalable Interaction Paradigms for Pervasive Computing Environments.

Disclosure of Interests. The authors have no competing interests to declare that are relevant to the content of this article.

A   Confusion Matrix for 4-Seconds Time-Window

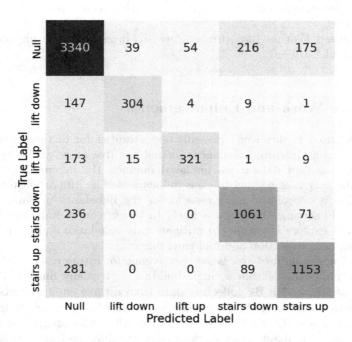

Fig. 7. Confusion Matrix for 4-second windows.

B   Evaluation Metrics for 20 Participants in 8-Seconds Time-Window

The following table presents evaluation metrics and also suitable hyperparameter values for random forest found by GridSearchCV for each participant in 8-second windows.

Table 3. The model evaluation metrics (Acc for Accuracy, Est.s for Estimators) for all 20 participants for 8-second time windows along with hyperparameter values.

No.	Acc.	macro F1	weighted F1	Depth	Est.s
1	0.84	0.83	0.84	None	200
2	0.85	0.82	0.85	None	250
3	0.90	0.89	0.90	None	250
4	0.82	0.81	0.83	15	275
5	0.96	0.94	0.96	15	250
6	0.87	0.86	0.87	20	200
7	0.81	0.79	0.81	15	225
8	0.89	0.80	0.88	20	200
9	0.90	0.87	0.90	None	275
10	0.91	0.85	0.90	20	250
11	0.92	0.91	0.92	None	300
12	0.90	0.90	0.90	20	200
13	0.87	0.87	0.86	20	300
14	0.89	0.88	0.89	None	250
15	0.87	0.87	0.87	15	350
16	0.88	0.89	0.88	None	300
17	0.86	0.82	0.86	None	300
18	0.88	0.89	0.88	20	300
19	0.86	0.79	0.86	20	275
20	0.85	0.84	0.85	20	225

C   Evaluation Metrics for 20 Participants in 4-Seconds Time-Window

The following table presents evaluation metrics and also suitable hyperparameter values for random forest found by GridSearchCV for each participant in 4-second windows.

Table 4. The model evaluation metrics (Acc for Accuracy, Est.s for Estimators) for all 20 participants for 4-second time windows along with hyperparameter values.

No.	Acc.	macro F1	weighted F1	Depth	Est.s
1	0.77	0.72	0.77	None	350
2	0.81	0.75	0.80	None	350
3	0.81	0.76	0.81	None	250
4	0.77	0.73	0.78	None	225
5	0.78	0.73	0.78	None	200
6	0.79	0.76	0.79	None	200
7	0.75	0.72	0.76	None	250
8	0.78	0.75	0.77	None	350
9	0.85	0.80	0.84	None	250
10	0.84	0.70	0.83	None	350
11	0.87	0.70	0.83	None	350
11	0.87	0.87	0.87	None	325
12	0.80	0.78	0.80	None	325
13	0.80	0.74	0.79	None	250
14	0.80	0.72	0.80	None	325
15	0.83	0.82	0.83	None	275
16	0.81	0.79	0.81	None	300
17	0.79	0.74	0.79	None	225
18	0.77	0.77	0.77	None	275
19	0.83	0.78	0.83	None	275
20	0.77	0.73	0.76	None	200

D   Total Time Duration for Each Class in Minutes

Table 5. Duration of data collected for each class in minutes

class	Minutes
Lift Down	77.60
Stairs Down	59.20
Stairs Up	39.88
Lift Up	75.36
Null	272.98

In total 152.95 min of data was collected for the lift classes and 99.08 min of data was collected for the stairs classes.

E   Feature-Scores for 26 Features Averaged over 20 Participants in 8-Seconds and 4-Seconds Time-Window

Table 6. Feature scores for all features extracted over 8-seconds and 4-seconds window

Feature	8-s	4-s
slope_pressure	0.313075423	0.24633301
var_magnitude	0.084037245	0.079129592
std_magnitude	0.082081804	0.072645593
max_magnitude	0.045221187	0.051749068
std_pressure	0.043930271	0.030623624
var_pressure	0.043276678	0.031141125
min_magnitude	0.036980905	0.032534554
kurtosis_pressure	0.036261681	0.029589955
min_accX	0.027751388	0.028021951
range_pressure	0.02538081	0.025415817
std_accX	0.023843761	0.034228149
var_accX	0.023416437	0.036206354
std_accZ	0.020009935	0.02788877
var_accZ	0.018040161	0.026410733
avg_accX	0.016969519	0.02231106
max_accX	0.016947775	0.022569319
avg_magnitude	0.0169168	0.027153292
skew_pressure	0.015893485	0.019383114
min_accZ	0.015800581	0.020498954
max_accY	0.015392096	0.020042188
std_accY	0.014100437	0.021778705
var_accY	0.01405132	0.021217197
avg_accZ	0.013379868	0.019155533
min_accY	0.013372234	0.017988043
avg_accY	0.012822567	0.017824296
max_accZ	0.011045632	0.018160005

References

1. Jovin, I.: Fitbit floors climbed not accurate? here's what to do. (2019). https://gadgetsandwearables.com/2019/07/28/fitbit-floor-count-too-high/. Accessed 26 June 2024
2. Anguita, D., Ghio, A., Oneto, L., Parra, X., Reyes-Ortiz, J.L., et al.: A public domain dataset for human activity recognition using smartphones. In: Esann, vol. 3, p. 3 (2013)

3. Atlas: Cardiovascular benefits of stair climbing: Fitness explained. https://atlasbars.com/blogs/fitness-explained/cardiovascular-benefits-of-stair-climbing-fitness-explained. Accessed 26 June 2024

4. Attal, F., Mohammed, S., Dedabrishvili, M., Chamroukhi, F., Oukhellou, L., Amirat, Y.: Physical human activity recognition using wearable sensors. Sensors **15**(12), 31314–31338 (2015)

5. Banos, O., et al.: mHealthDroid: a novel framework for agile development of mobile health applications. In: Pecchia, L., Chen, L.L., Nugent, C., Bravo, J. (eds.) IWAAL 2014. LNCS, vol. 8868, pp. 91–98. Springer, Cham (2014). https://doi.org/10.1007/978-3-319-13105-4_14

6. Captain calculator: Calories burned on stairs | calculator & formula (2020). https://captaincalculator.com/health/calorie/calories-burned-stairs-calculator/. Accessed 26 June 2024

7. Delahoz, Y.S., Labrador, M.A.: Survey on fall detection and fall prevention using wearable and external sensors. Sensors **14**(10), 19806–19842 (2014)

8. Kim, Y., Oh, J.H.: Recent progress in pressure sensors for wearable electronics: from design to applications. Appl. Sci. **10**(18), 6403 (2020)

9. Kritzler, M., Bäckman, M., Tenfält, A., Michahelles, F.: Wearable technology as a solution for workplace safety. In: Proceedings of the 14th International Conference on Mobile and Ubiquitous Multimedia, pp. 213–217 (2015)

10. Mattmann, C., Amft, O., Harms, H., Troster, G., Clemens, F.: Recognizing upper body postures using textile strain sensors. In: 2007 11th IEEE International Symposium on Wearable Computers, pp. 29–36. IEEE (2007)

11. Neves, P., Stachyra, M., Rodrigues, J.: Application of wireless sensor networks to healthcare promotion. J. Commun. Softw. Syst. **4**(3), 181–190 (2008)

12. Blackmer, N.: Here's how many stairs you should climb a day for a healthy heart (2023), https://www.verywellhealth.com/daily-stairs-for-a-healthy-heart-8349369. Accessed 26 June 2024

13. Ohtaki, Y., Susumago, M., Suzuki, A., Sagawa, K., Nagatomi, R., Inooka, H.: Automatic classification of ambulatory movements and evaluation of energy consumptions utilizing accelerometers and a barometer. Microsyst. Technol. **11**, 1034–1040 (2005)

14. Patel, S., Park, H., Bonato, P., Chan, L., Rodgers, M.: A review of wearable sensors and systems with application in rehabilitation. J. Neuroeng. Rehabil. **9**, 1–17 (2012)

15. Ramasamy Ramamurthy, S., Roy, N.: Recent trends in machine learning for human activity recognition-a survey. Wiley Interdisc. Rev. Data Mining Knowl. Discov. **8**(4), e1254 (2018)

16. Randell, C., Muller, H.: Context awareness by analysing accelerometer data. In: Digest of Papers. Fourth International Symposium on Wearable Computers, pp. 175–176. IEEE (2000)

17. Reiss, A., Stricker, D.: Introducing a new benchmarked dataset for activity monitoring. In: 2012 16th International Symposium on Wearable Computers, pp. 108–109 (2012). https://doi.org/10.1109/ISWC.2012.13

18. Rozalynn S. Frazier, C.P.T.: Do you have a sedentary lifestyle? Here are 8 signs and solutions (2024). https://www.realsimple.com/health/fitness-exercise/sedentary-lifestyle-signs. Accessed 26 June 2024

19. TheTechyLife: Which fitbits count stairs (2024). https://thetechylife.com/which-fitbits-count-stairs/. Accessed 20 June 2024

20. Thompson, W.R.: Worldwide survey of fitness trends for 2020. ACSM's Health Fitness J. **23**(6), 10–18 (2019)

21. Nielson, T.: [fix] fitbit not counting floors climbed or tracking incorrectly (2023). https://wearholic.com/fitbit-not-counting-floors/. Accessed 26 June 2024

22. Weiss, G.: Wisdm smartphone and smartwatch activity and biometrics dataset data set. UCI Machine Learning Repository (2019). https://archive.ics. uci. edu/ml/datasets/WISDM+ Smartphone+ and+ Smartwatch+ Activity+ and+ Biometrics+ Dataset+. Accessed 18 May 2022

23. Weiss, G.: WISDM Smartphone and Smartwatch Activity and Biometrics Dataset. UCI Machine Learning Repository (2019)

24. Wu, M., Luo, J.: Wearable technology applications in healthcare: a literature review. Online J. Nurs. Inform **23**(3) (2019)

25. Zhang, S., et al.: Deep learning in human activity recognition with wearable sensors: a review on advances. Sensors **22**(4), 1476 (2022)

Similarities of Motion Patterns in Skateboarding and Hydrofoil Pumping

Michael Zöllner$^{(\boxtimes)}$ (ID), Moritz Krause (ID), and Jan Gemeinhardt (ID)

Institute for Information Systems, Hof University, 95028 Hof, Germany
michael.zoellner@hof-university.de

Abstract. Like skateboarding acceleration in surfing on a hydrofoil with muscle power is achieved by a constant sinusoidal motion. Both are challenging sports to begin with because learning the complex up and down movements takes time, skill and reflexion. The interplay of rotating joints and applying forces at the right time is hard to perceive, understand and to transfer into muscle memory.

Since the motions in skateboarding on pump tracks and hydrofoil pumping are similar, we are comparing both motion sequences with inertial measurement units and 3D pose estimation. We postulate that learning the physically challenging and expensive hydrofoil pumping can be improved and accelerated by training with skateboards. Therefore, we are capturing forces with inertial measurement units and validate them with 3D pose estimation. Finally, we are comparing and visualizing the motions and forces of the boards and the skeleton to show the similarities within the y- and z-momentum.

Keywords: Machine Learning · Data Visualization · Pose Estimation · Interactive Systems

1 Introduction

Hydrofoil pumping is a rather new sport with its first commercial boards being made after Mango Carafino developed the first hydrofoil surfboard in 1999 [7]. Since then, the sport sparked the interest of surfers and athletes around the world, who had no access to surfable shores, beaches or rivers. Despite the low requirement - an open water area, that's deep enough for the mast to fit - the technical entry barrier is quite harsh: Successfully riding a hydrofoil surfboard and staying afloat requires decent experience, a certain amount of technical skill and some sort of sense or understanding of the board's physical behavior. In our previous research [12] we noticed a similarity between the motion sequences of hydrofoil pumping and skateboarding. With our research we want to empower athletes and those to gain a better understanding of the board and accelerate their training progress.

At the current stage of our research, we are further comparing the motion sequences of these sports to gain insight on how to elevate the training experience of learning how to foil pump.

O. Konak et al. (Eds.): iWOAR 2024, LNCS 15357, pp. 240–248, 2025.
https://doi.org/10.1007/978-3-031-80856-2_15

2 Related Work

2.1 Hardware Sensors

There is a range of small and integrated systems with 32-bit microcontrollers and sensors available with onboard machine learning functions like the BHI260AP [11]. The Arduino Nicla Sense ME [2], that we are using in our project, features a BHI260AP self-learning AI sensor with integrated IMU, a BME688 environmental sensor, a BMP390 pressure sensor and a BMM150 magnetometer. On the cheaper Adafruit Feather nRF52840 Sense we find an LSM6DS3TR-C accelerometer/gyroscope, an LIS3MDL magnetometer and a BMP280 temperature and barometric pressure sensor next to other sensors. Both micro-controllers can be programmed with the widely used open-source Arduino C++ in its own development environment with a very large community and libraries.

Unlike the mentioned development boards MBIENTLAB MetaMotionS [14] is a ready to use product with a gyroscope, accelerometer, magnetometer, barometric pressure sensor communicating like the forementioned devices via BluetoothLE.

We also worked with integrated solutions like Apple Watch and Google Pixel Watch but did not include the data at this time. Apple's latest Watch features several sensors like optical/electrical heart sensor, temperature sensor, blood oxygen sensor, GPS, compass, accelerometer and gyro sensor.

For our applications the Arduino Nicla Sense ME is currently one of the best solutions. With only $22 \times 22 \times 4$ mm, the development board fits under a skateboard truck and on a foil mount under a surfboard.

2.2 3D Pose Estimation

Machine learning based 3D pose estimation approaches eliminated the need for special hardware like time-of-flight cameras in favor of standard cameras. Carnegie Mellon University's OpenPose [4] is a robust solution for 2D and 3D skeleton reconstruction delivering 3D skeleton data in the BODY_25 pose topology. MeTRAbs Absolute 3D Human Pose Estimator [10] is also featuring 2D and 3D position data of the skeletons' joints in the SMPL-24 topology. As part of the Mediapipe framework BlazePose [3] (currently transitioning to Gemini branding) delivers 33 3D landmarks in the COCO [9] topology superset GHUM3D and also a background segmentation mask.

In our prior research [13] we evaluated these human pose estimation solutions in different sports situations. We found that OpenPose and MeTRAbs performed best regarding accuracy recognizing close and far bodies and correct approximation of hidden body parts. BlazePose unfortunately only works accurately on bodies closer than 4 m. In our experiment we were using MeTRAbs since the OpenPose model repository is not existent anymore.

2.3 Skateboarding

Physics of skateboarding are well documented since the 1970s. In an early publication Hubbard et al. [6] where analyzing the skateboard and rider parameters and described them with stability criteria in experimental validations. Kuleshov [8] constructed a mathematical model of the skateboard, describing the motion of the rider on a skateboard.

Several publications are describing on the detection and classification of skateboard tricks. There are algorithm-based approaches using IMU-sensors [5] and more recent machine learning-based classifications [1].

2.4 Hydrofoil Pumping

The history of hydrofoil surfing since the 1960s and the popular mechanic principles are well summarized by Red Bull [7] in an article about hydrofoil surfing. In a recent publication Kirill Rozhdestvensky [9] describes a simplified mathematical model of a pumped hydrofoil surfboard elevated above water. An in-depth description of the physics of a surf foil by analyzing the physical concepts behind hydrofoils using the principles of aircraft design and aerodynamic wing theory was published by Robin Chahal et al. [4].

3   Experiment Setup

3.1   Skateboard Track Facility

For collecting the skateboard data, we choose a skate park close by featuring a concrete pump track ideal for our measurement. The pump track consists of a drop in to gain speed to start the run, then two waves and a quarter at the right end (Fig. 1). Since the skate park is new the quality of our measurements benefits from the smooth concrete surfaces.

The skateboarder starts on the left side of the track. He drops in, stretches his legs and gains speed while moving downwards to the right. Climbing the first wave he loses speed while catching the momentum by bending the knees. This sequence repeats on the second wave and until the turn/exit on the end of the track.

We are using a skateboard with a standard popsicle shaped deck, trucks and soft wheels to dampen uneven ground and thus minimizing noise in the measurements.

3.2   Hydrofoil Facility

As stated previously, the only requirement of hydrofoil pumping regarding the location is water with a decent scale to ride and enough depth to not hit the ground with the mast and foil. We choose a natural public pool without any other visitors, which featured a footbridge at the edge of the pool for a good starting position.

The surfer starts on the footbridge, jumps on the board and begins with up and down body movements to create a forward momentum with the foil under water (see Fig. 2). He surfs a linear path while he is recorded and measured. Unlike in the skateboard setup the surfer on the hydrofoil has no terrain but must create the uniform sinusoidal path himself. Uneven curves, stalls or collisions with the water surface are interfering with the quality of the forward momentum.

We are using a short (4'0) foil surfboard with a 75 cm long mast and a wide carbon hydrofoil wing. Unlike in other hydrofoil sports in muscle based pumping a wide wing with a large surface is needed.

Fig. 1. A skater riding the concrete pump track.

Fig. 2. A hydrofoil surfer "pumping" on a lake.

3.3 Hardware

In our setup we are using two different sensing devices for motion data acquisition: One Arduino Nicla Sense ME and one Apple Watch Series 9, which was only used for background data validation in this paper at this time. The Apple Watch is worn by the athlete on the back foot's ankle facing inside. To ensure watertight and firm positioning of the microcontroller to the boards we designed and 3D-printed one universal case and two different mounts – one for hydrofoil boards' mast box (see Fig. 3) and one for skateboards in front of the back truck (see Fig. 4). For both boards the microcontroller is placed at the bottom directly under the athletes back foot when standing on the board, to minimize angular offsets in the data.

The microcontroller runs custom Arduino code logging the sensor data connected via BLE. For field recordings we are using an off the shelf Android smartphone which connects to the controller via WebBLE in a web-browser to trigger start, stop as well to receive the data. We captured the data of the sensors with different intervals of 20 and 60 Hz during several takes.

To better compare, validate and understand the motion sequences we additionally capture the skateboard runs with a GoPro Hero 5 Black at 1920 × 1080-pixel resolution and 60 frames per second and the hydrofoil runs with a DJI Mini 3 Pro at 2688 × 1512-pixel resolution and 60 frames per second.

Fig. 3. Arduino Nicla Sense ME mounted to the bottom of the hydrofoil board.

3.4 Pose Estimation

To get an even better understanding of the recorded datasets and for validation of the data points we then analyzed the recorded videos with the MeTRAbs pose estimation model. The skeleton data we received from the algorithm could then be combined with the sensory data to visualize the athletes' movements and corresponding forces (see Fig. 5). The visualization shows the forward momentum (red arrows) and the skeleton joints of the front hip, knee and ankle (grey lines and circles) on top of a rotoscope image of the video. The relation and angle of hip, knee and ankle represent the pushing movement with the up and down motion of the skater's body.

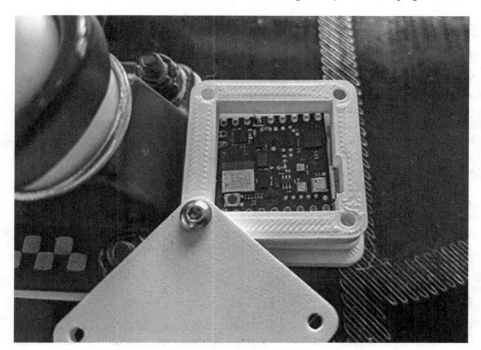

Fig. 4. Arduino Nicla Sense ME mounted to the bottom of the skateboard.

Fig. 5. Visualization of the captured data combined with the pose estimation data. (Color figure online)

4 Results and Interpretation

4.1 Data Quality Optimization

When we started to evaluate the recorded data, we noticed noise in the skateboard data which turned out to be originating from the different riding surface although we were using soft wheels to dampen the noise from the surface. Small gaps in the concrete and little stones created acceleration peaks. The unevenness of the concrete can be observed on the skateboard IMU data (see Fig. 6). In the hydrofoil board recordings are very smooth without noise, as the flow through the water only creates minor noise from the vibrations of the hydrofoil wing and mast which are also audible.

To compensate this issue and further refine data and the later plotted graphs, we applied a standard Kalman Filter algorithm with the process noise variable R at 0.01 and the measurement noise variable Q at 3 to the datasets. The resulting data exposes the sinusoidal motions. The noticeable difference in amplitude is resulting from the track dimensions for skateboarding and from the mast height and overall size of the hydrofoil board.

4.2 Visual Interpretation

In the following graph plots we would like to substantiate our thesis of the similarity in the motion patterns of skateboarding on pump tracks and hydrofoil surfing and the outlook of using it for training purposes. The graphs are displaying the filtered (foreground) and unfiltered accelerometer data. Color codes are distinguishing the axes of the accelerometer. The y axis of the graph displays the force measured in G. On the x axis the time of the take is visible in milliseconds from start.

The first graph (see Fig. 6) is displaying the accelerometer data of one skateboard run on the described track. Most relevant for our thesis are the Y values of the accelerometer representing the forward momentum of the skateboard and the Z value representing the height position on the skateboard track.

We are observing a strong acceleration at the start and a clear downward movement followed by a slowdown while climbing the first wave repeating over the track. The length of the wave and the amplitude corresponds to the concrete structure of the pump track.

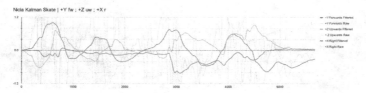

Fig. 6. Arduino Nicla Sense ME data of one skateboard run.

Figure 7 represents the motion patterns of the hydrofoil surfer on the lake. We are observing a similar sinusoidal pattern with a noticeable shorter wavelength and lower amplitude due to the physical characteristics of the foil mast and wing. The Z values are clearly displaying the motion path. The Y values representing the forward momentum are constituting the slower speed.

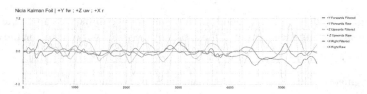

Fig. 7. Arduino Nicla Sense ME data of one hydrofoil board run.

In order to further compare the motion patterns, we combined in Fig. 8 the forward momentum and in Fig. 9 the vertical acceleration of the two sports. A clearer picture emerges and illustrates the similar patterns. Although there is noticeable a difference in wavelength and amplitude the sinusoidal patterns for generating forward momentum are clearly visible.

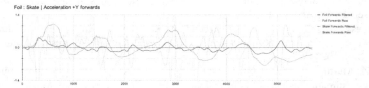

Fig. 8. Comparison of forward acceleration data of hydrofoil and skateboard. Positive equals forward acceleration.

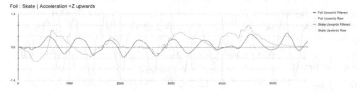

Fig. 9. Comparison of vertical acceleration data of hydrofoil and skateboard. Positive equals upwards acceleration.

5   Conclusion and Future Work

We recorded the acceleration forces of a skateboard in a concrete pump track and a hydrofoil surfboard in a lake and compared the resulting filtered data in combined graphs. Our theory of the similarity of the motion patterns of both sports and the emerging momentum is proven in the visualizations although differences in wavelength and amplitude.

In our next steps we will combine the acceleration data with the pose estimation data not only for visual validation but to automatically extend the observation on the motion of the bodies of the athletes. We will validate the data with additional sensors of smart watches on ankles and wrists. Our goal is to create complete models of the motion patterns.

With these models and embedded motion patterns we think we can create a watch application supporting the learning of the sports by drawing the attention on the different motions.

Acknowledgments. This work was partially supported by the European Regional Development Fund (EFRE) in cooperation with Blackriver GmbH supporting hardware and knowledge in the two sports.

References

1. Abdullah, M.A., Ibrahim, M.A.R., Shapiee, M.N.A.B., Mohd Razman, M.A., Musa, R.M., Abdul Majeed, A.P.P.: The classification of skateboarding trick manoeuvres through the integration of IMU and machine learning. Intell. Manuf. Mechatron. 67–74 (2020)
2. Arduino Nicla Sense ME. https://www.bosch-sensortec.com/software-tools/tools/arduino-nicla-sense-me/. Accessed 13 Mar 2024
3. Bazarevsky, V., Grishchenko, I., Raveendran, K., Zhu, T., Zhang, F., Grundmann, M.: BlazePose: On-device Real-time Body Pose tracking (2020). arXiv. https://doi.org/10.48550/arXiv.2006.10204
4. Cao, Z., Martinez, G.H., Simon, T., Wei, S., Sheikh, Y.A.: OpenPose: realtime multi-person 2D pose estimation using part affinity fields. IEEE Trans. Pattern Anal. Mach. Intell. (2019)
5. Groh, B.H., Kautz, T., Schuldhaus, D., Eskofier, B.M.: IMU-based trick classification in skateboarding. In: KDD Workshop on Large-Scale Sports Analytics (2015)
6. Hubbard, M.: Lateral dynamics and stability of the skateboard (1979)
7. Hydrofoil Surfing: The ultimate beginner's guide to getting started (2023). https://www.red bull.com/au-en/beginners-guide-to-hydrofoil-surfing. Accessed 20 Mar 2024
8. Kuleshov, A.S.: Mathematical model of the skateboard. In: ISBS-Conference Proceedings Archive (2006)
9. Rozhdestvensky, K.: A simplified mathematical model of pumped hydrofoils. J. Mar. Sci. Eng. **11**(5), 913 (2023). https://doi.org/10.3390/jmse11050913
10. Sárándi, I., Linder, T., Arras, K.O., Leibe, B.: MeTRAbs: metric-scale truncation-robust heatmaps for absolute 3D human pose estimation. IEEE Trans. Biometrics Behav. Identity Sci. **3**(1), 16–30 (2021). https://doi.org/10.1109/TBIOM.2020.3037257
11. Smart sensor BHI260AP. https://www.bosch-sensortec.com/products/smart-sensors/bhi 260ap/. Accessed 25 Mar 2023
12. Zöllner, M., Krause, M., Gemeinhardt, J.: Explaining sinusoidal oscillating motion of hydrofoil pumping by fusion of machine learning based human pose estimation and smart sensors. In: Integrating Machine Learning with Physics-based Modelling of Physiological Systems (2021)
13. Zöllner, M., Krause, M., Gemeinhardt, J., Döllinger, M., Kniesburges, S.: Preliminary studies and prototypes for machine learning based evaluation of surfers' performance on river waves. In: HCII 2023 - Late Breaking Work, Copenhagen (2023)
14. MetaMotionS – MBIENTLAB

Short Papers: Emerging Topics in Sensor-Based Systems

SurfSole: Demonstrating Real-Time Surface Identification via Capacitive Sensing with Neural Networks

Patrick Willnow[1], Max Sternitzke[1], Ruben Schlonsak[1,2(✉)],
Marco Gabrecht[1,2(✉)], and Denys J. C. Matthies[1,2(✉)]

[1] Technical University of Applied Sciences Lübeck, Lübeck, Germany
ruben.schlonsak@th-luebeck.de, denys.matthies@th-luebeck.demand
[2] Fraunhofer IMTE Lübeck, Lübeck, Germany

Abstract. In this paper we present SurfSole, an untethered mobile system combining a smart sole prototype and mobile app to achieve real-time surface identification. We solely rely on the technology of capacitive sensing while choosing a neural network approach for classification. We evaluated different machine learning models with different layer architectures of 3–4 layers with 32, 64, 128, and 256 filters. The theoretical overall accuracy reaches from 74.85% up to 87.11%. While we retrieve data with 40 Hz with a single window of 120 data points, we have a real-time detection delay of 3 s.

Keywords: Artificial Intelligence · Surface Detection · Neural Networks · CNN · Capacitive Sensing · Real-Time · Smart Insole

1 Introduction

Technological advancements are continuously transforming our daily lives, with wearable technology emerging as a crucial area of innovation. Current wearable technologies, such as smart insoles, also but slowly emerge. Currently, the primarily function of smart insoles is measuring pressure distribution for gait analysis, including a multitude of sensors, such as force-sensitive resistors [15], capacitive sensors [14], piezos [6], and other [7]. While these insoles are often in the stage of prototypes, they usually lack the capability to accurately identify the user's context, such as understanding the different surface types one is walking on. This may be a crucial information, while it can infer on the dynamic outdoor environment and the runner's energy expenditure. While there is a variety of sensors deployed with insoles, capacitive/electric field sensors [11], known for their sensitivity and versatility, offer a potential solution for this challenge by detecting subtle changes in capacitance caused by different surfaces.

Modern capacitive pressure sensors often utilize materials like polydimethylsiloxane (PDMS) and thermoplastic polyurethane (TPU) as dielectric layers

O. Konak et al. (Eds.): iWOAR 2024, LNCS 15357, pp. 251–259, 2025.
https://doi.org/10.1007/978-3-031-80856-2_16

Fig. 1. Demonstrating SurfSole: The insole prototype, consisting of 6 copper electrodes, and a small box of electronics is worn on the right foot, while our mobile app "Surf-Tastic", running on an Android Smartphone detects the current terrain surface one is walking or running on.

[19]. These materials provide the necessary flexibility and durability for wearable applications [24]. Advanced insoles incorporate arrays of capacitive sensors to capture detailed pressure distribution across the foot, allowing for high-resolution mapping of plantar pressure [17,22]. This is crucial for applications in gait analysis and posture correction [17,18]. Capacitive sensors are often integrated together with accelerometers and gyroscopes to provide comprehensive data on gait and movement, enhancing measurement accuracy and reliability [16]. Real-time feedback on plantar pressure is important for the wearer as it can invoke a direct behavior change, such as helping to correct posture and improving balance, benefiting athletes and individuals undergoing rehabilitation [20]. The most related works are "PneuShoe" [7] and "CapSoles" [14], mobile shoe/insole-based systems that enable surface detection using conventional machine learning and enabling the distinction between sand, lawn, paving stone, carpet, linoleum, and tartan.

This paper presents SurfSole, a prototype system that consists of a redesigned insole capable of collecting capacitive data from various surfaces during walking or running. The collected data is processed using a Convolutional Neural Network (CNN) to classify the terrain type in real-time. The key contributions of this work include:

- Development of a slim and lightweight insole integrated with capacitive sensors and a compact controller for seamless data collection,
- Implementation of a data collection protocol using a mobile application,
- Design of a CNN model capable of distinguishing between multiple surface types with high accuracy,
- and the integration of the model into a mobile application, providing real-time feedback on the terrain type one is walking and running on.

2 Implementation

The prototype consists of several hardware components, including the insole, controller & PCB, and housing & more. Moreover, a software was developed, which consisted of several distributed parts, running on the microcontroller, server, and on an android app (Fig. 2).

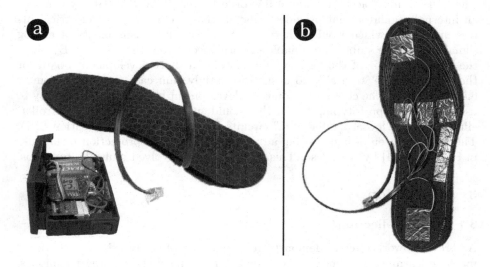

Fig. 2. a) Prototype with opened case, b) Opened insole displaying the copper electrodes.

2.1 Insole

We evaluated several materials for the insole as a basis. The soft insoles from Budni drugstore [4] satisfied our needs. We implemented a total of six copper patches to the bottom side of the insole with double-sided tape. The copper patches [3] are originally used for snail protection in gardening but do just fine as capacitive sensing. Six electrodes resulted in 6 wires, which we integrated into a 6-pin cable with an RJ12 connector, which is an easy attachment to the case.

2.2 Controller and Circuit Board

Our printed circuit board (PCB) was designed to accommodate the pin layout from the ESP32 microcontroller board. The ESP32 conveniently incorporates a Bluetooth LE module, enabling a connection to the smartphone. Since the prototyping breakout board, which matches the development board, has interconnected sides, the circuit had to be designed extremely carefully, using isolated bridges for some connections to avoid short circuits. Our custom OCB utilizes both sides due to the unavailability of a single ground port. The placement of the PCB is in close proximity to the controller, to ensure relatively high integration density. The bulkiest part however, is the 9 V battery.

2.3   Housing and More

The housing must accommodate a 9 V LiPo battery. This 9 V battery contains an internal regulator that provides a flat discharge curve against electrical jitters and noise, which would otherwise be present in measurements of analog signals, to ensure stable and reliable performance during the analysis. By using the compact shape of the battery and choosing a short development board for the controller, we were able to design a relativly slim case (approx. 4.5 cm × 6.5 cm × 2 cm). The choice of a compact development board led to the ability to use a matching prototyping board that could sit directly under the controller, eliminating the loosely "integrated" circuits for sensing and a notification LED. The case has been designed using advanced 3D modeling projection techniques in Fusion 360 [1] by Autodesk. This design process involved multiple iterations.

3   Evaluation

3.1   Data Collection

As previous work already demonstrated some sort of study using conventional machine learning, we aimed to focus on emerging machine learning techniques, namely training a neural network model. Our objective was to obtain a minimum of 10 min of data per person, with each individual walking or running on each surface. To collect the required vast amount data for training a neural network, we utilized a mobile application developed with the Flutter framework [9]. This application facilitates communication with the controller software, enabling the initiation and termination of data recording through the continuous transmission of data via Bluetooth, a measure designed to conserve energy. The user interface of the application allows for the configuration of multiple data labeling parameters, including the username, surface type, surface condition (dry or wet), and shoe type. Upon completion of the recording, the app transmits the data to the SurfSole Data App, as illustrated in Fig. 1. This web-based application enables real-time data verification, facilitating prompt detection and resolution of potential issues related to insole damage or Bluetooth connectivity disruptions.

With two participants, we collected around an hour of training data in total. This is an adequate quantity of data to commence the ml model training phase. Figure 4 shows the distribution of our collected data in terms of walking speed, and surface type. Due to the lower energy exposure, walking speed is slightly more prevalent than running, as well as the surface types, which include pavement, tartan, and lawn, which are slightly more prevalent than, for example, beaches. Upon downloading the data from the SurfSole Data App, a zip file containing 982 CSV files has been generated for further data processing.

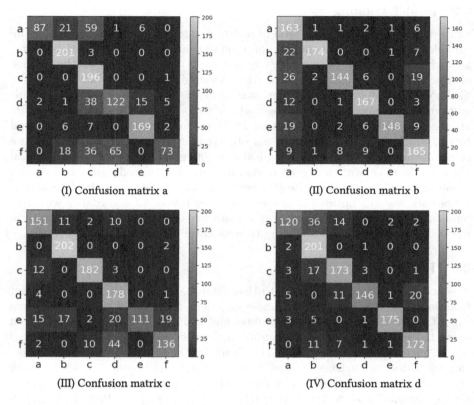

Fig. 3. Confusion matrices of different neural networks: (I) 3 layer CNN with 16, 32 & 64 filters, resulting in up to 74.85% accuracy; (II) 3 layer CNN with 32, 64 & 128 filters, resulting in up to 84.82% accuracy; (III) 4 layer CNN with 16, 32, 64 & 128 filters, resulting in up to 84.73% accuracy; (IV) 4 layer CNN with 32, 64, 128 & 256 filters, resulting in up to 87.11% accuracy. Classes: a) beach sand, b) clay turf, c) lawn, d) pavement, e) synthetic turf, and f) tartan.

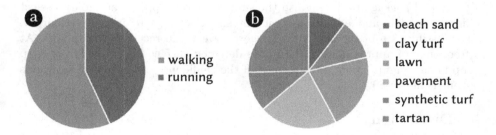

Fig. 4. Distribution of data collected: a) Distribution on walking style, b) Duration per surface type.

3.2 Model Training

Since we want to create some kind of real-time interaction, the network must be capable of performing classification on brief sequences. Additionally, the interrelation between two subsequent steps in a sequence may diminish with the passage of time. This is particularly evident when a step directly follows another, as the likelihood of them occurring on the same surface is high. In light of these considerations, a convolutional neural network (CNN) emerged as a promising initial approach, which is already indicated in literature [13]. We initially employed Keras, which precisely aligns with our objective, even though it requires the use of six channels [5]. As Keras is basically an integrated part of Tensorflow [23] nowadays and Tensorflow has an option to convert a trained model to a smartphone friendly TensorFlow Lite [12] model, it was evident that the TensorFlow framework was the optimal choice for implementation. In accordance with recommendations, such as from Towards Data Science [21], we evaluated several iterations of the original network until we identified four candidate networks.

3.3 Results

The networks with 3 to 4 layers with 16 or 32 initial filters with doubling amount from layer to layer were trained on sequences as short as 40 to 120 datapoints (about 1–3 seconds walking or running) and came to acceptable results on an extracted testing data set as the confusion matrices in Fig. 3 clearly show. Eventually, our models converged after 71 epochs. Our results confirm that the detection of 6 diverse surfaces is feasible with a relatively modest CNN on brief sequences. However, as shown in Fig. 3, the accuracy remains highly variable across our four models; I) 74.85%, II) 84.82%, III) 84.73%, IV) 87.11%, indicating that the training process may require further optimization or additional data for training.

4 Real-Time Application

The exported TensorFlow Lite [12] model has been packaged into a mobile app, built with the dart-based [8] framework Flutter [9]. Further, we used the Flutter TFLite [10] package to distinguish the surface. In our app, we are able to select different models and adjusting some threshold settings to improve accuracy. The classification of the surface is triggered every 120 received data points. At a frequency of approximately 40 Hz, the detected surface in the SurfTastic app is updated roughly every three seconds if the confidence of the neural network's output is above 80%.

5 Discussion

5.1 Benefits and Key Insights

Creating and putting SurfSole into action as a product would mean a major step forward in wearable tech and sports industry. For instance, identifying the terrain has a major impact when it comes to reduce running injuries and to optimize running performance.

The sleek case and compact development board improved the hardware design makes it comfortable for users and more reliable in comparison to most other prototypes demonstrated in literature. Using Bluetooth LE in combination with the SurfSole data collector app works perfectly with 40 Hz data. Having the data directly on the phone enables for many more applications than just identifying terrain. The smartphones' power nowadays enable our app's for real-time data labeling makes it a reliable platform for prototyping.

The evaluation of different neural network architectures revealed that modest CNN could effectively classify surfaces based on brief data sequences. However, the accuracy varied significantly under different conditions, indicating the necessity for further optimization and extensive training data.

5.2   Challenges and Limitations

One of the major challenges encountered was the variability in the collected data. Different walking speeds, surface types, and environmental conditions (e.g., wet or frozen surfaces) significantly impacted the model's accuracy. This variability underscores the need for a more extensive and diverse dataset to train the neural networks adequately.

The current models demonstrated acceptable performance under controlled conditions but struggled under variable real-world conditions. Future work should focus on enhancing the robustness of the models through extensive data collection and pre-processing techniques such as normalization.

6   Conclusion and Future Work

In conclusion, the SurfSole project demonstrates a significant step forward in wearable technology and surface detection. By leveraging capacitive sensing in conjunction with neural networks, the prototype successfully identifies various terrains in real-time with an accuarcy of up to 87.11%. In our real-time implementation we can see that these results may be not always obtainable. In reality, we face many varying variables that impact accuracy. For instance, one day we might have slightly different weather conditions than other days (e.g., the surface is wet, slightly frozen, and therefore a harder surface). As we performed our tests in winter, we exactly faced these issues.

One of the most urgent next steps is to collect a significantly larger dataset for training the NN models, as the currently trained models still exhibit weak robustness. A broader dataset will result in adjusting the current network architecture and optimizing training parameters to improve for generalization. Currently, we deal with raw data. It is an open question whether pre-processing techniques such as regularization, normalization, etc. can help to significantly improve the model. Bagnall et al. [2] suggests it might further enhance the models' robustness.

References

1. Autodesk Inc.: Fusion 360, version 2.0 (2024). https://www.autodesk.com/products/fusion-360/overview
2. Bagnall, A., Bostrom, A., Large, J., Lines, J.: The great time series classification bake off: an experimental evaluation of recently proposed algorithms. Extended version (2016). https://arxiv.org/abs/1602.01711
3. Bauhaus AG: Neudorff schneckenband (2024). https://www.bauhaus.info/schneckenkorn-schneckenzaeune/neudorff-schneckenband/p/24881296
4. BUDNI Handels-und Service GmbH & Co. KG: Dein drogeriemarkt in deiner nachbarschaft | alles gute für dich (2024). https://www.budni.de/
5. Chollet, F.: Timeseries classification from scratch (2023). https://keras.io/examples/timeseries/timeseries_classification_from_scratch/#introduction
6. de Fazio, R., Perrone, E., Velázquez, R., De Vittorio, M., Visconti, P.: Development of a self-powered piezo-resistive smart insole equipped with low-power BLE connectivity for remote gait monitoring. Sensors **21**(13), 4539 (2021)
7. Gabrecht, M.T., Wang, H., Matthies, D.J.C.: PneuShoe: a pneumatic smart shoe for activity recognition, terrain identification, and weight estimation. In: Proceedings of the 8th International Workshop on Sensor-Based Activity Recognition and Artificial Intelligence, pp. 1–5 (2023)
8. Google: Dart: A programming language for apps on multiple platforms (2024). https://dart.dev
9. Google: Flutter: A UI toolkit for building natively compiled applications for mobile, web, and desktop from a single codebase (2024). https://flutter.dev
10. Google: tflite: Tensorflow lite plugin for flutter (version 1.0.0) (2024). https://pub.dev/packages/tflite
11. Grosse-Puppendahl, T., et al.: Finding common ground: a survey of capacitive sensing in human-computer interaction. In: Proceedings of the 2017 CHI Conference on Human Factors in Computing Systems, CHI '17, pp. 3293–3315. Association for Computing Machinery, New York (2017)
12. Lite, T.: Timeseries classification from scratch (2023). https://keras.io/examples/timeseries/
13. Luwe, Y.J., Lee, C.P., Lim, K.M.: Wearable sensor-based human activity recognition with hybrid deep learning model. In: Informatics, vol. 9, p. 56. MDPI (2022)
14. Matthies, D.J.C., Roumen, T., Kuijper, A., Urban, B.: CapSoles: who is walking on what kind of floor? In: Proceedings of the 19th International Conference on Human-Computer Interaction with Mobile Devices and Services, MobileHCI '17. Association for Computing Machinery, New York (2017)
15. Matthies, D.J., Elvitigala, D.S., Fu, A., Yin, D., Nanayakkara, S.: MobiLLD: exploring the detection of leg length discrepancy and altering gait with mobile smart insoles. In: Proceedings of the 14th PErvasive Technologies Related to Assistive Environments Conference, pp. 37–47 (2021)
16. Nascimento, D., Magalhães, F., Sabino, G., Resende, R., Duarte, M., Vimieiro, C.S.: Design a custom resistive force sensors to optimize sensorized insoles. Sens. Rev. **43**(3), 179–189 (2023)
17. Paixão, L.M., de Morais, M.E., Bublitz, F.M., Bezerra, K.C.T., Franco, C.I.F.: The use of smart insoles for gait analysis: a systematic review. In: Machado, J., Soares, F., Trojanowska, J., Ottaviano, E. (eds.) Innovations in Mechanical Engineering, pp. 451–458. Springer, Cham (2022)

18. Qian, X., et al.: An intelligent insole based on wide-range flexible pressure sensor. AIP Adv. **14**(3), 035128 (2024)
19. Samarentsis, A.G., Makris, G., Spinthaki, S., Christodoulakis, G., Tsiknakis, M., Pantazis, A.K.: A 3D-printed capacitive smart insole for plantar pressure monitoring. Sensors **22**(24), 9725 (2022)
20. Santos, V.M., Gomes, B.B., Neto, M.A., Amaro, A.M.: A systematic review of insole sensor technology: recent studies and future directions. Appl. Sci. **14**(14), 6085 (2024)
21. Towards Data Science (2024). https://towardsdatascience.com/
22. Sorrentino, I., et al.: A novel sensorised insole for sensing feet pressure distributions. Sensors **20**(3), 747 (2020)
23. TensorFlow: Timeseries classification from scratch (2023). https://keras.io/examples/timeseries/
24. Wang, S., et al.: High sensitivity capacitive flexible pressure sensor based on PDMS double wrinkled microstructure. J. Mater. Sci.: Mater. Electron. **35**(1), 78 (2024)

ShoeTect2.0: Real-Time Activity Recognition Using MobileNet CNN with Multisensory Smart Footwear

Ruben Schlonsak[1,3]($\boxtimes$), Tengyunhao Yang[1,2], Marco Gabrecht[1,3]($\boxtimes$), and Denys J. C. Matthies[1,3]($\boxtimes$)

[1] Technical University of Applied Sciences Lübeck, Lübeck, Germany
ruben.schlonsak@th-luebeck.de, denys.matthies@th-luebeck.de
[2] East China University of Science and Technology, Shanghai, China
[3] Fraunhofer IMTE, Lübeck, Germany

Abstract. In this paper, we introduce a proof-of-concept multi-sensory footwear prototype with artificial intelligence to facilitate human activity recognition. We equipped a shoe with a force sensitive pressure sensor, an accelerometer, and a gyroscope in order to detect human activity. Such sensors allow the system to capture and analyze data about various physical movements, which are further processed in order to detect specific human activities. To achieve accurate activity recognition, we trained and compared several models, which are two types of convolutional neural networks (CNN) and a conventional support vector machine (SVM). The system's accuracy in identifying activities like standing, sitting, walking, running, and jumping was evaluated, and scored highest using a MobileNet CNN with 83.33% accuracy. With this work, we demonstrate that a somewhat robust real-time activity recognition is feasible with prototypical hardware.

Keywords: Artificial Intelligence · Gait Detection · Neural Networks · CNN · Smart Insole

1 Introduction

Wearable technology is revolutionizing our daily lives, with smart insoles emerging as a notable innovation. The most smart insoles are mainly designed for gait analysis with the help of a variety of sensor types.

Advanced sensing technologies that provide a number of enhanced sensing capabilities have been investigated and implemented. For example, force-sensitive [8] resistors provide accurate measurements of force or pressure through changes in resistance. Capacitive sensors [7] operate due to changes in capacitance, which can be highly sensitive to changes. Oppositely, piezoelectric sensors [3] generate an electrical charge under mechanical stress and hence are particularly applicable for insole measurements. Additionally, other innovative

O. Konak et al. (Eds.): iWOAR 2024, LNCS 15357, pp. 260–268, 2025.
https://doi.org/10.1007/978-3-031-80856-2_17

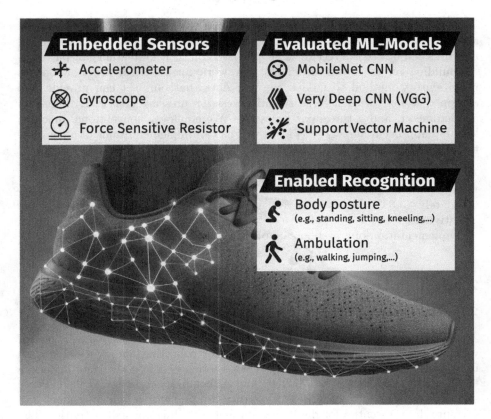

Fig. 1. Our prototype system features three sensors: Accelerometer, Gyroscope, and three FSRs. We then trained and compared three machine learning models, being a MobileNet CNN, VGG, and an SVM. We trained several models to detect body postures and ambulation activities in real-time.

technologies [4] continue to push the boundaries of sensor capabilities, integrating new materials and approaches to improve performance.

Recent advancements in smart insole technology have significantly enhanced the capabilities of gait analysis systems. Modern smart insoles have taken advantage of the integration of multiple sensor types, which has substantially improved the accuracy and reliability of gait assessments. For example, Choi et al. [2] highlight the advantages of combining various sensor technologies within smart insoles, offering a more comprehensive evaluation of gait patterns.

In parallel, the application of machine learning models has further advanced gait recognition capabilities. Shen et al. [10] provide an overview of how deep learning techniques are applied to analyze gait data from insole sensors, showcasing the potential of these advanced models to effectively interpret complex gait patterns.

In addition, recent research has highlighted the importance of personalized approaches to gait analysis. Several studies [14,15] have focused on how neural networks can be used to recognize people based on their individual gait patterns.

Building on these advancements, our work introduces a proof-of-concept multi-sensory method to unlock the rich data that our feet can provide. We equipped a shoe with a force sensitive resistor pressure sensor, a three-axis accelerometer, and a three-axis gyroscope. We employ a conventional machine learning approach, namely a SVM as well as two implementations of a convolutional neural network (CNN) for a typical data classification task.

The key contributions of this work include:

- Application of MobileNetV3 CNN for classifying activities, achieving approximately 83.33% accuracy in recognizing six postures and three movements activities.
- Implementation of a system capable of real-time activity recognition

2   System Design and Implementation

2.1   Hardware Setup

The smart shoe prototype was developed using an Arduino development board, which serves as the central processing unit for collecting and processing data from multiple sensors. The primary sensors integrated into the shoe include a three-axis accelerometer (MPU6050) and a membrane pressure sensor. These sensors were strategically placed to capture comprehensive foot movement and pressure data, essential for distinguishing between different gait activities. The MPU6050 sensor, located on the exterior of the shoe, measures acceleration and gyroscopic data. The membrane pressure sensor, positioned within the insole, has three sensing points at the big toe, fifth metatarsal, and heel, providing localized pressure data. The prototype is based on former work [6] and adjusted for this work. The smart shoe protoyp is presented in Fig. 2.

2.2   Software

The software for the smart shoe system was developed using the Arduino Integrated Development Environment (IDE) [1], which facilitates the programming and uploading of code to the Arduino board. The Arduino IDE is compatible with various programming languages, including C and Java, which allows flexible and efficient code development.

To ensure real-time data visualization and logging, SecureCRT [12] software was used. SecureCRT provides a terminal emulation interface for capturing serial data output from the Arduino board, enabling the storage of activity data in log files for subsequent analysis.

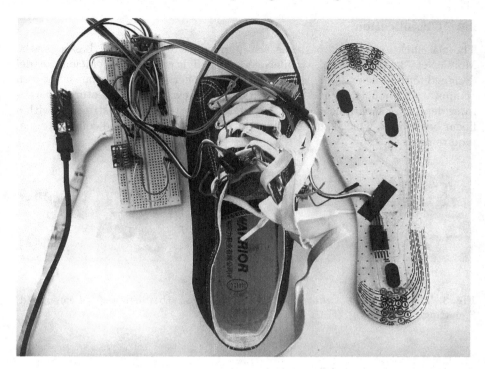

Fig. 2. The hardware prototype: a Converse-type shoe with low-level integration. We use breadboard prototyping with an Arduino Nano that streams the data via USB to a portable computer. Different to the previous version of ShoeTect [6], we waived on using the data gathered by the microphone and humidity sensor, although the sensors are still plugged. We believe the data not to be very meaningful for our activities.

2.3   Data Acquisition

Data collection for this study involved monitoring the activities of 11 participants (11 male subjects, age: 22 ± 1 years; height: 176 ± 5 cm; body mass: 80 ± 10 kg) wearing smart shoes equipped with sensors. Each participant had an average shoe size of 260 ± 5 mm. The participants performed a series of predefined body posture activities, including standing, sitting, kneeling, squatting, leaning, and cross-leg sitting. For each activity, participants were instructed to maintain the posture for approximately 25 s. The sensors in the smart shoes captured data on acceleration, angular velocity, and pressure distributions.

In total, 66 sets of gait data were collected, with 11 sets corresponding to each of the six body posture activities. Each of the 11 participants contributed one set of data for each activity, resulting in a total of 11 sets per activity.

2.4   Classification

The classification of gait patterns was performed using a CNN based on the MobileNetV3 architecture. MobileNetV3 is a lightweight and efficient model designed for mobile and embedded applications, offering a good balance between computational efficiency and classification accuracy. This architecture incorporates depthwise separable convolutions and an inverted residual structure with a linear bottleneck, which significantly reduces the model's size and computational requirements [5,9].

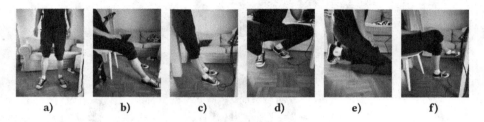

Fig. 3. The six body posture activities. (a) Standing. (b) Sitting. (c) Leaning. (d) Squatting. (e) Kneeling. (f) Cross-leg Sitting.

3   Evaluation and Results

3.1   Body Posture Recognition

The evaluation of the body posture recognition model was conducted using a dataset that included six distinct body postures: cross-leg sitting, kneeling, leaning, sitting, squatting, and standing. The model was trained over 100 epochs, and its performance was assessed using various metrics, including precision, recall, and F1 score. The results are shown in Table 1.

Table 1. Performance Metrics for different Body Postures

Class	Precision (%)	Recall (%)	F1 Score (%)
cross-leg_sitting	60.00	100.00	75.00
kneeling	100.00	100.00	100.00
leaning	75.00	100.00	85.71
sitting	100.00	66.67	80.00
squatting	100.00	66.67	80.00
standing	100.00	66.67	80.00

The model demonstrated high precision in identifying various postures, achieving perfect scores of 100% for kneeling, sitting, squatting, and standing.

However, cross-leg sitting exhibited a lower precision rate of 60%. In terms of recall, kneeling was perfectly identified with a 100% recall rate, while other postures showed a recall rate of 66.67%, except for cross-leg sitting, which achieved a perfect recall rate of 100%. The F1 scores, reflecting a balance between precision and recall, ranged from 75% to 100% across different postures. Overall, the model's performance was robust, with a mean precision of 89.17%, a mean recall of 83.33%, and a mean F1 score of 83.45%, highlighting its effectiveness in accurately distinguishing between various body postures.

3.2 Ambulation Recognition

For ambulation activities, the system was tested on three primary movements: jumping, running, and walking. Similar to body posture recognition, the model's performance was evaluated over 100 training epochs. The results for the trained model are shown in Table 2.

Table 2. Performance Metrics for different gaits

Class	Precision (%)	Recall (%)	F1 Score (%)
jumping	80.00	66.67	72.73
running	100.00	83.30	90.91
walking	75.00	100.00	85.71

The performance evaluation of the model in recognizing ambulation activities demonstrates robust accuracy and effectiveness. Running achieved the highest precision at 100%, indicating flawless identification, followed by jumping with a precision of 80% and walking at 75%. In terms of recall, walking excelled with a perfect recall rate of 100%, while jumping had the lowest recall at 66.67%. Regarding the F1 score, which balances precision and recall, running led with an impressive 90.91%, whereas jumping had the lowest score at 72.73%. Overall, the model exhibited strong performance across all three ambulation activities, with a mean precision of 85%, a mean recall of 83.33%, and a mean F1 score of 83.12%. This underscores the system's capability to accurately classify and differentiate between various types of movement.

3.3 Comparison with Other Classifiers

To benchmark the performance, the MobileNetV3 model was compared with other classifiers such as the VGG model [11] and Support Vector Machines (SVM) [13]. The results for all three classifiers is shown in Table 3. The results indicated that MobileNetV3 outperformed the other classifiers in both body posture and ambulation recognition tasks, achieving higher accuracy rates.

These results underscore the efficacy of the MobileNetV3 architecture in the context of foot data-based activity recognition, offering a promising solution for real-time posture and movement monitoring applications.

Table 3. Performance Metrics of Different Models

Category	MobileNetV3 (%)	VGG (%)	SVM (%)
ambulation	83.33	72.22	77.78
body gesture	83.33	83.33	72.22

4   Discussion

4.1   Benefits and Key Insights

The smart shoe prototype integrates multiple sensors, including a pressure sensor and an MPU6050 sensor, to capture comprehensive foot data. This combination provides a holistic view of foot dynamics in various postures, enhancing the accuracy of gait pattern recognition and mitigating the limitations of relying on a single type of data. The system employs real-time monitoring of gait activities using an Arduino development board, operating at an output frequency of 10 Hz. This allows for immediate feedback on foot posture and movement, facilitating quick adjustments and improving data accuracy. The use of SecureCRT software for serial port control allows for efficient storage of foot activity data. This system ensures the chronological and immediate saving of data, which reduces the manual workload and enhances the integrity of the experimental data. The MobileNetV3 is noted for its efficiency and accuracy in extracting relevant features from the data, outperforming traditional machine learning models like VGG and SVM in this context. The study highlights MobileNetV3's suitability for real-time applications and its potential for widespread use in gait analysis systems.

4.2   Challenges and Limitations

The smart shoe prototype used in the study was a custom-built solution rather than a commercially available product. This decision led to certain compromises in terms of appearance and sensor integration. The use of a single shoe size (260 mm) limited the participant pool and may not accurately represent broader population dynamics. The pressure sensors used in the prototype provided data from only three points on the sole (big toe, fifth metatarsal, and heel), which may not fully capture the complete force distribution across the foot, which could impact the accuracy of the detected gait pattern. The data transmission in the prototype was conducted via a wired USB connection, which, while secure, restricted the mobility of the users and the range of data collection. The data collection was conducted under controlled conditions with a uniform ground surface. Variations in ground conditions, which were not accounted for, could potentially influence the accuracy of the data collected. Furthermore, the study did not consider the possible asymmetries between the left and right feet, which could affect the accuracy of gait analysis if not addressed.

5 Conclusion and Future Work

The study developed a smart shoe prototype aimed at recognizing gait patterns through the integration of multiple sensors and the use of machine learning models. Key findings include the effectiveness of the MobileNetV3 model, which demonstrated superior accuracy in recognizing both body posture and ambulation activities compared to other classifiers like VGG and SVM. The smart shoe system, despite its limitations, successfully validated its hypotheses, achieving a high accuracy rate exceeding 80% for gait recognition tasks. This research highlights the potential of using lightweight neural networks and multi-sensor data fusion in wearable technology to provide accurate real-time monitoring and feedback. Such systems could play a crucial role in various applications, including health monitoring, rehabilitation, and athletic performance enhancement.

The future development of this smart shoe system will focus on addressing the current limitations and exploring new avenues for enhancement. A crucial next step involves developing a mobile application that enables real-time activity recognition and user feedback. This application will leverage the data collected from the sensors to provide users with immediate insights and recommendations, enhancing the system's utility in everyday settings and potentially aiding in health monitoring and athletic training. To increase the accuracy and usability of the smart shoe, future iterations will incorporate more advanced sensors capable of capturing finer details in pressure distribution and motion tracking. Efforts will also focus on miniaturizing these sensors and integrating them seamlessly into the shoe's design, which will help reduce user discomfort and make the device more practical for prolonged use. Replacing the current wired data transmission setup with wireless technologies is another key area for development. This change will significantly enhance the user's freedom of movement and allow for more natural data collection, particularly in dynamic environments. To validate the system's robustness and generalizability, extensive field testing in diverse environments and with a broader participant base will be necessary. This will involve assessing the system's performance on various surfaces and under different conditions, helping refine its adaptability and accuracy. Exploring cutting-edge machine learning techniques is crucial for enhancing the system's performance. This includes investigating advanced deep learning architectures, such as transfer learning, reinforcement learning, and ensemble methods, which can potentially improve classification accuracy and computational efficiency. Implementing these techniques will further optimize the system, making it more capable of handling diverse and complex data.

References

1. Arduino: Arduino integrated development environment (IDE). https://www.arduino.cc/en/software. Accessed 28 July 2024
2. Choi, S.I., Moon, J., Park, H.C., Choi, S.T.: User identification from gait analysis using multi-modal sensors in smart insole. Sensors **19**(17) (2019). https://doi.org/10.3390/s19173785. https://www.mdpi.com/1424-8220/19/17/3785

3. de Fazio, R., Perrone, E., Velázquez, R., De Vittorio, M., Visconti, P.: Development of a self-powered piezo-resistive smart insole equipped with low-power BLE connectivity for remote gait monitoring. Sensors **21**(13), 4539 (2021)

4. Gabrecht, M.T., Wang, H., Matthies, D.J.C.: PneuShoe: a pneumatic smart shoe for activity recognition, terrain identification, and weight estimation. In: Proceedings of the 8th International Workshop on Sensor-Based Activity Recognition and Artificial Intelligence, pp. 1–5 (2023)

5. Howard, A., et al.: Searching for MobileNetV3. arXiv preprint arXiv:1905.02244 (2019). https://arxiv.org/pdf/1905.02244

6. Li, X., Matthies, D.J.: ShoeTect: detecting body posture, ambulation activity, gait abnormalities, and terrain with multisensory smart footwear. In: Proceedings of the 7th International Workshop on Sensor-Based Activity Recognition and Artificial Intelligence, iWOAR '22. Association for Computing Machinery, New York (2023). https://doi.org/10.1145/3558884.3558904

7. Matthies, D.J.C., Roumen, T., Kuijper, A., Urban, B.: CapSoles: who is walking on what kind of floor? In: Proceedings of the 19th International Conference on Human-Computer Interaction with Mobile Devices and Services, MobileHCI '17. Association for Computing Machinery, New York (2017)

8. Matthies, D.J., Elvitigala, D.S., Fu, A., Yin, D., Nanayakkara, S.: MobiLLD: exploring the detection of leg length discrepancy and altering gait with mobile smart insoles. In: Proceedings of the 14th PErvasive Technologies Related to Assistive Environments Conference, pp. 37–47 (2021)

9. Sandler, M., Howard, A., Zhu, M., Zhmoginov, A., Chen, L.C.: MobileNetV2: inverted residuals and linear bottlenecks. arXiv preprint arXiv:1801.04381 (2018). https://arxiv.org/pdf/1801.04381

10. Shen, C., Yu, S., Wang, J., Huang, G.Q., Wang, L.: A comprehensive survey on deep gait recognition: algorithms, datasets and challenges (2023). https://arxiv.org/abs/2206.13732

11. Simonyan, K., Zisserman, A.: Very deep convolutional networks for large-scale image recognition. In: International Conference on Learning Representations (2015). https://arxiv.org/abs/1409.1556

12. VanDyke Software: Securecrt. https://www.vandyke.com/products/securecrt/. Accessed 28 July 2024

13. Steinwart, I., Christmann, A.: Support Vector Machines. Springer (2008). https://link.springer.com/book/10.1007/978-0-387-77242-4

14. Venkatachalam, S., Nair, H., Vellaisamy, P., Zhou, Y., Youssfi, Z., Shen, J.P.: Realtime person identification via gait analysis (2024). https://arxiv.org/abs/2404.15312

15. Yi, S., Mei, Z., Ivanov, K., Mei, Z., He, T., Zeng, H.: Gait-based identification using wearable multimodal sensing and attention neural networks. Sens. Actuators, A **374**, 115478 (2024). https://doi.org/10.1016/j.sna.2024.115478. https://www.sciencedirect.com/science/article/pii/S0924424724004722

Optimal 2D-LiDAR-Sensor Coverage of a Room

Noel D'Avis[1]([✉]) [iD] and Silvia Faquiri[1,2] [iD]

[1] RheinMain University of Applied Sciences, Wiesbaden, Germany
noel.davis@hs-rm.de
[2] Fraunhofer IGD, Darmstadt, Germany

Abstract. This work presents a novel concept for achieving optimal coverage of an unspecified room using 2D-LiDAR (Light Detection and Ranging) sensors. The primary goal is to maximize coverage with the fewest possible sensors. We present an algorithm that determines the ideal locations for these sensors, which are all mounted on the floor by the walls. By dividing the room into a grid with adjustable cell sizes (e.g., 10×10 cm), the algorithm marks all grid cells detected by each potential sensor location. This process is repeated for all possible locations. Based on the resulting coverage map, the algorithm calculates the minimum number of required sensors and their optimal positions. An application case for this approach is movement and fall detection using 2D-LiDAR.

Keywords: 2D-LiDAR · Optimal Coverage · Sensor Placement · Room Monitoring · Grid Mapping · Algorithm Optimization · Movement Detection · Fall Detection · Smart Environments · Indoor Monitoring

1 Introduction

Achieving comprehensive coverage of indoor spaces with minimal sensor usage is crucial for applications such as security, monitoring, and smart environments [1]. The advent of 2D-LiDAR sensors has opened new possibilities for efficient room monitoring due to their precise range-finding capabilities and wide field of view. However, placing these sensors optimally to maximize coverage while minimizing their number remains a significant challenge.

An exemplary application of this concept is in movement and fall detection within indoor environments, as discussed by Bouazizi et al. [1]. Their research highlights the use of multiple 2D-LiDAR sensors for activity detection, demonstrating the practical relevance of optimal sensor placement for efficient monitoring. In scenarios such as elderly care or security monitoring, accurately detecting movement is critical.

The proposed algorithm can ensure comprehensive coverage of rooms and common areas with minimal sensors, enabling quick detection and response to any incidents.

O. Konak et al. (Eds.): iWOAR 2024, LNCS 15357, pp. 269–276, 2025.
https://doi.org/10.1007/978-3-031-80856-2_18

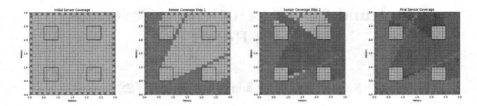

Fig. 1. The image shows the steps of the sensor coverage optimization algorithm, where three sensors (yellow, green, blue coverage area) are placed in a square room with four obstacles. The image on the right illustrates the final optimized sensor placement with a minimum number of sensors. Each sensor is strategically positioned to ensure maximum coverage despite obstacles. (Color figure online)

2   Related Work

Optimal sensor placement aims to maximize coverage with a minimal number of sensors, which is crucial for cost-effective and efficient monitoring. Various approaches have been proposed to address this challenge. For instance, Dhillon and Chakrabarty developed a framework for sensor placement in wireless sensor networks, focusing on coverage and connectivity issues [3]. Their approach utilizes a grid-based method to ensure that the sensors' coverage areas overlap sufficiently to detect all events of interest.

In the field of robotics, Gonzalez-Banos and Latombe (2001) introduced an art gallery approach to place sensors in a polygonal environment [4]. Their algorithm ensures that the entire area is covered by a minimal number of sensors, leveraging the visibility properties of polygons. This work has been foundational in developing algorithms for sensor placement in indoor environments.

Recent advancements in LiDAR technology have enabled more precise and flexible sensor placement strategies. Bouazizi et al. (2024) explored the use of multiple 2D-LiDAR sensors for activity detection in indoor environments, highlighting the importance of optimal sensor placement for efficient monitoring [1]. Their research demonstrates that strategically placed LiDAR sensors can provide comprehensive coverage and accurate activity detection with fewer sensors.

In this work, we present a conceptual approach to address this challenge by developing an algorithm that determines the ideal locations for 2D-LiDAR sensors placed on the floor of a room by the walls. The algorithm ensures that the entire room is covered with the fewest sensors possible, thus optimizing both cost and performance. The proposed approach leverages a centralized software system that records room dimensions and sensor positions, enabling efficient and effective room monitoring.

3   Sensor Placement Algorithm

The process of achieving optimal coverage by placing 2D-LiDAR sensors involves several steps: First, the dimensions of the room are entered into the software

(Listing 1.1). This system maintains a detailed map of the room and records all possible sensor locations. The sensors are then placed at the various potential positions along the room's walls. These positions are input into the software, and each sensor is initially marked as "non-essential". These virtual sensors perform a series of measurements to detect walls or obstacles at various angles.

Listing 1.1. Optimal 2D-LiDAR Sensor Placement Algorithm Pseudocode

```
# Input: Room dimensions, grid cell size, sensor range
# Output: Optimal sensor locations

# Initialize grid based on room dimensions and grid cell
    size
grid = initialize_grid(room_dimensions, grid_cell_size)
coverage_map = initialize_coverage_map(grid)

# Evaluate potential sensor positions
for each possible sensor location in room:
    for angle in sensor_angles:
        cells_covered = get_covered_cells(sensor_location,
            angle, sensor_range)
        update_coverage_map(coverage_map, sensor_location,
            cells_covered)

# Determine essential sensors
essential_sensors = []
for cell in grid:
    if is_covered_by_single_sensor(cell, coverage_map):
        sensor = get_covering_sensor(cell, coverage_map)
        mark_as_essential(sensor, essential_sensors)
        mark_cells_as_completed(cell, coverage_map)

# Optimize sensor placement
while not all_cells_covered(grid, coverage_map):
    sensor = get_sensor_with_most_coverage(coverage_map)
    mark_as_essential(sensor, essential_sensors)
    update_coverage_map_after_selection(sensor,
        coverage_map)

# Return optimal sensor locations
return essential_sensors
```

When a sensor detects an obstacle at a specific angle, all cells between the sensor and the obstacle at that angle are marked as covered. This data is fed back into the software, where each cell in the grid maintains an array of sensors that cover it. Additionally, each sensor is assigned a value based on the number of cells it covers. The algorithm evaluates all potential sensor positions to create a comprehensive coverage map. This involves iterating through each sensor and updating the coverage information for each cell in the grid.

Once the initial coverage map is created, the algorithm determines the necessary sensor locations through an optimization process. For cells covered by only one sensor, that sensor is marked as "essential" and the cells are marked as "completed." Using a "First Fit Decreasing" strategy, the sensor covering the most cells is then marked as "essential." After each step, the number of cells covered by each sensor is adjusted by subtracting cells already covered by other sensors. This process continues iteratively until all cells are covered.

The final outcome of the algorithm is a set of sensors, each with a specific optimal position. These positions ensure that the entire room is covered with the fewest number of sensors, optimizing both cost and performance. We refer to the pseudocode in Listing 1.1 for a detailed algorithmic representation of the optimal LiDAR sensor placement process.

3.1   Implementation Details

The implementation of the proposed algorithm involves several key steps, each critical to achieving optimal sensor placement.

Grid Division. The room is divided into a grid based on specified cell sizes. This grid forms the basis for all subsequent calculations and evaluations. Each cell in the grid represents a small section of the room, and the size of these cells can be adjusted based on the specific requirements of the environment and the capabilities of the sensors.

Sensor Range Calculation. For each potential sensor location, the algorithm calculates the range of cells that the sensor can cover. This calculation takes into account the sensor's maximum range and its angular field of view.

Coverage Map Update. As each sensor performs measurements and detects obstacles, the coverage map is updated. The software records which cells are covered by which sensors, and updates the array of sensors covering each cell. This ensures that the coverage map is accurate and up-to-date.

Optimization Algorithm. The optimization step is crucial for determining the minimal set of sensors needed to cover all cells. Techniques such as integer linear programming (ILP) or greedy algorithms can be employed to solve this problem. The "First Fit Decreasing" strategy is particularly effective, as it prioritizes sensors that cover the most cells, ensuring efficient coverage.

4   Preliminary Algorithm Validation

To validate the proposed algorithm, simulations were conducted in various obstacle configurations. The simulations involved different grid cell sizes and numbers
of obstacles. The results showed that the algorithm consistently identified the
optimal sensor placements, achieving full coverage with a minimal number of
sensors.

The simulations were performed in a virtual environment where grid cell
sizes, and number of obstacles were varied (Table 1). The algorithm was tested
for its ability to cover the entire room with the fewest sensors. Various scenarios
were simulated to account for different room shapes and obstacle placements.

Table 1. Simulation setups of square space with different cell grid sizes and variying
number of randomly placed obstacles

Room Size	Grid Cell Size	Number of Obstacles
3×3 m	5×5 cm	1
3×3 m	10×10 cm	1
3×3 m	25×25 cm	1
3×3 m	33×33 cm	1
3×3 m	5×5 cm	4
3×3 m	10×10 cm	4
3×3 m	25×25 cm	4
3×3 m	5×5 cm	7
3×3 m	10×10 cm	7
3×3 m	25×25 cm	7

The algorithm's performance was evaluated through a series of simulations
conducted in a square environment with varying numbers of obstacles: specifically, 1, 4, or 7. Determining sensor placement in an unobstructed square space
is straightforward. However, the introduction of obstacles significantly increases
the complexity of the problem.

Figure 2a, shows the initial plot of a 3 m × 3 m space with a single obstacle,
representing the second simulation configuration from Table 1. Potential sensor
locations are shown along the walls placed 20 cm apart, a total of 24 sensors in
this case. The space is divided into 10 cm grid cells. The algorithm checks if there
are cells that are only covered by one sensor. Due to the high resolution in this
simple simulation configuration, no such cells exist. In the next step (Fig. 2b),
the sensor with the highest number of covered cells is marked as "necessary". In
this case it is the sensor at position (0, 0), the red dot in left corner. All covered
cells are marked as covered, colored dark blue with 240 grid cells remaining
uncovered. This step is repeated identifying the sensor that covers the second
highest number of cells, in this case at position (30, 20). This area is colored
light blue. The process is repeated until all cells are covered. In this illustratory

example, the algorithm terminates after 2 steps. The plot of the final step, shown in Fig. 2c, displays the two sensors, along with the covered cells.

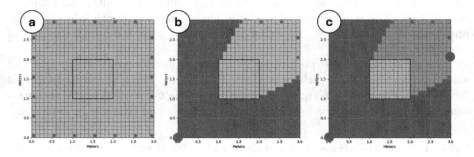

Fig. 2. Intermediary algorithm results (b), where 2 sensors are enough (c) to cover the area around the obstacle in the middle (a) (Color figure online)

The algorithm was also tested in more complex environments with four and seven obstacles, with results shown in Fig. 1 respectively Fig. 3. For the 4-obstacles environment three sensors are enough to cover the area. For the 7-obstacles environment five sensors need to be specifically placed.

5 Discussion

The results of the simulation cases indicate that the algorithm consistently produces favorable outcomes, achieving the minimal number of necessary sensors in all tested scenarios. These were validated against manual calculations and alternative optimization techniques. The "First Fit Decreasing" strategy, combined with efficient data structures, ensures that the algorithm runs efficiently even for large rooms with complex layouts.

A noteworthy aspect of the algorithm is its handling of scenarios where multiple sensor locations provide identical coverage. In such instances, rather than selecting an optimal angle, the algorithm employs a randomized selection process. This approach maintains the algorithm's flexibility and adaptability, even when faced with multiple equally optimal solutions.

The impact of variations in potential sensor locations and grid sizes on the results appears to be marginal. However, these variations warrant more thorough evaluation in future research to ensure a comprehensive understanding and robustness of the algorithm.

While the algorithm performs well in simulations, there are limitations to consider. The accuracy of the coverage map depends on the precision of the sensors and the resolution of the grid. Also, in real-world applications, factors such as sensor malfunctions or environmental changes could affect the performance of the system. Futhermore, there might be areas along the wall, where sensor placement is not allowed or not possible and thus scenarios might arise

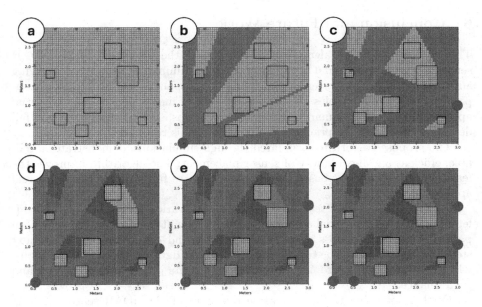

Fig. 3. Intermediary algorithm results (b–e) for a 7-obstacle environment (a), where five sensors are needed to cover all the areas between the randomly placed obstacles (f) (Color figure online)

where no full sensor coverage is achievable. Thus, strategies might be needed to tackle these situations based on context information such as path tracking and fall probability.

5.1 Complexity

In this section, we analyze the complexity of our algorithm with respect to both time and space.

Firstly, we consider the input parameters: the room size (L), which denotes the side length of the square room; the sensor spacing (S), representing the distance between sensors positioned along the walls; and the grid size (G), the dimension of the cells within the grid, for example, 10×10 cm.

For the time complexity, we evaluate three main components. The initialization of the room map and sensors has a complexity of $O\left(\left(\frac{L}{G}\right)^2\right)$. The calculation of line-of-sight and coverage per sensor has a complexity of $O\left(\frac{L^3}{S \cdot G^3}\right)$. The optimization process for selecting the minimal number of sensors has a complexity of $O\left(\frac{L^3}{S \cdot G^2}\right)$. The dominant term in these calculations is $O\left(\frac{L^3}{S \cdot G^2}\right)$, which represents the overall time complexity of the algorithm.

For the space complexity, we again evaluate two main components. The space required for the room map is $O\left(\left(\frac{L}{G}\right)^2\right)$, while the space needed for sensor coverage data is $O\left(\frac{L^3}{S \cdot G^2}\right)$. Therefore, the overall space complexity is $O\left(\frac{L^3}{S \cdot G^2}\right)$.

6   Conclusion and Future Work

This work proposes an algorithm for optimizing the placement of 2D-LiDAR sensors to achieve maximal room coverage with minimal sensors. By leveraging adjustable grid cell sizes, sensor range and angle span, as well as obstacle mapping, the algorithm enables effective monitoring of indoor spaces. The potential applications in various smart environment scenarios, such as movement and fall detection, highlight the practical significance of this research.

The proposed algorithm, validated through simulations, demonstrates a reliable, efficient and flexible way of sensor placement. The algorithm improves the feasibility of 2D LiDAR-based systems and ensures full sensor coverage in real applications.

Further research will test the algorithm with various room layouts and different numbers of potential sensor locations. This will ensure that the algorithm performs optimally across a range of scenarios and configurations. As a next step, the algorithm will be tested using real sensor data rather than simulations, which will provide a more accurate evaluation of its practical applicability and performance.

Furthermore, due to the increasing relevance of 3D-LiDAR sensors [2,5,6], exploring the placement of stationary 3D-LiDAR sensors will also be investigated to improve coverage and increase efficiency in complex environments.

References

1. Bouazizi, M., Mora, A.L., Feghoul, K., Ohtsuki, T.: Activity detection in indoor environments using multiple 2D lidars. Sensors **24**(626), 1–27 (2024). https://doi.org/10.3390/s24020626. https://www.mdpi.com/1424-8220/24/2/626. Academic Editor: Natividad Duro Carralero
2. Dewan, A., Caselitz, T., Tipaldi, G.D., Burgard, W.: Motion-based detection and tracking in 3D LiDAR scans. In: 2016 IEEE International Conference on Robotics and Automation (ICRA), Stockholm, pp. 4508–4513. IEEE (2016). https://doi.org/10.1109/ICRA.2016.7487649
3. Dhillon, S., Chakrabarty, K.: Sensor placement for effective coverage and surveillance in distributed sensor networks. IEEE Wireless Commun. Netw. **3**, 1609–1614 (2003)
4. Gonzalez-Banos, H., Latombe, J.C.: A randomized art-gallery algorithm for sensor placement. In: Proceedings of the Seventeenth Annual Symposium on Computational Geometry, pp. 232–240. ACM, Medford (2001)
5. Gómez, J., Aycard, O., Baber, J.: Efficient detection and tracking of human using 3D LiDAR sensor. Sensors **23**(10) (2023). https://doi.org/10.3390/s23104720. https://www.mdpi.com/1424-8220/23/10/4720
6. Thakur, A., Rajalakshmi, P.: L3D-OTVE: LiDAR-based 3-D object tracking and velocity estimation using LiDAR odometry. IEEE Sens. Lett. **8**(7), 1–4 (2024). https://doi.org/10.1109/LSENS.2024.3416411

Using Wearable Sensors in Stroke Rehabilitation

Justin Albert[1]([✉]), Lin Zhou[1], Kristina Kirsten[1], Nurcennet Kaynak[2],
Torsten Rackoll[2], Tim Walz[3], David Weese[3], Rok Kos[3],
Alexander Heinrich Nave[2], and Bert Arnrich[1]

[1] Digital Health – Connected Healthcare, Hasso Plattner Institute,
University of Potsdam, Potsdam, Germany
{justin.albert,lin.zhou,kristina.kirsten,bert.arnrich}@hpi.de
[2] Department of Neurology, Charité – Universitätsmedizin Berlin Center for Stroke
Research Berlin, Berlin, Germany
{nurcennet.kaynak,alexander-heinrich.nave}@charite.de,
torsten.rackoll@bih-charite.de
[3] D4L data4life gGmbH, Potsdam, Germany
{tim.walz,david.weese,rok.kos}@data4life.care

Abstract. Stroke is one of the major causes of disability worldwide, and
patients with residual neurological deficits are recommended to undergo
rehabilitation. Besides baseline medical conditions, many other factors
play a role in rehabilitation success, including patient engagement and
medical complications. Wearable technology allows objective and continuous monitoring of body functions and behavior. Furthermore, wearable
sensors could detect the risk of adverse events such as falls, infection and
mood disorders. In the past, we gained experience using wearable sensors for stroke gait analysis. For example, we have evaluated algorithms
to quantify gait patterns using inertial measurement units (IMUs) data
and demonstrated that we can quantify and visualize changes in gait
patterns in both healthy and stroke populations. As a next step, we
aim to combine multiple wearable sensors and data modalities to further
assess patient performance in rehabiliation. This planned study aims to
investigate the efficacy of wearable devices, including, continuous glucose
monitoring (CGM), and smartwatch devices. We will not only investigate the potential of wearable devices in quantifying the improvement in
neurological function and reducing complications during the early stroke
rehabilitation process, but also assess the effects of using wearables in
improving patient engagement and motivation during early stroke rehabilitation.

Keywords: Wearable Sensors · Inertial Measurement Units ·
Continuous Glucose Monitoring · Stroke Rehabilitation · Patient
Motivation

O. Konak et al. (Eds.): iWOAR 2024, LNCS 15357, pp. 277–282, 2025.
https://doi.org/10.1007/978-3-031-80856-2_19

1   Introduction

Stroke is the second most common cause of death and among the most common causes of disability globally [1]. Post-stroke disabilities such as impairments in the sensory and motor functions can have an impact on patients' mental states, eventually leading to an array of psychosocial issues [4]. Although disabilities might be reversible, the right form and dose of rehabilitation coupled with patient engagement is crucial. As marked in the literature, patient motivation in post-stroke rehabilitation is a major determinant of rehabilitation outcomes both mentally and physically [9].

The need for tools that enable remote patient monitoring led to the emergence of wearable sensors [5]. According to a study conducted in the USA, 30% of the general population and 25% of the patients with high cardiovascular risk reported using wearable devices [3]. The use of wearable sensors in post-stroke rehabilitation can impact the course of patients by improving motivation and helping medical professionals develop individualized, realistic and sustainable rehabilitation strategies [7]. Furthermore, new digital biomarkers can be identified which predict rehabilitation outcomes. Inertial Measurement Units (IMUs) are devices that measure acceleration and rotation rates. They are commonly used in gait and motion assessments. Continuous Glucose Monitorings (CGMs) are sensors used to measure blood glucose levels based on the interstitial fluid and can also be used to detect glucose levels, which is believed to have a deteriorating effect on stroke outcomes [6]. Finally, smartwatches have the ability to capture multiple health-related parameters, including but not limited to heart rate, respiratory rate, activity levels, and step counts.

In our previous work, we have proposed methods to select IMUs for mobility assessment [11], validated the performance of gait quantification algorithms using IMU data and opto-electric and pressure sensor-based reference systems [8], and demonstrated that we can quantify and visualize changes in gait patterns in both healthy and stroke populations [10,13]. Figure 1 shows the attachment of the IMUs sensors on the shoes of a participant.

However, it is worth emphasizing that a holistic approach that captures different aspects of a patient's health status is needed to comprehensively evaluate the stroke rehabilitation progress. Therefore, additional sensor modalities are necessary as a next step.

In an upcoming clinical study planned to be conducted with the Charité–Universitätsmedizin Berlin, we will implement the intervention of equipping patients with wearable sensors (IMU, CGM, and smartwatch) and providing them feedback about the data collected by the sensors in terms of daily and weekly reports in a designated mobile application. Further, we will let patients choose a personal rehabilitation goal and record their reflections and perceived progress as well as their setbacks in the mobile application. We hypothesize that receiving feedback and setting personal goals will increase patient engagement and motivation during stroke rehabilitation. This innovative approach aimed at improving the level of motivation can counteract disengagement from stroke rehabilitation and can be a milestone in stroke rehabilitation.

Fig. 1. IMU sensors that are attached to the laces at the top of shoes to measure spatio-temporal gait parameters.

2   Wearable Sensor Data Collection

Recording multiple sensor modalities simultaneously usually requires individual mobile applications for each sensor modality. To reduce the burden of having too many applications and to ensure good data quality, we rely on a mobile application that runs on a smartphone (Android OS). The initial development of this software was initiated at the research group Digital Health–Connected Healthcare at the Hasso Plattner Institute under the name SensorHub [2]. Now, the software is developed, provided, and managed by the non-profit organization D4L data4life gGmbH under the name D4L Collect. The mapping between the data collected through the native application and the clinical data is handled outside the application, ensuring that no PII (personally identifiable information) is accessible to anyone outside the medical team. All data collected by the mobile application are encrypted at rest and in transit and only stored on servers hosted in Germany, adhering to applicable data privacy laws. In the context of the study, the app will be used to connect to a Samsung Galaxy Watch 6, CGM device (Dexcom G7), and IMUs (Movella Dot). Figure 2 shows a screenshot from the D4L Collect application running on an Android smartphone.

The mobile application further allows for creating questionnaires that are delivered to the study participants, either one time at the beginning of the study, or in regular intervals during the study. Possible use cases for the planned study could be the assessment of patient's mood or motivation. In combination with the smartphone application, Data4Life developed a research platform to allow the design of study protocols, including planned questionnaires and mobility tests, and enables the configuration of sensor modalities such as acceleration and angular velocity of IMU sensors. Moreover, the platform has an integrated dashboard to display information about the ongoing study, including the number of participants enrolled, the results of the questionnaire uploaded and the recording sessions of sensors. The recorded sensor data can also be downloaded directly through the research platform.

Fig. 2. The D4L Collect Android application used to collect data from multiple sensor simultaneously.

3 Preliminary Data Analysis

To comprehensively assess the efficacy of the intervention using the sensors presented, we briefly describe planned data analysis methods that we will conduct on the collected data. We aim to assess rehabilitation progress utilizing subjective and objective measurements. The subjective measurements could be based on questionnaires, including motivation and patient-reported outcome measures. Objective measurements will comprise the assessment of data coming from the smartwatch, CGM, and IMU sensors. Smartwatch data can be used to gain insights into average daily heart rates, sleep, or general activity levels, whereas CGM provide insights into blood glucose levels. IMU sensors will be used to analyze movement of upper and lower limbs, e.g. during walking tasks or standard clinical tasks such as the timed-up-and-go test. For gait analysis, we will use an algorithm established in our previous studies to derive spatio-temporal gait parameters such as walking speed, stride length, and stride time, as well as variation and symmetry measures from these gait parameters [11,12]. The outcomes of those mentioned above will be collected, and subjective and objective

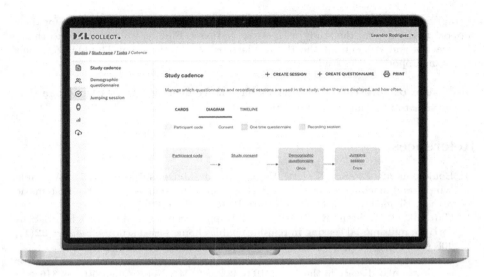

Fig. 3. The D4L Collect platform used to design, distribute, and monitor the study progress. Data collected from the participants will also be downloaded through the solution.

assessments from all planned visits will be used to evaluate the rehabilitation progress based on the longitudinal development of these outcomes and statistical tests for significant improvements (Fig. 3).

4   Conclusion

In this article, we have outlined the importance of wearable sensors in the context of stroke recovery. By using technologies like IMUs, CGMs devices, and smartwatches, we build on our experience of past studies and plan to conduct studies in the future to monitor patients' physiological and behavioral data continuously in an in-home setting. With the D4L Collect app, all data shall be collected through a single device and made available to researchers in a secure and harmonized format. In future studies, we not only plan to assess patients' rehabilitation progress but also want to assess the effect of patient engagement using these wearable technologies. Especially through real-time feedback and personalized health prompts, we hypothesize that this might foster a greater motivation for patient rehabilitation. In addition, these devices might help identify and mitigate complications such as falls and mood disorders.

Acknowledgements. The authors would like to acknowledge Deniz Büyükkaplan for his work on the literature review. We would also like to thank Claire Mouton, Florian Helmchen, Jan Huenges, Lars Rückert, Leandro Rodriguez, Prajakta Deshpande, Sarah Al-Saeedi, Sebastian Woinar, and Thomas Holst from D4L data4life gGmbH for their support in developing the data collection infrastructure in the planned study, and therapists at the Department of Neurology at the University Hospital Charité for their support in developing the study with stroke patients. Finally, we would like to thank the coaches and students at the Hasso Plattner School of Design Thinking for their efforts in supporting the study.

Disclosure of Interests. The authors have no competing interests to declare that are relevant to the content of this article.

References

1. Boukhennoufa, I., Zhai, X., Utti, V., Jackson, J., McDonald-Maier, K.D.: Wearable sensors and machine learning in post-stroke rehabilitation assessment: a systematic review. Biomed. Signal Process. Control **71**, 103197 (2022)
2. Chromik, J., Kirsten, K., Herdick, A., Kappattanavar, A.M., Arnrich, B.: SensorHub: multimodal sensing in real-life enables home-based studies. Sensors **22**(1), 408 (2022)
3. Dhingra, L.S., et al.: Use of wearable devices in individuals with or at risk for cardiovascular disease in the US, 2019 to 2020. JAMA Netw. Open **6**(6), e2316634–e2316634 (2023)
4. Perna, R., Harik, L.: The role of rehabilitation psychology in stroke care described through case examples. NeuroRehabilitation **46**(2), 195–204 (2020)
5. Spatz, E.S., Ginsburg, G.S., Rumsfeld, J.S., Turakhia, M.P.: Wearable digital health technologies for monitoring in cardiovascular medicine. N. Engl. J. Med. **390**(4), 346–356 (2024)
6. Steck, M., et al.: Evaluation of glycemic variability and discharge outcomes in patients with ischemic stroke following thrombolysis. The Neurohospitalist **14**(4), 373–378 (2023)
7. Stock, R., Gaarden, A.P., Langørgen, E.: The potential of wearable technology to support stroke survivors' motivation for home exercise-focus group discussions with stroke survivors and physiotherapists. Physiotherapy Theory Pract. **40**(8), 1779–1790 (2023)
8. Trautmann, J., et al.: Tripod-a treadmill walking dataset with IMU, pressure-distribution and photoelectric data for gait analysis. Data **6**(9), 95 (2021)
9. Verrienti, G., Raccagni, C., Lombardozzi, G., De Bartolo, D., Iosa, M.: Motivation as a measurable outcome in stroke rehabilitation: a systematic review of the literature. Int. J. Environ. Res. Public Health **20**(5), 4187 (2023)
10. Zhou, L., Fischer, E., Brahms, C.M., Granacher, U., Arnrich, B.: Using transparent neural networks and wearable inertial sensors to generate physiologically-relevant insights for gait. In: 2022 21st IEEE International Conference on Machine Learning and Applications (ICMLA), pp. 1274–1280. IEEE (2022)
11. Zhou, L., et al.: How we found our IMU: guidelines to IMU selection and a comparison of seven IMUs for pervasive healthcare applications. Sensors **20**(15), 4090 (2020)
12. Zhou, L., et al.: Monitoring and visualizing stroke rehabilitation progress using wearable sensors. In: 46th Annual International Conference of the IEEE Engineering in Medicine and Biology Society (2024)
13. Zhou, L., Schneider, J., Arnrich, B., Konigorski, S.: Analyzing population-level trials as N-of-1 trials: an application to gait. Contemp. Clin. Trials Commun. **38**, 101282 (2024)

Author Index

A

Albert, Justin 277
André, Elisabeth 169
Arnrich, Bert 181, 277

B

Bauer, Olesya 181
Bavadiya, Niravkumar 220
Benouis, Mohamed 169
Bieber, Gerald 111, 151
Burchard, Robin 55, 181, 220

C

Campos, David 124
Can, Yekta Said 169
Ciortuz, Gabriela 18
Contoli, Chiara 40
Cunningham, Douglas W. 81

D

D'Avis, Noel 269
Decker, Stefan 94
Duong-Trung, Nghia 94

E

El Hillali, Yassin 81
Endlicher, Erik 111, 151

F

Faquiri, Silvia 269
Fellmann, Michael 151
Fudickar, Sebastian 18

G

Gabrecht, Marco 251, 260
Gemeinhardt, Jan 240
Gross, Peter 111

H

Hadid, Abdenour 81
Haghbin, Iman 220
Hansen, Claus D. 124
Harkämper, Lena 18

J

Jaleel, Edda 151

K

Karande, Hrishikesh Balkrishna 220
Kaynak, Nurcennet 277
Kirsten, Kristina 181, 277
Kos, Rok 277
Krause, Cassandra 18
Krause, Moritz 240
Kubsch, Bastian 111

L

La Porta, Nicolò 3
Laerhoven, Kristof Van 181, 220
Lattanzi, Emanuele 40
Le, Thuy Hai 124
Lieb, Roselind 181

M

Matthies, Denys J. C. 199, 251, 260
Miché, Marcel 181
Minardi, Luca 3

N

Nave, Alexander Heinrich 277
Nekhviadovich, Aleksandra 94

O. Konak et al. (Eds.): iWOAR 2024, LNCS 15357, pp. 283–284, 2025.
https://doi.org/10.1007/978-3-031-80856-2

O
Opris, Adonis   169

P
Papandrea, Michela   3
Peretti, Susanna   40
Pöhler, Jonas   69

R
Rackoll, Torsten   277

S
Saadi, Ibtissam   81
Schlonsak, Ruben   199, 251, 260
Schmidt, Angelina   151
Scholl, Philipp   181
Shivalingappa, Ravikiran Arasur
         Thippeswamy   220
Slupczynski, Michal   94
Song, Rui   199
Sternitzke, Max   251

T
Taleb-Ahmed, Abdelmalik   81

V
Van Laerhoven, Kristof   55, 69

W
Wahl, Karina   181
Wald, Christopher   111
Walz, Tim   277
Weese, David   277
Willnow, Patrick   251

Y
Yaici, Abdelhafid Nassim   220
Yang, Tengyunhao   260

Z
Zhou, Lin   277
Zhuang, Hanzhi   199
Zöllner, Michael   240

Printed in the United States
by Baker & Taylor Publisher Services